Fixation

Fixation

Jack Pulman

Book Club Associates
London

First published in Great Britain 1978
by Hamish Hamilton Limited

Copyright © 1978 by Jack Pulman

This edition published 1978 by
Book Club Associates
By arrangement with Hamish Hamilton Limited

Printed in Great Britain by
Willmer Brothers Limited, Rock Ferry, Merseyside

*For Barbara — and
all the good times*

Chapter One

The city lay in the narrowly circling bay like a doughnut with a bite in it. It sparkled in the sunlight. Clean and white, tall buildings rose in the smokeless air like healthy, well-watered plants. The canopy of blue sky draped itself lazily behind. Even the docks were clean. It was a clean city. Industry had not spoiled it. Men of vigour and men of conscience had seen to that. They had dug the earth, attacked it, rather, but put everything back in its place, except the minerals. They drew patterns, laid out lines, landscaped. Where nature had blossomed lazily, mindlessly, in her own time, of which she had plenty, men, shorter lived, with the pressure of mortality upon them, feverishly, impatiently, ordered everything into a garden.

Crime had grown with the city, as weeds will grow in any garden. Once, and not so long ago, they had threatened to take the garden over altogether, spreading everywhere, crowding out the flowers, breaking through the neat, stone paths and destroying their lovely, ordered symmetry. Hurried conferences had been held, investigations carried out. Weeds were found to be growing where none had been thought to flourish. The gardeners, or some of them, were found to be actually cultivating them.

It was then that the city found Edward Groczek, Captain Groczek, vigorously gardening in his own patch, weeding, pruning, keeping his own section of the city a pleasure to stroll in. A policeman of some experience, a man, as near as a man can be, incorruptible, they made him Chief Groczek and gave him his head. He swept through the city and its surrounding county like a clean, fresh wind.

First, he weeded his gardeners. There was much anguish.

1

Cries of rage and pain filled the air for many months, as ruthlessly he pulled them out, one by one. He found them growing everywhere, in low places and in high. And the higher they were the harder he plucked, regardless of opposition, indifferent to threats on his life. Then he turned on the weeds. Relentlessly he searched them out. No matter what shaded, hidden corners they clustered in, he found them. None was safe. His instinct for them was sure and swift. Beneath the fairest blossoms his fingers found them and dragged them, protestingly, into the light. Within two years, the city breathed again. The weeds that had threatened to choke it had been thinned. Everyone relaxed. Groczek paused to draw breath.

All that was some time ago. Since then he had sat back a little, resting comfortably on his laurels. His reputation had spread in ripples through the vast continent. His methods were studied and copied. On the one side, he was asked everywhere to lecture and to talk. He spoke well. He had a sharp mind and a sharp tongue and had not neglected to read. And he did not believe in the policeman who had never read a book. On the other hand, the criminal fraternity noted his success and stayed away. Not that crime was absent. Crime there certainly was. Groczek knew about it and had it well in hand. The syndicates, however, had not moved in. They had visited, looked around and gone away again. It didn't smell right. Groczek met them – sometimes personally, sometimes allowing his presence to be felt rather than seen – always smiling, always confident. No muddy foot ever planted itself inside his door without feeling his steely eye upon it, inviting it to withdraw.

He was a handsome man, large and in his prime – like the city itself. In his frame there was always the sense of great strength, beautifully controlled, an athlete's, that could move into top gear at the first crack of a gun. He had not been born in the county but in a city, far away where the buildings were not tall and white but grey and grimed, and the smell of rotting garbage was always in the air in summer. He had found the

2

police by instinct. Some men are born to it. He was one. It was his natural home and he found it early.

Early, too, he had found his country's involvement in Vietnam, before others had found it, before the general public were even aware that such a place existed on the earth or had any significance for them. And long before long-haired, over-indulged youths had used it as a stick to beat their betters with. Restless, he had sought a new horizon to enlarge his mind and widen the scope of his experience. He had found it in the Military Police, first in Saigon and then elsewhere in that God-forsaken country. He had learned a lot there, though he rarely spoke of it. Well, that was all in another country. Today, he could look back with satisfaction on a successful career.

His colleagues stood in silence around his room, watching him with something akin to awe, as he paced up and down, his hands clasped behind his back, glancing, each time he turned, at the radio, willing it to speak again. It had already spoken several times over the last few hours but the wait in between was always too long for him. Since early morning he had been listening, waiting, moving his pieces into prepared positions. From the moment the ship had docked, every movement, every activity had been relayed to him. But still he must wait. The time was not quite yet.

For months he had been watching the growth of this ring, spreading like a small stain on a new tablecloth. He had seen it begin – nothing escaped him. He had marked it, pointed it out to his colleagues and for a while ignored it. There were many other things to occupy his mind. But little by little it had been brought to his attention again, not merely by his own colleagues but by the narcotics' division of the FBI. They had urged him to move in earlier but he had judged the time not right, and such was his reputation they had held their hand, deferred to him.

Drugs now led the league table of crime, above prostitution above even gambling. There was more money invested in it

3

more crime attached to it. A whole new industry of crime had come into being to prop up the fractured youth of the country. The kids now carried the needle in their school bags as they once carried the French letter. The results, of course, were different. But not in his city. Here they had been clean of it, relatively. Some of the softer stuff was peddled, grass of various sorts, but all on a fairly amateur level. This little ring, though, was different. It was new. When he saw it he knew it was trying to establish itself here, in his city, either to market or to set up a new route to the north. He thought the latter more likely. He let it grow a while. When he struck, the news would resound throughout the country. It would be good for the city to have his name bandied about the country again.

Schuster's voice came over the radio, halting Groczek in his tracks to listen. 'He's putting it in a truck. I can't see the number plate from here. Cooper's getting out to have a look.'

Groczek snatched the microphone off the desk. 'Schuster? This is Chief Groczek.'

'Yes, sir?'

'Tell Cooper if they get one whiff of fuzz in that area I'll put him through the shredder.'

'Yes, sir. I'll tell him. It's all right, I think. The place is crawling with people. No reason to pick him out.'

In the car, sitting within the area of the docks, Schuster looked at Cooper who had the car door open and one leg on the ground. He nodded. He had heard. 'For Christ's sake,' Schuster said, 'don't blow it now.'

Cooper got out and closed the door. He slipped his hands into his pockets and slouched along the road towards the dock. The ship, a Japanese vessel, was berthed in number four. Dockers swarmed all over it, cranes raised frail arms into the sky and swung heavy loads from ship to shore. Cooper strolled into the thick of it. He knew what he was looking for, what they were all looking for. He paused behind the truck, noted the license plate and walked on. He saw the last of the boxes

4

going to the back of the truck as he described a wide circle back to the car again.

Schuster sat behind the wheel of his red Plymouth glancing through the morning paper. Cooper got back into the car and picked up his microphone. 'The number plate of the truck,' he said, 'is 7AU 333. It looks about ready to move off.'

'Stay with him,' Groczek's voice crackled, 'and don't lose him.'

Schuster picked a bar of chocolate up from below the dashboard, snapped off a square and gave it to Cooper. They were both young, neither smoked, but they did eat a great deal of chocolate. They sat in silence, munching. They had the truck just in the side mirror. It had to come out this way so they were pointing in the right direction. Schuster sat with his eyes glued to the mirror. Cooper picked up the morning paper and looked through it.

Groczek stood and stared out of the window on the fourth floor of the building onto the city. He could see the outlines of cranes at the docks from there. In his mind he could see exactly what had gone on and what was going on. He saw the off-loading of the boxes of water chestnuts stamped 'Oriental Spice Company.' He saw them put on the wheeler trolley and moved down to the waiting truck. He saw them being loaded onto the truck. He couldn't see the truck driver in his mind – he had no known record. Perhaps he was, perhaps he wasn't part of the ring. They would see. The Oriental Spice Company he knew. Mr. Tai, a respectable gentleman who owned the company had been providing Chinese restaurants in the city with delicacies for nearly forty years. No, it was the others he wanted. He knew who they were, most of them, but they had to be taken with the stuff in their hands. That's why they waited. That's why, at that moment, there was silence.

He turned from the window as Schuster's voice came over the radio again. 'The truck's moving. It's on its way past. Here we go.' Groczek looked at Fallon, his deputy, a slight, quiet, efficient man in his late thirties. Fallon smiled slightly. They were on their way. Groczek nodded as he read the smile and turned back to the window again. The other officers in the room shifted on their feet a little, sensing a rising excitement in their chief.

Down town, Schuster kept the truck just a little ahead of them. It was always a tricky business following another car. The trouble was there was too much of it on television. The public thought it was easy but let them try it. Any cop could tell them that in heavy traffic over a reasonable period it was a damned difficult thing to do without being noticed. You could be separated by other traffic, by the lights, by pedestrian crossings, by a sudden turn of the other car – and God help you if you knocked a pedestrian down or crashed a car trying not to lose sight of your quarry. Fortunately, the truck in front was big and in no hurry.

Periodically, Cooper spoke into the radio, giving their position street by street, not only to Chief Groczek waiting in the office, but to other cars parked at various points in the city and waiting instructions to move. The truck turned at an intersection and then almost immediately turned left again and pulled into the kerb. Schuster swore as he had to make the sudden left turn and almost as suddenly swerve to avoid the truck that had come to a halt. That was typical of the kind of thing that could happen to give you away for sure. He certainly couldn't stop behind the truck so he drove on down the street and then deliberately pulled over to the other side of the road and parked. He was sure he hadn't been noticed.

They turned in their seats and looked back. The truck had parked behind a small green van. A young man with long fair hair was leaning against the hood, smoking. The truck driver jumped down and greeted the young man with a wave and a pat on the back. They both walked round to the back of the truck and the truck driver pulled the back down and climbed in. He pulled several boxes down onto the tailboard and the young man started carrying them to the green van.

6

Groczek listened to Schuster's voice describing the scene over the radio. 'Green van, city license plate 3XJ 896. Driver fair-haired, shoulder length, about five eight medium build, wearing zip-up green nylon jacket. He's putting the boxes onto the van.'

Groczek nodded, satisfied. He spoke into the radio. 'What about the truck driver, Schuster? He's in on it, too, isn't he? It's not a chance meeting, I take it, of old school friends? Let's have a description.' He waited while Schuster's voice gave out a description of the truck and the driver and then he called the nearest car which was a couple of blocks away from where Schuster was sitting. 'Fairfax, you heard all that? Move in. Schuster's following the green van. Let the van get out of sight before you pick up the driver of the truck. Move.'

Groczek turned to the waiting officers. 'Now, listen to me. If our information is correct, that van is going to Young's Chinese. They'll all be there – and I want them all, not just one or two. We could have had one or two if we'd moved in six months ago when the FBI started to make noises. But we knew better than the FBI, didn't we?' There were smiles all round. It was nice of the chief to include them all. 'And we'd better know better, O.K.?' Groczek added.

He paused to listen again as Schuster's voice came in over the radio, describing the whereabouts of the van and the direction in which it was moving. It confirmed what he already knew. He turned to lead them out of the office when Detective Sergeant O'Malley entered, carrying in his hand a paper. He looked white and sick. He opened his mouth. The voice seemed to take a long while to emerge from it. 'The search warrant expired yesterday. We forgot to renew it.'

Fallon could hear the clock tick. He looked at Groczek who had gone quite still and whose eyes glittered. There was no other word that occurred to Fallon to describe the look in them. He heard the voice come out in a soft, breathy hiss. 'Who's "we"?'

7

O'Malley swallowed hard for a moment. 'Colson – I suppose, sir.'

Groczek stared at him, and the muscles in his jaw twitched. It was, of course, the strike. He had applied for the warrant a week ago, knowing the date the ship was due to dock, but a dispute among the dockers had led to a strike and delayed the unloading for twenty-four hours. It hadn't occurred to him, he had so many things on his mind. And it was Colson's job to watch that – Colson and even, perhaps, O'Malley. Fallon felt a twinge of sympathy for Colson, mixed with his own irritation at the slip-up. 'We'll have to take the stuff off the van,' he said to Groczek.

'We'll take it inside the premises,' Groczek replied. 'Warrant or no warrant, we'll take it inside the premises. Let them squeal in court.' He turned and walked out of the office, followed, after a pause for some raising of eyebrows, by the others.

He had done it, or something like it, more than once, lately – sailed very close to the wind. Fallon had noticed it. It wasn't much, but enough to notice, a tendency to act without due process or turn a blind eye to others doing it. There was, about Groczek, a growing impatience with the law's delays and growing, if humorous, contempt for its elaborate provisions. It wasn't much, but Fallon had noticed it.

They piled into the car. Schuster's voice could be heard on the radio giving a street-by-street account of where the van was. Groczek and Fallon settled back in the car. They moved away sedately. There was no hurry. They knew where they were going and they couldn't arrive before the little green van.

The little green van turned down Front Street and came to a halt outside Young's Chinese. The driver got down and went round to the back of the van and opened the doors. At the far end of the street, Schuster's red Plymouth drew up at the kerb and came to a halt. Schuster picked up the microphone. 'He's stopped outside the restaurant. He's starting to unload.'

8

Fallon tapped the driver on the shoulder and the driver put his foot down. The car leapt forward and the cars stationed at various positions around Front Street did the same. They were all no more than a few blocks away. As they approached Front Street they slowed to normal pace, turned the corner into the street and came to a halt, one behind the other, at the kerb.

Groczek leaned forward and looked down the street. The young man was carrying the boxes into the restaurant. Further up, on the other side, he could see Schuster's car, waiting. He looked again at the van. The driver had disappeared inside and was now coming out again to take another load in. Fallon put his hand on the door handle but Groczek laid a restraining hand on him and he paused.

The driver had the last of the cardboard boxes in his arms. Groczek waited for him to carry them inside. The moment he disappeared, the police would emerge quietly from the waiting cars and walking swiftly across the road, follow him into the restaurant. But the driver had paused on the kerb, as if sensing that something was not quite right. He looked further down the road.

Three cars were sitting there, one behind the other. Although not obviously police cars, there was something not quite right about them. He couldn't say precisely what but, like many more of his generation, he had a nose for fuzz. He turned and looked at the other end of the street, and saw the red Plymouth. Once again, it looked innocent enough – and yet? He was undecided. He put the last of the cardboard boxes back inside the van and casually closed the doors. He walked towards the front of the van and lit a cigarette but his eyes were probing the three cars ahead of him. He could see, now, that they were fully occupied. Parked cars were usually not – not that occupied. Across the street, directly opposite the restaurant, a small alleyway led down to the main shopping thoroughfare. Casually, he began crossing the road towards it.

9

'He's seen us. Out!' Groczek said. Almost simultaneously, twelve doors in the cars opened and policemen leaped out on both sides. The young man bolted for the alleyway. Schuster and Cooper leaped from their Plymouth and made after him. 'Take the restaurant,' Groczek shouted at Fallon and left him like a bullet in hot pursuit of the van driver.

Schuster and Cooper turned into the alleyway well ahead of Groczek, their arms moving like pistons in an effort to close the gap on the young man who was running like a hare in front of them. He burst into the crowded thoroughfare, racing down a line of shops, knocking people right and left as they got in his way.

Schuster and Cooper panted wildly behind, trying to make up ground. Waves of gawping shoppers parted like the Red Sea before them as they careered wildly down the sidewalk. Behind them, making ground quickly, his action as smooth and his destruction of distance as ruthless as a 1,500-metre champion, Groczek drew abreast of them and passed them without a glance, his eyes glued on the fleeting figure in front.

He drew close, almost tripping over the flying heels in front of him. He got a hand on the young man's collar. The young man twisted and turned and leaped like a fish on a line. The young man was lifted from his feet and flung against the wall with a force that almost broke his back. He slithered down, panting, gasping agonisedly for breath. In almost the same state of agony, Schuster and Cooper arrived.

Groczek looked at them witheringly. He was scarcely puffed. 'They run faster than that in a girls' school,' he said, 'with a pound of cotton wool inside them.' The young man had slithered to one side and made a sudden break for it but Groczek hammered him against the wall again. 'Stop it, son, stop it. You've been nabbed. Don't make it hard on yourself. Be philosophic about it. Learn to accept these little setbacks gracefully.' He slammed him back against the wall again and the young man gasped. Groczek turned to Schuster and said, 'Put him in the car.'

Schuster and Cooper grabbed him, put the handcuffs on him and led him back to the car. Groczek walked briskly back down the main thoroughfare, turned into the alley and walked on down to the restaurant.

The dining room was swarming with police. Bewildered diners sat before half-eaten spare-ribs and spring rolls, rapidly cooling, staring at the intruders as if they had suddenly gone mad with hunger and were about to use their authority to take over the restaurant. Mr. Young, a middle-aged Asiatic, shaking either from fear or indignation, stood with a group of his white-coated staff just in front of the bar. All were decidedly inscrutable and determined to give little away. Piled on the floor were several cardboard boxes which had been brought in from the rear of the restaurant where the young van driver had deposited them. A tape of Chinese music was playing quietly in the background. Groczek pushed his way into the restaurant and stood looking round for a moment, with a quiet satisfaction. His eye fell on Young. 'Mr. Young, I believe?'

'Do you have a warrant for this intrusion?' Young asked.

'Ah, yes – a warrant. I thought you'd ask me that, somehow. You people learn your rights before you get off the boat.'

'I was born here,' Young answered, coldly. 'May I see the warrant?'

'O'Malley, show Mr. Young the warrant.'

'Sir?' O'Malley said, looking at Groczek.

'The warrant, O'Malley,' Groczek repeated, 'you brought it with you, I presume? You know a policeman can't enter a premises without a warrant. Show him the warrant, O'Malley.'

O'Malley took out the warrant and handed it to Young. Groczek looked at the pile of cardboard boxes on the floor, then looked around the restaurant for a can-opener. 'Anyone got a can-opener?' he asked.

No one moved. Groczek looked at Young who was reading the warrant. 'Mr. Young – a can-opener? We came with a warrant but no can-opener. Could you oblige?' Young lifted his eyes from the warrant and stared at him stolidly but said

nothing. Groczek turned and looked at a young waiter standing near. He went up to him and put his hand in the top
pocket of his white coat and pulled out a corkscrew and can-
opener combined. He walked over to the cardboard boxes and
ripped the top one open. Young watched him. Groczek pulled
out one of the cans and looked at the label 'Made in Hong
Kong. What isn't, these days?' He inserted the can-opener
into the can and prised off the lid. All the diners stared at him
in silent curiosity. He looked at the whitish powder inside and
sniffed at it. He took a pinch and placed it on his tongue, tasting it. He smiled, and held the can out to Young. 'What do
you think that is?' Young didn't answer, neither did he look at
it. 'Smell it,' Groczek said to him, 'smell it.' He held the can
out to him but Young made no move towards it. 'Smell it,'
Groczek said, even more quietly but thrusting the can violently
under Young's nose.

Dutifully, Young sniffed at the contents and then shrugged.
'I don't know what it is.'

'Really?' Groczek said. 'Well, tell me what it obviously is
not? Like water chestnuts, like it says on the label?'

There was no answer, again. A quiet stillness hung over the
restaurant. No one moved or spoke. Groczek took the warrant
from Young's unresisting hand and passed it to O'Malley
without a word. Then he looked round at the diners. His gaze
came to rest on a table at which three smartly dressed men
sat – like the rest, their dinners congealing on the plates in
front of them. Groczek tossed the can-opener to Fallon. 'Try
some of the other cases,' he said to him, and walked over to the
table where the three men sat. He looked at the smooth, dark-
haired younger one facing him. 'Well, well – Mr. Adleman.
Fancy meeting you here. Do you come here often?'

'Now and then,' Adleman said.

'And just for the water chestnuts.' Groczek shook his head
and smiled. 'You gourmets.'

'Water chestnuts?' Adleman said. 'I never eat them. They
give me indigestion.'

12

'You'll get more than indigestion from what's in those cases, Adleman,' Groczek replied, 'I promise you that.' He glanced beneath the table. A brief-case lay propped against the leg of the chair. He picked it up and looked at it, then looked at Adleman. 'Yours?' Adleman didn't answer. Groczek extended his hand. 'The key?' Again there was no response. 'Come on,' Groczek coaxed, 'do you want me to use the can-opener on it? Why spoil a beautiful case like this? Pig-skin, isn't it? You know I hate vandalism.'

Adleman put his hand in his pocket and brought out a key. Groczek took it, inserted it in the lock and opened the case. It was stuffed full of dollar bills of very large denominations. 'What were you going to do, play monopoly after lunch?' Groczek asked.

'I was going to the races.'

Groczek nodded easily and snapped the case shut. He tossed it to a policeman. He walked round the table, bent down and picked up another brief-case. He held it up to his ear and shook it. It rattled. 'I wonder what could possibly be in there,' he said. He looked at its owner. 'You were going to the races, too, I suppose? Who'd do business with you? You'd frighten all the bookies away, don't you know that? It would be like playing poker with the Chase National Bank.' He threw the case to another policeman and picked up the third. He shook it. It made a familiar rattle. He smiled benignly at its owner and tossed it yet again to another waiting pair of hands.

'I'd like to phone my lawyer,' Adleman said.

'And so you shall,' Groczek answered, 'what do you think this is, a police state? But not now,' he went on, as Adleman rose, 'it's lunch time. Why spoil his lunch? Do it from the station. You get it free. That's part of your rights.' He turned to the waiting officers. 'Take them outside. And him.' He indicated Young. 'And the staff. The rest can go.' He turned to the waiting diners. 'I'm sorry to spoil your lunch, ladies and gentlemen, but this place is closed. As you see, Mr. Young is going out of business for a while. It's all very sudden. But what

13

can you do? Life is just full of one damned thing after another.'

There was a general movement all around the restaurant as the diners gathered their things together. Groczek walked back to Fallon who had selected a can from each pack, opened it and investigated its contents. Fallon said, 'It's all junk. I've never seen so much. There must be $10,000,000 worth of it. It looks pure, too, uncut.'

Groczek turned to Young. 'What were you going to do – buy South America and retire? I know – all you did was order some cases of water chestnuts.' He turned to O'Malley. 'Take them all down to the station and book them. Put all that junk in the green van and bring it with them.'

O'Malley ushered Young and the others out through the door. Groczek turned to Fallon. Fallon said, 'You took a bit of a risk giving him that warrant to read.'

Groczek shook his head. 'Have you ever known a man in a state of shock to read anything properly? The last thing he's likely to look at is the date. Well, come on. The smell of this food is making me hungry.' He turned and walked out. He felt good. They had challenged him and lost. The city was clean again. It would be a warning to all others who might look at his city and think to find there easy pickings.

Chapter Two

Slovak got into his car and drove it south. The day was fine. The hood of the blue Ferrari was folded back and the warm air rushed passed his face joyously. The tyres sang. He laughed out loud, so fine was the day, so warm and tender the wind, so dark the place he left behind. Dark. The waves had suddenly parted for him and he had rushed through. Oh, it had been a long tunnel back there, but he was through it now,

14

and the future stretched like the highway in front of him.

He drove the car south. There was 400 miles of road between him and there but he did not mind. Driving relaxed him. The air was heady. He might have taken a plane but that was not what he needed. He needed distance and time and their effect on the human body. Air travel knew none of that. Pick you up and put you down. You were the same in L.A. as you were in New York. He had to be different. He had to be what he once was, not what he had recently become. No, that had frightened him. He had not recognised himself. Yes, that aptly described it. He had not recognised himself at all, had not been himself.

Odd how such a common phrase could so aptly describe the human condition. Phrases one had used over and over in a thousand different, trivial ways suddenly stood up and revealed their true meaning, what they had meant to mean, meant all the time. 'Had not been himself.' Then who had he been? Someone else?

'It is not an uncommon experience,' the young doctor had said to him, 'in your condition. The young animal, the young child, is unaware of his own "self"; he is part of his environment, is blended with it. But as he grows, he separates himself from his environment and stands in opposition to it. Then he becomes a man. The connecting tissue is broken, usually for all time. But sometimes, in periods of mental stress, the tissue begins to grow again, thread by thread, re-establishing its connection with the outer world as if expressing some deep, atavistic longing to blend back with it again, as if the separation had been too hard to bear and could not be supported any longer.'

He was an erudite, softly spoken young man, younger than he, younger by far. He had probed him gently, urging him to talk about himself but this he had been unable to do, unable to do easily, at any rate. 'What is your profession?' he had asked him.

15

'I have none.'

'No profession?'

'I am of independent means.' And he was – rich beyond the dreams of this young man in front of him. But he would not tell him his profession. No, that was not possible. 'Am I ill?"

'No, no – not ill."

'Then why am I here?'

'Well, you came to me.'

'Would I have done so if I weren't?'

'Well, a little bit ill, if you want to use such terms.' The young man shrugged and smiled to show what he thought of such terms.

'How would you describe it, then? My condition, I mean.'

'I'm not sure. Not yet. When I can describe it, I can cure it. Try not to worry about it, though. Your case is not exceptional.'

'How do you know if you can't describe it?'

The young man smiled again but deigned not to answer. 'We'll meet again tomorrow. You may go now.' He had gone, and returned many times.

The young man had said to him at one point, 'To a certain extent you have lost sight of yourself,' and this had been the only remark to make any sense to him. He responded immediately to that, recognising the germ of truth in it at once. He had often, in the recent past, felt this to be true, and pondered on it curiously, for his mind hated unsolved problems. He had looked into his life for the cause of such an event but had been unable to trace it. Of course, he understood and it was clear to him that, in a way, his whole life had been a conflict between a desire to be wholly known and a desire to be concealed, to be, if you like, unseen, and he dimly perceived that there was a connection there, somewhere. That conflict was, to some extent, inevitable, given the nature of his life and his work, but there was, he was certain, a deeper connection he could not trace.

16

He drove the car on south. The signs on the highway floated past him like ghosts from another world. Mile after mile he drove and the more he drove the more relaxed and happy he felt. He had been brought to an awareness of the conflict that had been troubling him for a while and in becoming aware of it had triumphed over it. The young man had done that for him. He could forget it now.

He saw the needle of the gas tank hovering low and drove off the highway onto the road that led to the complex of buildings offering refreshment and refuelling services. He stopped at the gas station and sat patiently while the attendant filled the tank. He paid him and drove into the parking lot. He left the car and went up the stairs to the main refreshment building. He had no desire to eat, though he hadn't eaten since morning. He wanted only to arrive at the city as quickly as possible.

He went into the washroom. It was empty. He walked over to the basin and washed his hands and face. He dried them on the towel and stood, for a moment, staring down at them, as if he were not sure that they were his. Something, however, was throbbing at the back of his mind as he stared down at his hands, turning them this way and that.

Slowly, he raised his eyes to the mirror on the wall. He had a dark foreboding of what he might see there or might *not* see there, which was more to the point. But in the end he could not avoid looking, the compulsion was so strong. But all he saw in the mirror was the empty washroom reflected in it and himself looking at himself.

It reassured him. He was observed, seen by that other self in the mirror. He smiled. It was slightly comical to be observed by oneself and yet, in the absence of others, it was reassuring. It was odd how that idea teased him now and then, the extent to which one existed only through the constant observation of others. To be an object in the perceived world of other people was the greatest insurance that one existed at all. Without Man

Friday, for instance, would not Crusoe have come so to doubt his own existence as to seem entirely invisible? Would it have been a true invisibility? Did it matter? Did it not come to the same thing?

'Hi, there? You O.K.? You look beat up. Been driving long?' The truck driver rolled up his sleeves, exposing thick, brown arms and giving him a sideways look turned on the taps and splashed water all over himself. 'These turnpikes play hell with your eyes.'

'I'm fine, thanks.'

The driver shook his head and cleared his ear with his little finger, splashing more water over his face and hair. 'Drive, drive, drive, mile after goddamned mile. Foot down, staring at the road. Ain't really natural, you know? Not for a man. Machine could do it, but not a man.' He took the towel and dried himself. 'You look all in. You look how I feel. Late night last night. Too many cans of beer, too much poker. You shouldn't do it when you're driving. I tell myself that everytime but I still do it. Have you eaten?'

'I'm not hungry.'

'You shouldn't drive on an empty stomach, though what you get here won't do you much good – plastic wrapped garbage, that's all it is. All so goddamned refined it just disappears inside you and leaves nothing to come out the other end. You know what the result is? Constipation – occupational hazard of truck drivers. A doctor told me that. Well, so long.' He gave him a friendly wave, turned and went out, leaving the door swinging to and fro. The washroom was empty again, except for himself.

He drove the car on south, mile after steady mile, while the blue of the sky turned a deeper and deeper hue and the sun descended in a slow arc behind him. As the tyres burned the miles he felt a growing impatience to be there and beginning again, an impatience mixed with a rising exhilaration. It was the thought of beginning again that had brought him through.

18

The idea had brought him forth from that dark lethargy, overcome his weariness, imbuing him with a new energy. Work was a therapy to him, the only therapy, and here was work on a grand scale to test him as never before. It was the testing that he rose to, that made him laugh out loud when he thought of it. What he proposed to do was outrageous. That it had never been done before only added to the appeal. That it might be considered impossible only made it all the more desirable to achieve.

He had it all clear in his mind, every piece of the plan was in place and laid out like a well ordered room. He had seen it at once and laughed. He had seen the shape. It had appeared in his mind with the familiarity of something already accomplished. He knew, instantly, that it could be done. It revived him all the more as it proved to him that his mind was as fertile as ever and that the period of loss of confidence in himself was over. All that was no more than a depressing backwater he had floated into. Now he had paddled himself out and was clean away again. His impatience burned inside him.

There was more to it though, than just the beauty of the idea itself, its diamond symmetry. It was the location, the city which drew him and fevered his impatience more than the idea alone would have done. The city was familiar to him. Though he had never been there, he felt, when he had read about it, that everything was familiar to him. He could not explain that, but so strongly was his feeling of it that when he left the highway around dusk and took the smaller road that was to lead him there, he stopped the car on the brow of a hill and felt impelled to get out and look.

From where he stood he could see the circling bay below him and the city, white, like icing sugar sprinkled all along the top of the curve from tip to tip so that where the two pincers of the bay ended in the white foam of the sea it truly looked like a doughnut with a bite in it as the travel book had said. But he knew it would look exactly like this.

19

He stood, in the gathering dusk, staring down at the winking lights of the city. He felt drawn by it. It was as if his destiny lay somewhere in it and that he had but to step into its streets to be confronted by it in some form, he wasn't sure what. That, of course, was absurd. Yet he had the distinct feeling that in a way the city represented for him the end of a road.

He noted to himself that he did not say 'the' road. It was not that sort of feeling, but the end of *something*, he wasn't sure what – but an end. It roused in him an excitement. His impatience, which had begun to diminish as evening fell and he approached nearer and nearer his destination, became fevered again as he saw, from that distance, the city waiting for him. He turned from the view and got back into the car. The car started with a roar from the exhaust and leapt away as if it, too, could no longer wait.

Within fifteen minutes he was in the heart of the city. He stopped off at the hotel, the Latham, and checked in. He had a bath and changed his clothes. He took out the street map of the city he had picked up from the desk and took from his wallet a small piece of paper on which he had written an address. He found the street in the south-west corner of the city. He looked at his watch and debated whether to telephone first. He decided against it. He wrote the address on the top of the map, then left his room and walked out of the hotel again. He went round to the car park, got into his car again, put the street map on the seat beside him and drove off.

The city was clearly laid out and well signed and by glancing from time to time at the map he had no difficulty in finding his way. As he drove, he looked about him curiously. The city was lit with a softness that was unusual, most pleasant. There was none of the raucousness of New York, neither did he pass through any obviously poor quarters. It seemed a model city.

Hill Towers apartment block overlooked the only major park

in the city, and the trees that had once occupied its site had not all been cut and cleared to build it. He parked the car and went into the heavily carpeted entrance. He crossed to the elevator which was waiting on the ground floor and got in. He closed the doors and pressed the button for the fourth floor. The elevator rose noiselessly and came to a halt. He got out, closing the doors behind him, and walked along the corridor to apartment forty-two. He pressed the bell and waited. He heard her voice calling from inside, 'Coming!' and then her light footsteps running towards the door. The door opened and she stood there, staring at him.

A long stalk of neck rose from a small, shapely figure to a small, delicately pale oval face framed by tumbling masses of red hair. So delicate and pale was the skin, so stretched like parchment on a lampshade that tints of blue coloured the white and slightly freckled the area under the large eyes. She stood looking at him, head to one side, a puzzled smile on her lips, doubting, at first, the evidence of her own eyes. 'Frank?' she asked, 'Frank?'

'Hello, Maggie?'

She laughed, a little breathless, and shook her head. 'Frank?' Her hand went automatically to her hair and combed it back with her fingers off her forehead.

'Can I come in?' he asked.

'Well, of course!' She laughed again, and stepped back a little, opening the door wider for him. 'I don't know what to say. Come in! Of course, come in. How wonderful to see you.' He came into the apartment and she closed the door and once again stood looking at him, lifting her hands wide in a helpless gesture and smiling at him at the same time. 'You've got me all confused, Frank. You're the last person I expected to see.' She led the way into the living room and he followed her. She turned and looked at him again. 'When did you arrive?'

'About an hour ago. I checked in at the Latham and had a bath.' He stared at her. Her presence filled him with a

21

warmth he thought he had remembered but he saw now, that his memory had played him false. He had forgotten how much he had once basked in all that warmth, how reviving it had been for him. He felt an immense urge to pull her slim body against his own, to reunite them. He ached for this union as a man might ache for a limb no longer there. Something stopped him, however, going towards her. He sensed it wasn't right, that she would have resisted. Instead, he said, 'How have you been?'

'All right.' She nodded. Yes, all things considered she had been all right. 'And you?'

'Well – yes, the same, really.' He shrugged. 'I've missed you.' She nodded again but said nothing. There was a certain embarrassment, it was inevitable. 'Let's go and eat,' he went on, 'I haven't eaten all day.'

'Well, Frank, I'm – I'm going out to dinner.'

'Oh.' There was a pause. He looked disappointed, though he could see now, that she was, in fact, dressed for going out. 'Couldn't you change it?'

'Well, no. No, I couldn't!' She laughed at the little-boy simplicity of the question. 'And you shouldn't ask me to.'

He felt a wave of irritation cross him but he didn't want her to see it. He looked around the apartment, nodding approvingly. 'It's very nice.'

'Thanks.'

'You always knew how to do up a place. Have you had it long?'

'About two years – ever since I came back.' She stared at him a moment. 'How did you find my address?'

'You've got a phone.'

'I'm not listed, though.'

'No.'

He smiled at her and she nodded. 'I see. Open any door?' She should've known. There was little he couldn't do if he wanted to.

22

'You've got time for a drink before dinner, haven't you? What time's your dinner?'

'Well, nine, but . . .'

'That's time for several.' He grinned, and looked more cheerful. 'Come on. We'll go back to the hotel, have a drink and I'll put you in a cab for wherever you want to go.' He was persuasive and all boyish charm. 'I've driven a long way,' he added.

It was hard to refuse. He seemed oddly helpless, lost. She hadn't seen him quite like that before. She nodded. 'All right. I won't be a minute,' she said, and went off into the bedroom.

As the door closed on her he felt himself collapse inside. He hadn't realised, fully, the effort it had cost coming there, seeing her, not knowing quite what he might find or what her attitude would be. And now he was in the room alone again he felt deflated, spent, and yet also a curious sense of relief, as if seeing her had confirmed something to him that he had been doubtful of. It was as though in her very observation of him he had thrived again, picked up a little. He felt like a plant freshly watered by her gaze. He had not come for that. He had come for a different reason altogether but his battle to exist had received support from an unexpected quarter.

This battle that he had fought in the recent past was not entirely over. He knew that. He had confidence now, that he would win it finally but he did not delude himself that it was already won. To this end he constantly directed his gaze inward, subjecting his inner self to searching scrutiny, heightening his awareness of his own self in the belief that while he remained aware, became more and more aware of the being that pulsed inside him, he held at bay the possible disappearance of that being altogether.

He stood for a moment in the room, drained and yet reassured. He crossed the room to the telephone and as he approached it heard it tinkle as the extension was put down in Maggie's bedroom. Clearly she had made a call, perhaps to

23

the person she was to meet for dinner that night. He picked up the phone. He had a call himself to make. He took out a small notebook, looked for a number, found it and dialled. He heard the phone ringing at the other end and then heard the receiver picked up. A woman's voice said, 'Hello?'

'Is Mr. Bellis there?'

'No, he's not. Who wants him?'

'What time will he be back?'

'In about an hour. Who is that?'

He replaced the receiver and stood for a moment staring down into it. Once again he felt his eyes being drawn to something and he was reluctant to look. But such was the power exerted upon him that he felt his eyes lift towards the mirror above the phone. *He* was in it, *him*, observing him, watching him. In a way, the reflection comforted him.

He turned away and wandered around the room, picking up ornaments, examining them with only a casual interest. It was, indeed, an attractive apartment. He paused by an armchair. Lying on the seat was the evening paper, still crisp and new as if it had just been brought in and dropped into the chair and left. On the front page the photograph of a man stared up at him. The caption identified him as 'Chief Groczek' and below gave an account of the largest haul of heroin ever made and the arrest of those concerned. Chief Groczek would be talking to the press tomorrow.

He stared down at the photograph, examining every feature of the face. It was a strong face, a broad expanse of forehead and a thick head of hair. The eyes were clear and set wide apart, the mouth firm with just the suspicion of humour at the corners. It was a face, strangely, not unlike his own. For a long while he stared down at it, as if trying to imprint every detail of it in his mind. He felt an odd, mysterious need to. He felt that the face was, in some way, inextricably mixed up in the pattern of his life at that moment. Of course, in one way, it was and he understood that and was not puzzled by it. That

24

was a connection he would have expected, by the nature of things, by the purpose of his visit, but that connection was no more than at the very periphery. He would have expected the contact to be no more than tangential but this other feeling went deeper, much deeper. It was as if he felt him to be at the very heart and core of his life.

It was an absurd feeling and he shook it off in a moment. He had no connection with this man, though it was true he had heard of him. Many people had heard of him. His fame had spread throughout the country, sending the bubble of his reputation floating across the continent for people to gaze at in wonder. He would prick that bubble, but only in the course of accomplishing what he had come to do. The bubble was of no importance to him, except that it would burst as a consequence of what he had to do and that lent a little added piquancy to it all. He smiled at that.

'Shall we go?' He turned and saw Maggie standing in the room, beautifully wrapped like a package newly bought from a store and waiting to be opened. He took her arm and guided her out through the front door. He drove her down to the hotel. They said little on the way but every now and then he turned and smiled at her and she returned the smile warmly, reassuring him that she, too, was pleased to see him. But he saw that the smile was carefully measured. He saw that it defined precisely the extent of her pleasure and her expectation that his should be no more than hers. It placed him in the balance opposite her and expected neither scale to tip. Without saying a word, she had prescribed the exact weight the meeting could bear. He would overload it at his peril.

He guided her through the foyer and into the bar. They found a table and sat opposite one another. He ordered drinks and then, for the first time, they gave themselves up to the inevitable acknowledgement of their confrontation. They knew they could not avoid it for ever. She went in sideways. 'You don't look well, Frank.'

'You look great.'

'I mean it.'

'So do I.'

He grinned at her. The charm was immense. She remembered, suddenly, just how powerful it could be, as he had done earlier. She felt it behind her knees where she had always felt it and in the pit of her stomach. A wave of irritation swept over her, but she allowed it to subside before going on. 'What did you come here for?'

'To see you.'

She waited stolidly. She would not be drawn and thus expose herself. Her barriers were still firmly up and she felt too secure behind them to emerge. He grinned again when he saw she could not be tricked out of her position. 'Well,' he added, 'mainly to see you. Why not?'

'You do nothing "mainly", Frank. Whatever you do, you do entirely for one reason or another but never partly for both.'

He shrugged. 'It's true, I've got business here, but it was made all the more attractive by the thought of seeing you.'

She stared at him for a moment. 'Business?' He nodded. 'What sort of business?' He smiled but said nothing. He was pleased with himself, she could see that. She felt something fall to the bottom of her stomach and she dropped her eyes and stared down into her drink. 'Haven't you made enough?'

'I'm too young to retire.' They both sat sipping their drinks for a while, but his eyes never left her face. He could see that he had depressed her and he made a real effort to bring her out of it. 'Hey,' he said, 'I'll bet you really could break this date tonight, and have dinner with me. What about it? We'll do the town, like we used to. Come on, make a phone call. I've driven a long way, Maggie. It took me eight hours to get here.'

'It seemed more like two years to me.'

The punch landed well below the belt and his smile faded somewhat. It was true, it was more than two years since he

26

had made any effort to contact her. But he had been hurt, grievously hurt by her abrupt departure. He had waited for her to return or phone or write but she never had. He had found that hard to forgive. She was the only woman he had ever loved. 'Who is he,' he asked, 'this date of yours? It's not serious, is it?'

She nodded. 'Yes.'

'Do I know him?'

'No.'

'What's his name?'

'Phillip Baron. He's a doctor. My doctor.'

'He knows what he's getting, then?'

The joke fell rather flat and he wished he hadn't said it. There was a short silence. This wasn't going as well as he'd hoped. He'd assumed too much, he could see that. He sat there for a moment, turning it over in his mind. Oddly, it was the one hurdle he hadn't expected. He had thought that, like him, she would have formed no new attachments.

'Is this thing you're down here for – big?' she asked, after a while. He nodded slowly. He had no qualms about telling her. He would have trusted her with his life. No one else – but her. 'Christ,' she said, finally, 'you frighten me.'

He smiled. The waiter brought fresh drinks but she scarcely looked at hers. 'They're building a picture of you, you know that, don't you,' she said, quietly, 'they've been building it for a long time. They'll know you're down here for something.'

'They'll think,' he said, and he grinned, 'if they think at all, that I came down to see you.' She nodded. It was true, they probably would. 'And it's true, Maggie, whatever else the reason, you've got to believe that. The fact that it's convenient doesn't make it any the less true.'

'They'll get you one day, Frank.'

'No.' He shook his head. 'Not me. They're not clever enough. Sure, they're building a file, I know that. They've

27

been doing it for years. But a file, that's one thing. Proof is something else.' He paused for a moment before going on. 'I'd like to move in, Maggie.'

She looked at him and shook her head. 'No, that's not possible.'

'Why not? Because of your doctor?'

'I just don't want to be involved.'

'You wouldn't have to be. All that's needed . . .'

'No!'

It was firm and final. He bit his lip and thought for a moment. 'Well, what about the house? You had a house, as I remember, just out of town somewhere. Your grandmother left it to you, didn't she? Is it empty?' She nodded. 'I'll rent it from you.'

She was reluctant, he could see that, but he had to press her. He needed somewhere to live, somewhere quiet, unobtrusive. He could have rented an apartment but he didn't want to do that unless he had to. 'All right,' she said, 'but you don't have to rent it. Mother's friends were there a week ago but they've gone.' She paused and looked at him. 'What is it this time?'

'I thought you didn't want to be involved?' She looked away. She didn't want to be involved. She didn't want to know anything and yet she had to satisfy her curiosity. He spared her, though, the trouble of asking again. 'It's heroin,' he said, quietly. 'A quantity came into the port the other day.'

She felt an enormous sense of relief flow through her and she laughed. 'You're too late, Frank. The police got it, didn't you know? Haven't you read?' He nodded, slowly. Of course he knew, what did she take him for? Would he have come all this way without knowing? She stared at him incredulously, taking in the look on his face, his steady eyes, the calm assurance with which he sat there. 'Are you serious?' she asked in a low voice. 'Rob the police?'

'It's a beautiful idea, Maggie,' he said, softly, 'I know it'll

28

work. I've thought it clear through from beginning to end. I've written the whole script.'

She didn't answer. He frightened her. He'd done so in the past which was why she had left him. When she had finally realised what he was she had been shattered. Then, as she got used to the idea – and he had brilliantly made her get used to it – it had seemed romantic in a way. He was not at all what she ever imagined such a man would be. And then, after all, she had loved him, been hopelessly in love with him.

He saw that she was concerned, concerned for him and that pleased him. He felt the urge to meet her a little. He said, 'You're right, they're getting too close, I've felt it for some time. That's why I've been thinking this one will be the last. Would that mean anything to you? Would it, Maggie?'

'I'd be glad for your sake.'

'That's not what I mean.' She looked away. She knew what he meant. 'Maggie, things would be different. There wouldn't be the strain anymore. We could start all over.'

She was looking for her bag and pulling the coat she had let fall on the seat up around her shoulders. He was losing her, he could see that. 'I have to go, I don't want to talk about it, now.'

'*Talk* to me!' It came out in a sudden, unexpectedly violent whisper and the hand that had moved to the edge of the table to shift it aside was gripped at the wrist so tight a pain shot through it. 'Talk to me,' he whispered, 'for Christ's sake!'

She stared down at his hand holding her wrist, refusing to look at him until he had let it go. He saw that he was hurting her and slowly relaxed his grip. She turned and stared at him. 'I'm getting married, Frank.'

'But if I gave it up?'

She shook her head. 'You wouldn't. You might try, but – you're too clever, Frank, you need the challenge.'

'No. No, I mean it. I've had enough.'

29

'Give it up now then?'

There was a pause. Then he shook his head. He sounded desperate. 'I can't. Not this one. This one I have to do, Maggie. I can't explain it but – it's beautiful.' She was silent. Then he said, 'Would you marry me if I did?'

She looked at him and shook her head. She would not make bargains, there was no profit in that. 'Give it up for your sake, Frank, not mine.'

'But *would* you?' She looked away. It wasn't only that. She knew it and he knew it. 'It's something else, isn't it? Tell me?'

It was hard to put into words. She wasn't sure of it herself, she never had been. But she had to try. Perhaps she should have tried before. It would have been more honest, but it was all so mixed up and different and he wouldn't have understood. But now she had to try, try to say it. 'There was a side of you I never knew at all. It frightened me. I can't explain it properly, but – it was like there were two of you, and one of you was a stranger. It wasn't like that in the beginning, but it got like that. I don't know why – and I began to blame myself and think it was my fault in some way, that I had made you like that, that somehow – this may sound silly – I'd forced you to find another side to present to me that wasn't you at all.' She paused, and shook her head. 'There were times when I simply didn't know who you were.'

There was a long pause. She had touched a naked nerve of truth and it was vibrating violently inside him. He had to wait for it to quieten before he could speak again. When he did, he said the only thing that mattered to him at that moment, the only thing in all this that seemed worth saying, in short, the simple truth of it all that appeared to him then as it had never appeared to him before. But he couldn't look at her when he said it. 'I need you, Maggie.'

He stared across the floor of the bar as if there were something of interest going on there but there was nothing he was interested in. It was only that he knew she was looking at him

30

and he could not, at that moment, bear her gaze upon him. It seemed to him a pressure on an open wound that was unbearable, as if her gaze, if he met it, would scorch him. He waited and waited for her reply but none came. Abruptly, he said, 'I have to make a phone call.' He rose quickly and crossed the room to the phone in the lobby outside.

He put a coin in the box and punched out the number. He heard the phone ringing at the other end. The ringing stopped as the receiver was picked up and a woman's voice said, 'Hello?' It was the voice that had answered before.

'Is Mr. Bellis there?'

'He's not back yet. He should be back any minute. Is that the person who called before? Hello? Would you like to leave a message? Hello? Hello?'

He hung up. He stood for a moment, thinking. There was no hurry. He would phone tomorrow. He left the lobby and went back into the bar. He crossed the floor towards his table and stopped, staring at it. A middle-aged couple were sitting at the table, deep in conversation. Maggie was not there. He looked around the room for her. Perhaps he had come back in by a different door? The bar was now crowded but Maggie was nowhere to be seen. He felt a tide of panic rise up in him and a choking sensation in his throat. He was disorientated. The room had suddenly taken on an air of unreality, as it might in a dream, familiar and yet unreal. He felt he had been abruptly transferred to another setting, as one does in a dream, for no reason and arising from no volition of his own. The noise in the bar seemed distant and though everyone was engaged in his own conversation he felt they were watching him covertly, as if there were something special about him, something that made him stand out in some way. He felt that he was the focus of attention and that although people were deliberately not looking at him they were, in fact, talking about him. He wanted to cry out, 'Why are you looking at me? Don't pretend that you aren't because I know that you are!

31

You have your eyes on each other but that is just a ruse, you're looking at *me*! Why? What have I done?' But nothing came out. His lips moved but no sound came out. He had to get out of this room. He knew that if he was to be safe he must leave. He turned – and blundered straight into a waiter crossing the bar with a tray. 'Are you looking for the lady, sir? She left. She asked me to say she'd call you tomorrow – about the house. Is that right, sir?'

He stared at the waiter and nodded. 'Yes, yes,' he said, 'that's right. I understand. Yes.'

Chapter Three

Chief Groczek sat in the main reception room of the City Hall behind a long table, flanked by officials of the administration. Normally, they would not have bothered to put in an appearance but the haul of heroin had been so large and the news of its seizure had created such a stir, not only in the city but throughout the country, that they were there to bask in some of the limelight and partake of the general euphoria. They presented to the gentlemen of the press a wall of solidity that would have given confidence to the citizens of any town. Looking along the table there were good citizens from commerce, industry and the unions, burghers and guildsmen who, in spirit at least, might have traced their ancestry back to the proud and respected towns of the middle ages.

Groczek, however, took no great satisfaction from this occasion. He had held too many press conferences since first he had taken over his post and was well aware that the press was more interested in having something to complain about than having something to celebrate. When the city was unclean they had clamoured for new brooms, and now that it *was* clean they complained that the brooms swept too energetically and made too much dust.

They had come, therefore, to the conference, if not to bury Groczek at least to damage his infernally robust good health. They would not be seen to flatter slavishly. They would give praise where praise was due, and where there were grounds for complaint they would point them out, and where they were hard to find they would spare no effort in looking for them.

One of those grounds for complaint was the matter of the warrant. Inevitably, they had discovered that it had expired the day before its use. Groczek was not entirely surprised that they had discovered it, though he was none the less irritated by it. Even in the most well run of police departments it seemed impossible to prevent leaks of this sort. Information was either sold or carelessly dropped. He was under no illusions. He knew he had policemen on his force still willing to supplement their incomes in this way, as well as policemen too foolish to know when to keep their mouths shut. That was inevitable. Neither was he greatly put out that the leak had occurred, though he made a mental note to discuss the whole question of leaks with Fallon once again. He knew that it had to emerge, eventually, that the warrant should not have been acted on, since the documents in the case would all have to be submitted and examined. What irritated him was that the incident should be used as the basis for another attack upon the probity of his force.

He resented these attacks. He took them for what they were, or seemed to him, as attacks upon himself. Such attacks made him bristle and at such moments he was inclined to make matters worse for himself by attacking the other side with too much vigour. That was a fault he had learned to live with. He was at times, he knew, impulsive, inclined to over-hasty action. He embarked on troubled waters too impatiently and without a sufficient supply of the necessary oil. Often he regretted it

33

but by then had rowed too far out and found himself left with nothing but brute strength to do battle with.

The man from the *Star* was on his feet and stabbing the air with his finger. 'You were in charge of this operation yourself! This is not another occasion, sir, when you can deplore the method while welcoming the result. You can't, in this case, ascribe the infringement to the incompetence of subordinates over whom you had no personal supervision. This is not another occasion when you can plead, like Napoleon after Trafalgar, the impossibility of being everywhere at once. You were there, yourself!'

He was a young man, with spectacles and a mop of red hair, clearly well educated. At least, he knew who Napoleon was and what he said after Trafalgar. He had probably been educated at the city's expense at one of the better universities, where he had acquired a taste for crusading in a world devoid of infidels. He had a knack for rhetoric that would doubtless lead him, in time, into city politics. Groczek took to this kind less than he took to the others, the kind that went straight from school to begin their journalistic careers by running errands and becoming the second strings of some established, older reporter. He, himself, had never been through university, though he considered himself no less literate than most of those who had. He had a faint contempt for most of them, bred, he admitted cheerfully to himself, out of envy. Had the opportunity presented itself to him to enter one of those institutions of higher learning, who knows what heights he might not have scaled?

'This conference,' Groczek said, when the young man had paused for breath, 'is a press conference, not a political rally. I'll take questions. Rhetoric you can keep for election year.'

'I've put a question,' the young man from the *Star* answered. 'We'd like an answer.'

'You'd better put it again then, because I've forgotten it. You speak so well,' he added with a smile, 'your listeners must

34

always be in danger of losing the thread while admiring the cloth.'

'Did you know the warrant was out of date when you acted on it?'

'Of course I knew. I'd be a damned poor police officer if I didn't.'

The city burghers beside him winced. Why, on earth, did he have to be so aggressive about his faults? Would it not have been better to admit he had erred? Feed the press something and they would go away appeased, but for heaven's sake give them something. They stared dismally in front of them as the *Star* man scored his inevitable point.

'Don't you think knowing about it, sir, makes you a damned sight poorer police officer?'

'No, I don't. I'd regard myself as poor indeed if I allowed the date on a scrap of paper to make me forget my duty to the citizens of this county.'

The young man smiled and put his thumb and forefinger over the frame of his glasses and pushed them firmly onto the bridge of his nose. His voice and his smile were sweetness itself. 'Do you regard a warrant that gives you the right of forcible entry as no more than a scrap of paper?'

'What else is it, if it's out of date?'

There was a burst of laughter among the journalists, some of whom thought the young man from the *Star* was pressing too hard on too little. The young man scowled. He removed his glasses and pointed them in the direction of the Chief of Police. 'It seems to me, Chief Groczek, that what you reveal at this conference and what you have revealed in the past is a growing contempt for the legal rights of the citizens of this county.'

Groczek rose to his feet and fixed the young man with a glittering eye. 'My concern,' he said, tightly, 'can be read in my record. I suggest you go back and look at the pages of the *Star* in any week you care to pick before I took office. You will

35

see how the facts of crime were making nonsense of the rights of the citizens of this county.' There were murmurs of assent from some of the journalists present. Groczek went on, 'However, I am not here to defend myself but to answer questions. I'd just like to say this, though,' he continued doggedly, as the man from the *Post* started to ask one, 'your police force has brought off a major coup that is the envy of police departments up and down the country. It was brought off by diligent police work and careful preparation . . .'

'Except in the case of the warrant!'

'Mistakes can be made. I'm not prepared to go into that again. Its significance will be settled in court. If my reputation suffers for it, that's my business and I'll take the consequences. It won't be the first time I've laid my reputation on the line in defence of law and order and I daresay it won't be the last. What has to be remembered is that a major drug ring has been broken and the extent of the haul and the efficiency of the operation will serve notice on any major syndicate that they enter this territory at the very gravest risk to themselves.'

There was some sporadic applause at the forthrightness of this statement. 'To what extent,' the man from the *Post* asked, 'would you regard the very establishment of this ring as significant? I mean, is it a foretaste of things to come? Is it your impression that the hoods are moving into the city on a large scale?'

'No, it's not my impression and I don't advise them to try.' Groczek smiled grimly round at them all. He was on safer ground now, more secure for everyone, and the city burghers breathed in deeply and visibly relaxed.

The young man from the *Star* replaced his glasses and returned to the fray. 'The whole country's losing control of the drugs situation. What gives you the right to think it can't happen here?'

'We are not losing control and will not lose control. I think I can promise you that.'

36

'How? How can you make such a promise? What grounds do you have? Don't you think such statements smack of complacency?'

Groczek rose once more to his feet. His patience was now expiring rapidly. He took a deep breath. 'I would ask you,' he responded, 'to compare the crime rate for every type of crime in this city with the figures for the country as a whole. You'll find they move in different directions. I'm not talking about one rate of increase that is lower than another. I'm talking about the total *arrest* of a rate of increase, a holding of it steady in the last two years, which is unprecedented anywhere in this country in this century! Well, that's been done here during my administration of the force and I am here to see that it continues. I believe it will. I repeat, we have not lost control. We have maintained control and will continue to maintain it.'

He stared round at them. In this mood, sombre, practical, reassuring, he was always at his best. 'But I have to warn you,' he went on, 'the struggle grows daily more difficult. The amount of cash invested in crime increases year by year. Cash commands resources. Everything then becomes a commodity that can be bought – labour, tools, information, the most sophisticated devices and, worst of all, the loyalty of otherwise trustworthy men in key positions and without whom much large-scale crime could not be committed. It will soon become commonplace for ruthless and enterprising men to invest two million dollars in the preparation and execution of a crime. As the rewards of decency daily diminish and the rewards of crime daily increase, it becomes harder and harder for men possessing key information in banks, in offices, in industry, at airports and so on to resist the temptations of large untaxed rewards. To counter this, the police department itself needs more money, more resources. But it needs something else, too. It needs the unqualified support of the people of this community and not the constant carping criticism of everything it does.'

'A free hand, in other words?'

'I'm not asking for a free hand,' Groczek replied with a touch of exasperation, 'but I am asking for some realism on the part of those who expect us to work efficiently with our hands and feet tied.'

'Are you asking for more police powers?'

'No, we've got enough. What I am asking for is the same consideration for the problems of the police that is so readily conferred on those apprehended in the commission of crimes. Every year the state legislation, spurred on by the press and by law reform societies, produce new laws circumscribing the powers of the police to operate efficiently. The rights of men of doubtful character, found in situations implying clear criminal intent, are constantly looked at with a view to making their conviction more and more unlikely.'

'They're not criminals until they've been convicted, sir,' the young man from the *Star* pointed out with exaggerated politeness. 'This is not a police state – yet.'

'Neither is it going to be a state run by criminals and crime syndicates, as some are.' Groczek glowered at the young man who remained unabashed and continued to make his notes as soon as he had made his point. 'We need a higher conviction rate,' Groczek went on. 'The rate of detection and apprehension is good, but we need a higher conviction rate, and you won't get it unless certain sections of the public stop hampering the police and pampering the criminal.'

The worthy men beside Groczek groaned again. He'd been doing well until then, why did he have to spoil it? The headlines were already writing themselves – 'PUBLIC MUST STOP PAMPERING THE CRIMINAL, says Police Chief.' Why, when he had been in such fine voice must he hit such a sour note? Had he no ear?

Stover, the young man from the District Attorney's office, rose to his feet, smooth and careful in his grey flannel suit. He fastened the top button and switched instantly, like a good

38

translator, into the language he had learned for occasions such as these. 'Chief Groczek is right,' he said. 'I'm sure most of you will agree that it is somewhat irresponsible for the press to talk about police states. Of course there is no intention, here, of trampling on any rights. Due process of law will always be observed. That is paramount. What Chief Groczek meant was no more than this, that it is sometimes possible, and with absolutely the right intentions, in our pursuit of the ideal – and God knows, we could do with some more idealism in this world – in the pursuit of an ideal to go too far in one direction, producing an imbalance between the rights of the public and the rights of the criminal.'

There was a general murmur of satisfied assent in which Groczek joined in. 'Exactly,' he said, 'a proper balance is everything, in nature and society. And now, gentlemen, if there are no more questions – we are all busy men.'

The conference broke up. The men from the press drifted out. Groczek turned to Stover and gave him a brief nod in acknowledgement of his contribution. Stover shrugged, 'What the hell do they want?'

'They want causes,' Groczek said. 'If crime is too successful, campaigns against crime. If the police are too successful, campaigns against the police. They're there to make sure the pendulum never stops swinging. What about the trial?'

'We're going through the evidence now. It shouldn't take long.'

'Any problems?'

Stover shook his head. 'You'll get your knuckles rapped over the warrant, but we'll get convictions. You can leave it all to us now.'

'Well, that's that,' Groczek said, satisfied. He picked up his papers and together they walked out of the hall.

'I've got to hand it to you,' Stover said as they walked out to the street, 'it was one hell of a haul. That's a lot of heroin.'

Groczek nodded and paused on the sidewalk outside. 'What

are you going to do with it?' he asked. 'After the trial, I mean?'

'Destroy it. Isn't that what we always do?'

'Is there a law that says we must?'

Stover thought for a moment. 'There's got to be, somewhere, I suppose. Anyway, the Federal Government will be involved, it being narcotics. Why?'

Groczek thought for a moment. 'There's 220 pounds of pure heroin lying in the vaults. The taxpayer spends millions on research into the problems of addiction and pumping dope into registered addicts on maintenance. Why shouldn't the public reap some of the benefits?'

'How?'

'Let Health and Welfare make use of the stuff. It makes sense, doesn't it? We could send the stuff to the labs in Boston for processing. It'll make a contribution to the cost of the operation, at least.'

Stover thought for a moment. 'Let me look into it,' he said, opening the car door. 'I'll call you.' He got into his car and drove off.

Groczek drove back to his office. By the time he reached it he had put the whole heroin haul out of his mind along with the press conference. The operation had provided, for him, a welcome interlude from the obligations of administrative work which was now his chief preoccupation. He had seen from the beginning that the solution to the city's problems lay there and he had applied himself to that end with vigour and resolve. In the early days he had worked sixteen hours a day at it. Lately, the pressure had relaxed and an element of restlessness had crept into him.

He had been used to great activity all his life and now there were even times when he stood at the window of his office and gazed out on the city below, waiting for the phone to ring or for Fallon to come in with some new problem that had arisen. He recognised that this feeling of descent, slow and lazy as it was, had been the real motive for his personal involvement in the heroin operation recently concluded. He had felt an urge to make a comeback, to step into the ring again, to show those who had stepped into his shoes how unfit they were to wear them – by comparison, of course.

How often could he do that? Not often, not without antagonising the people whose function he was usurping. But he missed the challenge. He admitted that to no one, not even his wife, though she privately sensed it. He recognised that this was partly the cause of his tendency to provoke the press and other organisations of self-righteous citizens. It was a feeling, when he thought about it, not too far distant from those brash kids he had seen swaggering along a crowded sidewalk and bumping the shoulders of unsuspecting shoppers as they passed. He understood them. They had nothing worthy to engage them, to test them or their manhood. They were bored out of their minds. They were not looking for a fight but if one came their spirits would leap, they knew not why. He understood them, but to understand was not, for Groczek, to pardon. His police had strict instructions to pick them up and charge them with a breach of the peace. Their protestations fell on deaf ears.

He looked through his diary and found little there of interest for the week. Fallon came in to remind him that he was due at the Police Academy after lunch to give his usual introductory lecture to new recruits about to embark on training, though he had already seen it in the diary. 'I'll come along, if you don't mind,' Fallon said.

'You've heard it all before.'

'Well, it's never the same two years running. Besides, I enjoy it.' He grinned. He genuinely did; Groczek could see he wasn't flattering. 'What's it to be about this year?'

'I don't know. I'll think of something. Let's have some lunch and then go.'

On the way out to the Academy, Groczek discussed the question of leaks. 'Nothing ever happens in this department on

41

a Monday that isn't known outside on Tuesday. There's too much information being sold, either to the press or to crooks.'

'Won't it always be the same, till the copper earns a decent wage?'

Groczek shook his head. 'No. That's the usual beef. I don't go for it. No matter what they get paid, some guys are going to want to make a little more. The fact is, the cop is often out of the same mould as the crook. We'd never admit it to ourselves but it's true.' He thought for a moment. ' And maybe I might just say something about that this afternoon. *Jesus Christ* !'

The car made a sudden swerve, throwing Groczek violently across the car against Fallon. At the same time, there was a squeal of brakes and a harsh rending sound as the car collided with something. 'Jesus Christ,' said Groczek again, 'what the hell . . .?' He pulled himself off Fallon, flung the car door open and got out. The front wing of the police car was badly dented. The front wing of the blue Ferrari that had struck was less so.

Scott, Groczek's driver, came hurrying round, white-faced. 'I'm sorry, sir, I didn't see him until it was too late!'

Groczek pushed past him furiously and stepped over to the blue Ferrari. 'What the hell do you think you're doing?' he shouted. 'Is that the way to come round a corner? *You* !' He rapped on the window. He could see the driver sitting at the wheel, staring fixedly in front of him. He made no effort to wind down the window. Groczek rapped on the window again. 'You! You in there! Wind this window down! Do you hear me?'

Slowly, the window slid down. 'What are you, some kind of nut,' Groczek snarled, 'don't you know how to turn into a street? What kind of driving do you call that?'

The man turned and looked at him. He seemed to take all the time in the world to do so. When the face had finally turned a full quarter circle, Groczek found himself staring into a pair of piercing blue eyes. There was something disconcerting about them. They had the odd and unaccountable effect of calming Groczek down. The thrust of his anger seemed to falter, its direction became uncertain. The eyes that held his seemed to lock them together for a moment and the accident was temporarily put out of his mind.

There was a long pause. Then the man said, 'I'm sorry. There was a van parked on the corner. I couldn't see.' The remark elicited no response from Groczek. He was still staring into the face. Rivulets of sweat had started to run down it, though the man seemed unaware of it.

The girl sitting on the seat next to him leaned across and said to Groczek, 'It was very difficult to see. The van shouldn't be there. We waited quite a while before entering.'

Groczek's eyes moved from the man to the girl and then back again. He had suddenly lost all interest in the accident. Abruptly, he turned to Scott and said, 'Get the details,' and walked back to his car.

He opened the door of his car and got back in, sinking down into the seat beside Fallon. Fallon looked amused. He laughed softly and shook his head. 'Of all the cars in this city he had to pick yours. Poor bastard! You've just got to feel sorry for a guy who runs into a police car.'

Groczek said nothing. He sat in the seat staring out of the side window at the blue Ferrari. Scott was scribbling in his notebook. The man was staring directly in front of him with an almost monumental patience waiting for the procedure to be gone through. Groczek said, 'I know that man.'

Fallon looked past Groczek to the man in the seat of the blue Ferrari. 'Who is it?' he asked.

'I don't know, but I've seen the face somewhere.'

'Where?'

'I don't know.'

Groczek turned once again and stared out of the window. Scott was writing away, asking questions. The man made some

43

reply, then turned, slowly, and looked across the intervening space between the cars at Groczek. Once again their eyes locked together like the horns of two fighting stags. It was Groczek who turned away. He felt an unaccountable shiver pass through him. He recognised it as a moment of fear. It was quite irrational. He couldn't explain it yet he was in no doubt that he had felt it.

Scott closed his notebook and got back into the car. 'Sorry about that, sir,' he said, apologising again.

'Who was that in the car?'

'A Mr. Frank Slovak, sir.'

Slovak? Slovak? The name bounced across the circuits of Groczek's brain, knocking on a thousand doors in an effort to open one. He nodded. 'Slovak. Of course. I remember now. I saw his photo in a file in New York. What address did he give?'

Scott consulted his notebook. 'He's staying at the Latham, sir.'

Groczek nodded. 'All right,' he said, 'drive on.'

Scott started the engine again and the car pulled away. Fallon looked at Groczek. 'Who's Slovak?'

Groczek was silent for a moment. 'Do you remember the gold bullion heist at Kennedy some years ago?' Fallon nodded. 'They reckon that was him. And the safe deposits at the Bank of America in Chicago a couple of years later?'

Fallon pursed his lips and whistled. 'Him, too?'

'And maybe half a dozen more over the last ten years.'

Fallon looked impressed. The bullion robbery had been so perfectly planned and so daringly carried out it had tickled the public's imagination and even the police had admired it. 'How did you come to see the file?' Fallon asked.

'Rosetti showed it to me in New York. They're building files on a number of people – maybe six in the whole country. He's one of them – men who plan and organise crime but are never involved in it directly. Rosetti calls him "an engineer".

44

He gets brilliant ideas, researches them, writes a script on it and sells it on the open market.'

'Never does the job himself?'

'Not that they know. Of course, it doesn't rule out the possibility, but usually he takes a fee for the script and a very large cut of the take.'

'I see,' said Fallon, and was silent for a moment. Then he said, 'I wonder what he's doing down here.'

'Exactly,' Groczek replied, pulling at his lip, 'that's exactly what I'm wondering.'

They sat in the car in silence for a while as it sped on towards the Academy. Groczek felt troubled. He felt the man spelled trouble for him and for the city but chiefly for him in an odd way. He felt he was being involved in a personal way. He could not explain that, but he felt it strongly. 'He's down here for something,' he said finally, 'I can tell you that.'

'Perhaps he just came down to see the girl that was with him in the car?'

'No.' Groczek shook his head. 'He's down here to do a job. I can feel it in my copper's bones. I don't know what it is, but that's why he's here.'

He leaned forward and tapped Scott on the shoulder. 'Give me the mike,' he said. Scott handed him the mike. Groczek pressed the switch and spoke into it. 'This is Chief Groczek. There's a man staying at the Latham – middle forties, fair hair, large build. His name is Slovak, Frank Slovak. I want him watched. I want to know all his movements, how he comes, how he goes. Put Schuster onto it. Tell him not to make himself obvious but if he's spotted not to worry. I don't mind if he knows we know he's here.'

He handed the mike back to Scott and leaned back again in his seat. 'He's down here for something,' he repeated, 'but what?'

'It could be anything,' Fallon mused. 'There are enough banks and payrolls in the city to make it worth anybody's while – that is, if they want to take us on.' He grinned at Groczek. He shared his chief's satisfaction in the reputation they had built for themselves.

Groczek nodded, thoughtfully. 'There may be something of that in it, too.''

'Something of what?'

Groczek pulled at his lower lip even harder. He had a notion, yet it was hard to put into words or, rather, to speak those words. Finally, he said, ' "He's the best there is," Rosetti said to me, "they simply don't come any better." And the best has always got to beat the best, nothing less will do. And do you know what I think? I think he's heard of me. I think he wants to prove himself and that's also why he's here.'

Fallon looked sideways at him. 'That's a bit fanciful, isn't it?'

'Is it?' Groczek thought for a moment. 'Maybe. We'll see. But if he's looking for a contest, he's got one. He may be the best there is to Rosetti, but to me he's just scum like the rest.'

Chapter Four

Slovak sat in the car with the sweat pouring down his face and hearing, from what seemed a long way off, Maggie's voice calling to him. It was not that he had been stunned by the collision. What he felt had to do with the face that had thrust itself at him on the other side of the glass.

He had recognised the face at once. It was unmistakable. He had seen it staring at him out of the front page of the newspaper in Maggie's apartment. It was Groczek and, when he thought about it, it seemed like the hand of destiny reaching out, that of all the cars he should accidentally come into collision with it should have been Groczek's and no one else's.

46

That was strange, but it was not the strangest thing about it. What had upset him, what had momentarily unnerved him, was the flash of intuition that this man, of all men, represented, for him, an enormous threat.

This threat had nothing to do with the operation he had come to this city to perform. There was no way that Groczek could know that, for no one, apart from himself and Maggie, were, as yet, party to that information. Further, there was no reason why a police chief, as eminent and as preoccupied as Groczek undoubtedly was, should find himself directly involved with a robbery and the actions that would subsequently and inevitably be taken by the police.

No, it was not that. It had, if anything, more to do with the question of whether Groczek had recognised *him*. That, in itself, seemed unlikely, though it was not beyond the bounds of possibility. He had been aware of a growing police interest in him over the last few years. He had been conscious of being followed at odd times and of cameras being clicked in unlikely places and he had, once, pointed this out to Maggie. Not that it had ever worried him. He had always conducted himself in such a way as to put himself well beyond their reach, but that they were 'building a picture' of him, as Maggie had put it, he was not in doubt, and Groczek might have encountered that picture at some time. If that were so, he would certainly be wondering, at this very moment, what he was doing in this city or, more to the point, what he intended to do.

And yet, as he sat there, rigidly, the sweat pouring down his face and running like open head wounds into his eyes, he knew, as clearly as he had ever known anything, that *that* recognition and its possible consequences were not the source of the disturbance going on inside him. It was something else, something that had to do with the premonition that had instantly flowed into him at the moment of the collision, that the face he would see when he wound down the window would be Groczek's. He could not understand why he should have

47

known that. It was as if the collision had bumped his brain onto a new level of intuition, jerked him, literally, to the highest peak from where he had a thrillingly new view of himself and his life that would have been impossible before. And with it he saw, as though looking out from that peak across the whole world to the very horizon of his life and beyond, all the dangers that lay ahead of him. For the first time in his life his nerve had failed.

He looked across the space that separated the two cars and stared straight into Groczek's eyes. And just as he had felt revived by the warmth of Maggie's gaze in the apartment the day before, and reassured, so he felt Groczek's scrutiny wither something momentarily inside him, as if that gaze were announcing the very opposite of the thing that her gaze had confirmed, were challenging it, in effect, so that he felt a warring of two opposite forces contending inside him, the one pledged to his survival and the other to his total destruction.

He had met that gaze of Groczek's and conceded victory to it. He had recognised in it, in one collapsing moment of weakness, his match. It was as if his own gaze had separated at last, finally and irrevocably, from himself and was staring now, across that intervening space at him. The gaze and the object of the gaze were no longer one. There was no sympathy, therefore, in the gaze, no humorous irony any more, born of old affection and intimacy. The scrutiny was no longer directed at his inward self but at his whole being. It no longer protected him by being aware of the existence of his inner self, but threatened him, in some way. It was, without doubt, this sudden and total separation that unnerved him and made him see, instantly, the danger.

He felt his shoulder being pushed and pulled and he heard Maggie's voice penetrating through the cloud of thoughts that swirled about in his brain and he nodded and said, 'Yes, yes, I'm all right, I'm all right.'

'What is it, Frank?'

'Nothing, nothing.' He took a handkerchief out and wiped his face, turning and smiling at her at the same time. 'I'm O.K. Really. I felt dizzy for a moment, that's all. Must be some bug I picked up.' He opened the car door and got out. He went round to the front of the car and looked at the damage. It was relatively small. He got back in the car and shook his head. 'It's nothing to worry about. I'll get it fixed.' He started the car again, gave her a quick smile and drove off.

The city thinned out as they drove towards the outskirts, the clean white roads and buildings giving way to open country. 'How far is it?' he asked.

'It's about ten miles out of town,' Maggie replied, 'I think you'll like it.'

'Why don't you live there?'

'It's too quiet for me, too lonely. When grandmother was alive, I was there a lot – as a child. I loved the house. That's why she left it to me, I guess. But it really needs a family. Maybe one day I'll go back there.'

'With your doctor?'

She nodded. 'Perhaps. It would be convenient for Phillip.'

He said nothing. He could not come to terms with this new idea of her being married, married to someone else, that is. She had loved him, once. A woman doesn't change. She had broken away from the rich, upper-crust background of her family and come up from the city to a world that presented itself in many more colours than were to be found at home. She had been wilder then. She had plunged into that neon-lit world with all the recklessness of her nature, with all the enthusiasm, as he once said to her, of a suicide reaching a river bank. He had found her and led her gently out of it. He had shown her how to drink without draining the glass. She had surrendered utterly to him. She had never been so happy and neither had he. How had he let her slip through his fingers? Why, when she had left, had he not gone straight after her?

The house appeared at the top of the hill, growing amid the

trees. It was not large and had been built on two stories with old timbers among the brick giving it a colonial style that once might have been pretentious but now, weathered with the years, might have passed for much older than it was.

He turned into the drive and halted the car. They got out. 'Well,' Maggie said, slamming the car door, 'this is it.' He stared round. Rolling green fields surrounded the house. A horse was grazing some way off. Birds rose from neat white fences at the sound of the car doors to settle higher on trees. Nearby was a barn with its door swinging on its hinge. 'Come on in,' Maggie said, putting her key in the lock. He turned and followed her.

They entered the hall. A fine staircase led to the rooms upstairs. Off the hall ran the living room, large and comfortable and running the length of the house. Off it, and what could have been a later addition, was the kitchen. The silence was impressive. He felt instantly at home.

He walked over to the window and stared out onto the country beyond. 'You never told me it was like this,' he said.

'I told you,' Maggie answered, 'but you never listened.'

He nodded. It was true. She had told him many times about her house, the one her grandmother had left her, but he had not listened properly. But then, at that time, such a house or the description of such a house would have meant little to him. He had no mind to retreat from the world, not even in the periods of his inactivity. 'Well, you were right,' he said, 'we should have come down here sometimes, instead of chasing around the world.' He looked at her and smiled. 'Why did we do that? I guess I must have thought it would amuse you.'

'Well, it did. I'm not complaining.'

'Did for a while?' She nodded and then shrugged. He understood she was not blaming him but he had failed to see that there had come a time when she was moving into a new phase. Perhaps that had been his mistake, in not sensing it. 'Who's going to look after me?' he asked.

50

'I'll find you some staff.'

'No, thanks,' he answered, drily, 'no strangers.'

'The house is yours, Frank,' she said, quietly, 'I don't go with it.'

He nodded. He wouldn't press her yet. He turned and looked out of the window again. 'It's just fine,' he said, 'it'll suit me. I feel as if I've – come home.' And he did. How curiously calming that feeling was. He felt safe here, that nothing would harm him. He could work here, make his plans and carry them through. The thought of it lifted up his spirits and he nodded again and said, 'Yes, I'll be fine here.'

He turned and smiled at her. 'How's your mother?' she asked him.

He nodded. 'O.K.'

'Still living in Brooklyn?'

'Where else?'

'Have you seen her lately?'

'Yes, I saw her. About six months ago.'

'Did you quarrel?'

'No. We don't quarrel any more. I gave that up. How can you quarrel with someone who doesn't understand what you're talking about?' He shrugged. 'She cooked me sauerkraut and meatballs and after dinner brought out all my old school reports.'

Maggie smiled. 'She showed them all to me once.'

He nodded. 'She brings them out every time I go there, all tied up like a bundle of old love letters.'

'Well, I can understand that, can't you?'

He didn't answer at once, but turned away again. He felt that old wound nagging at him once more. 'I could buy the street she lives in,' he said, finally, 'but she still prefers three rooms and a kitchen over a delicatessen.'

His voice had an edge of bitterness in it she had heard before when he spoke of his mother. 'She's happy there,' Maggie said, 'she knows everyone.'

51

'I guess so.' He was silent for a moment, and then he said, more to himself than to her, 'I don't know what she ever got out of life to make her so high-minded.'

'Do you think she knows?' Maggie asked, hesitantly.

'What about?'

'Well, about you?'

He stared at her a while and then grinned. 'You mean what I do for a living?' She nodded. 'Well, you can come out and say it, Maggie, it doesn't bother me, you know, provided there's no one in earshot.'

'I don't want to say it.'

She looked uncomfortable. He wanted to take her up in his arms and tell her everything would be all right. 'Funny how that upsets you,' he said. He smiled at her and she looked away. 'You know what the old song says, Maggie? "Some men'll rob you with a six-gun and some with a fountain pen." It's never seemed to me to make much difference which way you get rich. Everybody's robbing somebody."

'*Does* she know?'

'Who knows what she knows? She knows something, I guess. Mothers know their sons. She's never talked about it but, well, yes, maybe she knows something.'

'I liked her.'

'She liked you. You were the only woman I ever took to see her. "Whatever happened to that nice girl you brought here once?" she said to me. I said I didn't know but I'd ask you. Whatever happened to you, Maggie?'

She stared at him. He was smiling but he was serious. She looked away again. She was annoyed with herself at the way her heart had begun to pound. 'Well, that's the house,' she said.

'You haven't shown me the bedrooms.'

'They're upstairs.'

He laughed out loud, the reply came so flat and so final. 'Don't you trust me?'

'Not within sight of a spring mattress,' she answered. 'You can look the bedrooms over when I'm not here. You can drive me back now.'

'What's the hurry?'

'I've got things to do. It's good to see you, Frank, but I can't spend all day . . .'

'Are you afraid?'

The question jolted her. Yes, she was afraid and it annoyed her. She was afraid to stay here too long, afraid of him, and what his effect might be on her. She loathed herself for this cowardice, hated the sudden pulse in her throat when she looked at him and the stab inside her womb. She thought she had done with all that, left it all back there. She had never wanted to feel all that over again. She couldn't trust it. It meant nothing, nothing she could rely on.

'Oh, Maggie,' he said, 'if you're afraid, that should tell you something.'

She saw him coming towards her, smiling, and she panicked. 'Tell me something,' she said, 'do you know Groczek?'

The question stopped him dead for a moment. 'Groczek? No, why?'

'You looked as if you did. I wondered if you'd met somewhere before?'

'No,' he replied, and grinned. 'I just know his type.'

'He's a big man down here. He's cleaned this county up. It's his pride and joy.'

'He won't bother me.'

'He's no ordinary man, Frank, believe me. He'll never let you get away with what you're planning.'

He was standing quite close to her now. 'Maggie . . .' His hand came up to her neck and caressed the lobe of her ear. His voice was gentle, she had forgotten how gentle it could be. 'Maggie – what is Groczek to me or I to him, for that matter? He's a cop. He'll do what he has to do and I'll do what I have to. It's no more than that.'

53

As he said it, he had a sense of someone walking on his grave and the echo of a laugh he could not hear but felt, like a cold wind, blow over him. But her beautiful porcelain face looking up at him with wide eyes was filling his mind now, taking possession of him, and the yearning that was in him to merge himself in her was overwhelming. Overwhelming, it was, for her, too. His desire for her was like a sea she had been swimming in and doing battle with, and now she felt an immense longing to give herself up to it, to let it have her, if having her was what it so desperately wanted. But one last flame of survival licked up through her and she pushed him violently away from her and backed up against the wall. 'No,' she cried, 'no, NO!'

They stared at one another, measuring, for a moment, the strength of will in each. She shook her head slowly at him. 'I'm getting married, Frank, I told you.'

He nodded. He was pressing too hard he could see. 'You're right,' he said, 'come on. I'll drive you home, then pick up my things from the hotel.'

He held out his hand to her. It was a friendly gesture. She looked at it a little uncertainly, at first, and then took it. He smiled at her. The first touch of her hand after so long an interval, the cool flesh against his own sent a small shiver through him. And it sent a shiver through her too. He saw it happen, the quick intake of breath, the eyes that suddenly became liquid. To a certain extent he had gambled on it, tricked her, momentarily, into dropping her guard. But he had no qualms about it. He led her out of the room and into the hall.

He paused at the foot of the stairs that led to the upper rooms. Her own momentum was to the front door but he hung back and she felt the pull of his hand as he stopped and his unspoken wish to go the other way. She turned and looked at him. He saw that the battle was over. He stood there, waiting for her, knowing it was now only a moment before she would

54

give herself up entirely and come of her own free will. He moved towards her and stood quite close. She stared down at her hand entwined in his. She couldn't bring herself to look him in the face. There was a certain shame in her total loss of will but there was nothing she could do about it. She leaned her head wearily on his chest. He stroked her hair and kissed her lightly on the lips and then, together, they walked on up the stairs.

For a while they lay together, side by side in the bed, not speaking, and scarcely moving. Their bodies had no need of haste. It was, rather, for them like a home-coming after a long journey, where the sight of the hearth exerts a greater pull than the sight of food and where the appetite must wait on peace and recovery and rest. At least it was for him. For her it was, perhaps, not quite that. Having finally given up and allowed herself to be swept away, she was ready for him at once but took a greater, perverse pleasure in denying herself while waiting for him. When, finally, he reached out for her and into her, the earth didn't shake as it once did but seemed, more, to receive them both into its bosom.

She fell asleep afterwards, and lay with her face on his chest and his arm around her shoulders. He did not sleep. His mind turned almost at once to the plan he had. To bring it off would require all his ingenuity and strength of mind. The thought excited him and he smiled to himself. If he had suffered lately a loss of confidence, this would certainly restore it. Nothing would stop him, not even Groczek. It was odd how the man's face floated into his mind at that moment, as if triggered off by the thought that he must not fail. Why did that happen? Why was that face associated with the thought of failure? Who was Groczek to assume suddenly such importance in his life. When had he, of all people, needed to take account of the actions of a cop? He couldn't understand that, nor why the face persisted in floating in front of him. Perhaps it was the effect of the collision? Perhaps the face had been 'bumped' into his brain. He had that sense of it. There had been the bump and then the face and somehow the two went together; that was why the face had made a much stronger impression on him than it might otherwise have done. Yes, that was it. It was a trick of the mind, an association of two effects, one seen and one felt, and they were indissolubly bound together. He must wipe it from his mind once and for all, and as if to do so, he passed his hand across his own face, touching his brow with his finger tips. He saw, then, that his hand was trembling but he couldn't trace the thought or the fear that had started it.

He eased his arm out from under her, gently, not wishing to disturb her sleep. He got out of bed and put on his trousers and shirt. He went downstairs to the living room, picked up the phone and dialled a number. It was the number he had called before, once in Maggie's apartment and once in the hotel. He heard it ringing at the other end.

The phone was picked up and a man's voice answered, 'Hello?'

'Mr. Bellis?' he asked.

'Who's that?'

'Frank Slovak.'

There was a pause at the other end. Then he heard the voice saying to someone else who was in the room with him, 'Go out and close the door.' He heard a door close in the background and then the voice returned to the phone. It sounded unctuous, eager to please. 'Frank! It's good to hear you. It's been a long time. Where are you? Where are you calling from?'

'I'm in town.'

'Jesus, it's good to hear you. Can I do something for you? Is that why you called?'

'I need some information. Inside information."

'I see.' There was a slight pause. 'Inside inside?'

He smiled slightly. 'Yes, inside inside. Can you lay it on?'

56

'Sure, Frank, sure. Give me twenty-four hours. Where can I reach you?'

'I'll call you. Goodbye.' He hung up. He stood for a moment thinking. He'd made a start. It felt good. He turned to go back up to the room when his eye caught the mirror above the phone and he saw, reflected in it, the whole room behind him and the door into the hall but he, himself, was absent. It was the oddest of sensations. He stared at the glass, examining it, looking into every corner of the room reflected in it and then, as if by a trick of photography, he was there again, staring at himself. He must have imagined it, but it had given him a shock. It was as though, for a moment, he had ceased to exist. He laughed. Now that really would be something, to disappear. But not yet.

He walked back upstairs to the bedroom. Maggie was sitting on the bed putting on her stockings. She had on her skirt but no top. When he entered the room she didn't look at him but went on dressing. He could see from her face that something had happened while he had been downstairs. 'I – had a call to make,' he said, by way of apology and of saying, at least, something.

She nodded, but the nod dismissed the remark as an irrelevance rather than acknowledged it. Her situation was clear to him at once. She had woken up and confronted the image of herself lying naked in the bed and hadn't liked what she had seen or what it made of her. He could see, too, that she had no intention of discussing it with him. She had, in fact, removed herself from him as effectively as if she were in the next room.

He came and sat down on the edge of the bed beside her. She got up, moving away from him and went to stand in the mirror while she put the finishing touches to herself. Finally, she said to him, 'You're a real, hard habit to break, aren't you?' He didn't answer. She finished brushing her hair and put the brush down on the dressing table. She turned and

57

looked at him, for the first time. 'Don't get any ideas, Frank,' she said, 'as far as I'm concerned, that was just the hair of the dog that bit me.' She picked up her bag and walked out of the room. From the bedroom window overlooking the drive he saw her get into the blue Ferrari and sit there, waiting for him to drive her home.

He finished dressing, came out of the house and locked it. He got into the car beside her and started the engine. He glanced at her once but she refused to look at him. He drove the car back into town.

He dropped her outside her apartment block and she said to him, 'There's no need for us to meet again, Frank. I'd rather you didn't call me.'

'Why?'

'You know why. I'm getting married, I told you. Don't spoil it.'

'I won't spoil it,' he said, 'if that's what you really want, I promise you, Maggie, I won't spoil it. Only, I may need to call you now and then.' He trailed off, looking slightly embarrassed, as if he would like to say more but felt he couldn't or perhaps didn't quite know how. 'All the same, if I call you,' he went on, not looking at her, 'don't not answer.' He laughed. 'Jesus, Maggie, I'd do the same for you.'

There was a touch of desperation in his face and in his smile that puzzled her. 'Well,' she said, nodding, 'so long as we understand each other. Goodbye, Frank.' He waved a hand at her, put his foot down and drove off.

He drove back to the Latham. He asked the clerk at the desk to prepare his bill and went up to his room. He packed the one and only bag he had brought with him and went down again. He paid his bill at the desk and went out to his car.

He drove through the city and the suburbs, passing the spot where earlier he had had the collision with the police car. The mood that that had induced in him was quite gone. He felt only the excitement of the plan that was unfolding more and more clearly in his head.

He had picked up the red Plymouth in his driving mirror some way back. He couldn't decide why he had noted it or how long it had been behind him. A picture kept floating into his mind that related the car to the hotel and he wondered if he had subconsciously noticed it as he had left. Perhaps it had been waiting outside. He couldn't be sure. He knew how the mind could play tricks in this respect. He was too old a hand to worry about every car behind him that happened to be going in the same direction as he was. On the other hand, his mind had an extra fine tuning in these matters. Perhaps it was, perhaps it was not following him.

He left the city behind and drove out onto the open road. He switched on the radio and for a while listened to the music. When it ended he listened to the local news. The leading item was a report on the news conference held by Groczek earlier in the day. He listened attentively. It told him nothing new, but he smiled at the report of the widespread criticism some of Groczek's remarks had aroused. It would be as nothing to the furore that would be aroused shortly when he had accomplished what he had come here to do.

He drove off the road and up the drive towards the house again. He halted the car and got out. As he did so, he noticed the red Plymouth pass on the road below him and disappear round the bend. He had forgotten about it on the drive out, his mind having been preoccupied with the music. Of course, it could be nothing more than a car going in the same direction and, on the face of it, this seemed the most likely explanation. On the other hand, Groczek might already have put someone on his tail. He didn't know. It would depend upon whether Groczek had recognised him or not. Either way it was of little importance to him. They may watch him, that was their privilege, but they would not stop him.

59

He took his case from the boot of the car and went into the house. Its aspect pleased him as much as it had done when he had been in it earlier with Maggie. It seemed utterly familiar to him. He sat down in a chair opposite the window and his mind, with what seemed a growing and surprising predictability, turned to Groczek.

Groczek reached out his hand and took the glass of water on the table, sipped it, and put it back. He looked round at the twenty or so eager, youthful faces before him, hanging on his every word. They had all come there expecting to be told in the course of an hour all there was to know about becoming the perfect cop. They had, of course, been disappointed. He had not treated them to a string of anecdotes carefully culled from a lifetime's experience and as carefully distilled into the essence of police wisdom. Instead, he had offered them a glimpse into a future in which they might, if they chose, enlarge their minds as well as their feet. Groczek did not believe in the cop who threw away his mind when he joined the force.

'Never let it be said,' he had remarked earlier, 'that the policeman is a man who never reads a book,' and had gone on to dazzle them with an array of titles of books they might profitably read. He, himself, he had told them, 'was not exactly a literary man,' but his life had been much improved by the cultivation of books. This had led him into a discussion of the role of crime in literature from Edgar Allan Poe to the later offerings of Raymond Chandler and Micky Spillane. He seldom, in this respect, went beyond the books of his youth. His tone was good humoured, bantering, drawing considerable laughter at strategic intervals. As he warmed to his subject, he found himself drawing more and more fascinating comparisons between the policeman and the criminal. And, the more he spoke, the more he found himself confronting the image of Slovak in his mind.

Fallon, sitting on the side, listened with fascination and

60

some envy to his chief who could talk, for so practical and efficient a man, with all the enthusiasm of the amateur criminologist. Of course, it was all quite useless, as far as the recruits were concerned, pitched way over their heads, but there was no doubt it impressed them and even more than that gave them, for the moment, an extremely good opinion of themselves, which could not be a bad thing. But Fallon's chief impression, on such occasions, was always that Groczek was really using the occasion to work out some problem of his own, that his discourse was actually with himself.

Today he was not far wrong. When the face of Slovak had entered Groczek's mind, taking possession of it, as it were, the whole drift of his talk had taken on a new direction, a direction he had begun to explore in terms of the concept of the 'super-criminal', or, as he qualified it instantly, the man who believed himself to be one. 'Do such men really exist,' he had asked, 'outside the realms of fiction? Men who recognise none of the laws that govern mankind but continually operate above them, as if for them they did not exist? To what extent, for instance, was the mind of a Napoleon or a Hitler, the mind of a super-criminal given, for the moment, public approval instead of public condemnation?' It was, he considered, a fascinating thought, bringing him, quite logically, to Raskolnikov in *Crime and Punishment*. 'Another book I recommend.'

He had paused, then, to take his sip of water and stare round at his class. Clearly none of them had read the book and only a few had ever heard of it. 'A Russian student,' he went on, 'kills an old woman, apparently for her jewellery, but really because the idea fascinates him, the idea of the superman, the man whom nature has endowed with the right to "get away with it", a man not accountable to the ordinary laws that restrict and bind the rest of us. "I didn't kill her," he says, "for the money. I killed her because I wanted to know if I was a worm like everyone else or a man. Am I a trembling creature?" as he put it, "or have I a special right?" '

' "A special right",' Groczek echoed, ' "a special right". I believe there's an element of that in every criminal, the need to dare, to assert his special place above the herd. It's a tantalising notion. One might even say it tantalises each and every one of us. Yes,' he emphasised, 'each and every one. You'll notice I don't confine myself to the criminal. Or, rather, let me say that what we call criminal may not be entirely confined to what we are used to calling crime. Napoleon and Hitler may be a case in point and, on a lesser scale, we'd be pretty foolish to ignore certain types of policeman.'

He paused for a while to let the point sink home and to pursue, privately, the train of thought he had set in motion. He was thinking, he knew, of Slovak. The man's face was in front of him as he spoke, hovering provocatively in his mind's eye. It had been with him, on and off, since the collision and he knew why. The man's reputation had irked him. Groczek had been placed on his mettle, he had felt challenged. It was not an entirely rational feeling but then none of us was wholly rational. His response had been instinctive, an instinctive arching of his back. He had felt threatened, not so much as to his territory as to his status, his reputation. The man's presence had seemed instantly an affront. The aura of untouchability that seemed to surround him aroused, in Groczek, an immediate desire to blot it out and the desire, he recognised, had to do with his own ego which seemed, suddenly, to have monstrously inflated itself. It had happened once before, he remembered.

'I call to mind,' he continued, picking up the thread of his argument, 'in Saigon during the early days, long before the war was actually declared officially, a young M.P., a dedicated soldier, frustrated by the law's delays, by rules and regulations and laid-down procedures, walked into a hut in a native village, emptied his gun into a known terrorist and walked out again. The terrorist had been known to army intelligence for some time, been responsible for countless murders and the

62

destruction of a great deal of property. Yet no one could touch him for lack of evidence and so this young M.P. walked into that hut and walked out again. Believe me, it caused quite a stir. The young man was arrested, an enquiry held, but nothing came of it.

'Those days, of course, are over, and the conditions of war can make acceptable rules of behaviour that have no place in other times, though some might argue that crime has moved, in this country anyway, into the realms of civil war.

'Be that as it may; I mention it to illustrate a point, to illuminate what may be said to be a policeman's greatest temptation – when he *knows* but cannot prove. His mind, then, most nearly approaches the criminal's. He gets, like Raskolnikov, delusions of grandeur, a growing belief that the truly great man is a law unto himself, that he can make, in effect, his own rules.'

Groczek paused again and looked round. Every eye was fixed upon him, every ear tuned not to miss a word of what he said. 'I don't recommend it,' he went on. 'First, to the policeman, the law should be a saint not an ass – though it must be said that saints are a bit hard to live with sometimes. And secondly, I know of no truly great man ever found in the ranks of the police. I leave you with that thought.'

There was a spontaneous burst of laughter at the final, ironic thrust and considerable applause. Groczek stepped down from the platform, smiling, and joined Fallon. Fallon shook his head admiringly. 'That was the best yet,' he said, 'I'm glad I came. Tell me, do you really believe all that stuff?'

'It's not important,' Groczek answered. 'What's important is that they shouldn't get the idea that the minute they become a cop the uniform'll do all their thinking for them.'

'What about that Vietnam story? I never heard you tell that before.'

'No.'

'Is it true?'

'It's true.'

'I had the impression that the young M.P. might have been – just might have been – you?'

They were walking down the corridor towards the front exit. Groczek didn't answer. It was almost as if he hadn't heard but Fallon knew that he had. He glanced at him. 'Was it?'

'It might have been anybody,' Groczek replied, 'what does it matter who it was?'

A policewoman slipped out of an office in front of them and said, 'Your call from New York, sir. Captain Rosetti's on the line.'

'Thank you.' He and Fallon followed her into the office. He had called Rosetti when they arrived at the Academy but Rosetti had been in conference and Groczek had left a message for him to call him there if he got through in time. He picked up the phone where it was lying on the desk. 'Rosetti,' he said, 'this is Groczek. How are things up there? How's business?'

'Booming,' Rosetti replied, 'we're in an expanding industry, didn't you know? The order books are full and deliveries way behind as usual. What about you?'

'We're ticking over. Listen, you showed me a file when I was in New York last, a file on a man named Slovak.'

'That's right. What about it?'

'He's here. I just ran into him – literally.'

There was a slight pause. Then, Rosetti said, 'Well, then, you may have a problem.'

'That's what I figured.'

'On the other hand, you may not. The fact that he's down there doesn't mean anything in itself.'

'He's down here to do a job.'

'You got any evidence?'

'I don't need evidence. I know. I know because I've been a cop long enough to know.'

'Look, Groczek, if you'll take my advice, you'll play this real cool. He's not someone to tangle with lightly, believe me.'

'I believe you.' Groczek's mouth tightened and his voice took on a metallic ring.

'It's a billion dollar brain you're dealing with.'

Groczek kept his voice even, suppressing a wave of irritation that swept over him. 'Mine didn't exactly come from Woolworth's,' he said. 'Look, I appreciate your advice and your concern, but all I really wanted was the file. I'd like to look at it. I'd like to know my man. Could you photostat everything in it and put it on the next plane?'

'Sure, if that's what you want. But he could just be down there visiting or on vacation.'

'He could be, but let's have the file all the same, I'd much appreciate it.'

He hung up. He looked at Fallon and nodded. Fallon could see that he was irritated and said nothing. Together they walked out of the building to the waiting car. They got in and the car drove off back towards the city. Groczek sat in brooding silence for a while. Rosetti's tone of respect for Slovak had riled him. It was out of place and in some way a reflection on him and his own capacity.

'What are you going to do about him?' Fallon asked.

'I don't know,' Groczek replied thoughtfully. He stared out of the window for a moment at the passing scenery. ' "The billion dollar brain!" Rosetti called him.' He looked at Fallon. 'Do you believe in the brilliant criminal mind, Fallon?'

Fallon shrugged. 'Some are better than others.'

'I'll tell you what I think. I think it's a theory invented to excuse shoddy police work.' He was silent for a moment, and then he continued, 'And I'll tell you something else, too. He'll regret the day he ever chose my patch to piss on.'

65

Chapter Five

Slovak locked up the house, got into the car and drove towards the city. He was to meet a man called O'Malley, a policeman who had been on the force for many years and had served both his office and mammon. Bellis had, within twenty-four hours, arranged the meeting. 'It wasn't easy,' he said, 'things aren't quite the same here, Frank, as they are everywhere else. But I've found someone. It'll be O.K.'

Slovak was satisfied. He wasn't interested in how easy or how difficult things were. They could always be done if there were enough will and imagination. He'd learned that, learned it early. It was he, of course, who most of the time, had to supply the imagination. Money supplied the will.

Bellis had been involved in the robbery at the airport where he worked as a loader. His role had been small but vital. He had been required to do no more than leave a trolley against a door marked, 'Keep Clear At All Times', but it had to be jammed. The fee offered had been staggering by his standards and he had agreed. Long after the robbery he had received no money. The man who was to have paid it to him had disappeared. He had been bitter about this, but unable to do anything about it; he had kept his mouth shut and suffered the loss. Then, one day, a man appeared at his house. He brought with him a bundle of investments in Bellis's name and worth a great deal. His name was Slovak. He said very little but when he left, Bellis was in no doubt that this was the man who had engineered the robbery. He never saw him again or had heard from him until the phone call.

It was in ways such as this, extending over a period of twenty years that Slovak had made a strange reputation for

66

himself. He was known and yet not known. People felt his presence behind certain capers that had been pulled but could not be sure. Others had met him, like Bellis, in circumstances that gave them food for thought but they valued their own lives too much to articulate them. There was a feeling – it could be no more than that – that he was ruthless in the preservation of his own privacy.

Thus Slovak knew that whoever it was that he was about to meet would be the very best that was available. It might not be good enough. He would have to judge that when he got there. If it were good enough, he would proceed. If not, it would entail a small change of plan, but that he had had to do many times.

He drove the car on towards the city. He was in good time and had no need to hurry. The meeting had been arranged at the Botanical Gardens which was in the eastern part of the city. It would take him just half an hour at this speed to get there.

He heard the siren wailing behind him and glanced in his rear view mirror. He saw the police car a hundred yards back and picking up speed all the time. He looked ahead of him. The road was clear. It had probably been summoned to some emergency in the city. He glanced in the mirror again. The car was coming behind him at great speed and now pulling out to overtake him. Or was it? He saw the faces behind the windscreen and he had the impression that their focus of attention was himself. He glanced down at his speedometer. He was doing no more than thirty.

The police car had drawn alongside him now, and the co-driver was signalling him to pull over. He pulled the car into the side of the road and halted it. The police car drew up in front of him and switched off its engine. Two policemen got out and walked with the studied slowness of their profession towards him.

The co-driver, a short, burly man, stopped by the side

67

window and leaned nonchalantly in. 'What do you think this is,' he asked, 'a race track?'

Slovak stared at him, puzzled. 'I don't follow you,' he said.

'Don't you know this is a restricted area?'

'Of course I know.'

' "Of course he knows",' the policeman echoed sarcastically, turning to his friend, ' "of course he knows". It's restricted to thirty, that's why he does fifty.' He turned back to Slovak. 'You been drinking?' he asked.

Slovak looked at the face, dumb beyond description. 'I was doing thirty,' he said, 'no more. There must be something wrong with your speedometer.'

'Do you hear that, Dave?' he asked his friend, 'there must be something wrong with our speedometer.'

'Some joker,' Dave replied.

His friend turned back once more to Slovak. 'I asked you a question,' he repeated, his voice taking on a slightly more menacing note.

'No,' said Slovak, patiently, after a pause, 'I am not drunk.'

'Let me smell your breath.' He pushed his face a little closer to Slovak's. Slovak turned and stared at it. Their noses almost touched. Clearly, the man expected him to breathe out. He was puzzled. What were they, a couple of jokers trying to relieve the boredom of a long afternoon? Or perhaps they hadn't given out any tickets lately, and felt they were falling behind. But enough was enough.

'If you want to give me a ticket,' he said, 'I think you'd better write it out and let me get on. You may not be busy today, but I am.'

The policeman remained perfectly still while Slovak spoke, his face still within an inch of his. Then, when Slovak had finished speaking, he said, without turning round, 'Dave, get the bag out.' And then he added to Slovak, 'Switch off.'

Slovak switched off the engine. He felt a great surge of rage sweep over him. Any further delay could make him late for his meeting. The policeman had withdrawn his face from the window and Slovak could see the other one, Dave, getting the breathalyser equipment out of the car. He broke off the end of the glass tube and fixed it in the mouthpiece. There was no doubt of their seriousness. They intended to breathalyse him. 'You're wasting your time,' he said to them, 'I haven't had a drink in twenty-four hours.'

They ignored him. Dave came over and offered him the nozzle. 'Blow into it for ten seconds,' he said.

Slovak hesitated. He had nothing to lose by blowing into the bag but he felt, besides a sense of outrage, a certain loss of dignity in doing so. However, it would obviously save time and trouble if he complied with the request. Dignity could be restored later. He blew into the bag.

Dave took the bag and examined the crystals. He showed them to his partner who nodded. Dave turned back to Slovak. 'Better come down to the station for a blood test.'

Slovak stared at them. The yellow crystals had remained yellow. There had been no change at all in their colour. What was the matter with these two? Hadn't the joke gone far enough? 'Those crystals are supposed to turn green,' he said.

Dave looked at his friend. 'They look green to me,' he answered, 'what colour do they look to you, Pat?'

'They look green to me,' Pat answered. 'You ought not to be driving that car,' he went on, turning to Slovak, 'if you're colour blind. Don't you know there's a law about that? Especially these foreign cars. They're built for speed, more speed than a guy with colour blindness can safely handle. Must have set you back a heap of gold, this car. What do you think of the car, Dave?' he asked.

'Beautiful,' Dave replied, putting the equipment back in his own.

Pat opened the door of the Ferrari. 'Get out,' he said. Slowly, Slovak got out of the car, taking the keys with him. 'Get in,' Pat said, opening the rear door of his own.

'What about my car?' Slovak asked.

'Well, now, you can't drive it. Seems to me you're in no fit state to handle a car, what with being drunk and colour blind as well.' He laughed. 'We'll leave it here.'

Slovak locked his car, got into the back of the police car and sat quite still. He was seething with anger and he took a firm grip on himself. This was the kind of small situation that, oddly, he was not used to handling. He recognised that what was causing him the most anger was the assault upon his ego, his identity. Here were two ordinary cops with the power to stop him, haul him out of his car and drag him down to the station on the basis of nothing more than a whim. Had they known who he was, they would have no more touched him than they would a red hot stove, but of course, they didn't and couldn't. Who was he? Few knew that. To them, he was just another motorist in a foreign car. Perhaps they had a down on foreign cars? People of low intelligence, such as these obviously were, had hang-ups that were strange and made no sense to him. It all came back to this question of his identity again. It revolved, in some way, around that. But it must not become a fixation with him. There was a price one must pay for everything in this world and he paid a price for the life-style he had chosen. It was, he could see, an aspect of that old conflict he had spoken of to the young doctor, the conflict between the desire to conceal oneself and the desire to be wholly known. What he must do was to put this in perspective. They had him in the car now, as if he were no one in particular, a pebble, like any other, picked up off the beach and flung carelessly into the sea. If they had failed to note its unique markings, so much the worse for them. He would endure it all meekly.

He sat impassively in the car, looking neither to right nor left and refusing to be provoked into any kind of conversation. When they got to the station it would be time enough to make his complaint to the sergeant or the captain of the city precinct, if he were there. He would have no more truck with these two.

70

With any luck, he would be able to pick up a cab and still keep his appointment. They were, after all, taking him in the direction he needed to go.

They arrived at the station and he got out. He walked up the steps and into the building with them. They turned into the squad room, pushing open the door. It was, like all stations, a shabby green, darker below the waist than on top. There was a main charge desk on which sat a typewriter. On another was a telephone. A smaller desk belonging to the sergeant was in a further corner. A big, burly man sat in it attending to paperwork. He looked up as they came in. Dave held up the bag of crystals. 'Blood test,' he said. The sergeant nodded and went back to his papers.

Slovak said, 'Are you in charge here?'

The sergeant looked up. 'Why?' he asked.

'I was stopped on the highway,' Slovak replied, 'on the pretence that I was speeding, breathalysed, and brought down here on the pretence the crystals had turned green.'

'Pretence?' The sergeant raised his eyebrows.

'I'd sort it out if I were you,' Slovak said, 'before I start calling lawyers and suing.'

'Where are the crystals, Dave?' the sergeant asked.

Dave, who had been rolling a charge sheet into the typewriter paused, picked up the bag and tossed it over to the sergeant. The sergeant looked at it. 'They look green to me,' he said, and held them up for Slovak to see.

Slovak stared at them. They were now green. The bag must have been switched in the car. 'That's not the bag I breathed into,' he said, coldly. 'That's someone else's bag.'

The sergeant looked across at Dave. 'You hear that, Dave?'

'I heard.'

'Well, what have you got to say about it?'

'I'd say that that is a very familiar story to me, sergeant, and I'd guess that it's a very familiar story to you too.'

The sergeant sighed and looked at Slovak. 'He's right, sir.

We hear that all the time. Well, it's natural, I suppose, but what would you do in my place, sir? I've got two officers here, that say it is your bag. Now why would they go to all the trouble of breathalysing a guy just for the fun of it? Doesn't make much sense to me. Does it to you, sir?'

He paused. The room had gone quiet and the two or three other people in it had ceased work and were looking at him. Slovak stared at the sergeant. He couldn't quite make out whether he was being serious or was, in fact, part of the whole elaborate charade. But then, why should he be? To assume that he was would be to assume that the joke had been plotted at a much higher level, and that it was, therefore, more sinister in its import than he had previously thought. This seemed un-likely. It made no sense. He was the victim of a couple of bored cops, nothing else. It could have been anyone. They had, unfortunately, picked on him.

'If you'll just give all the details to the officer there,' the sergeant went on, indicating Dave behind his desk, 'I'll see if I can't hassle up the police surgeon.'

With meticulous care and exaggerated slowness, Dave filled out the charge sheet. He seemed in no hurry. When he had finished he handed it over to the sergeant and went out, leav-ing Slovak sitting there. The time ticked away. No one paid any attention to him. Policemen came in and went out again. At one point, growing impatient, Slovak asked, 'How much longer is this comedy going to take?'

'We're waiting for the police surgeon, sir,' the sergeant re-plied, without looking up.

There was nothing he could do but wait. He had missed his meeting. He would have to arrange another. The time went by, the room gradually became quieter and quieter. Very little seemed to be happening. After a while, the room itself began to take on an unreal aspect and he found himself won-dering if he were actually there at all and not sitting in the house imagining it all. It was only with the greatest effort of

72

will that he managed to prevent himself from getting up and walking out of the door.

It was an hour and a half before the police surgeon returned. The sergeant spoke to him quietly and Slovak saw them both looking across the room at him. The conversation seemed to go on far longer than was necessary but eventually the police surgeon nodded and said to Slovak, 'Would you follow me?'

Slovak followed him into a small adjoining room where he was asked to remove his coat and roll up his sleeve. The surgeon then took a blood sample and emptied the contents of the syringe into three porcelain cups which he took outside and gave to the sergeant. Slovak followed him out. Apart from being asked to remove his coat and roll up his sleeve not a word had been spoken to him.

The sergeant sealed the cups and signed them and asked Slovak to sign them too. He did so. The sergeant put two of the cups in one can and the third he put in another which he handed to Slovak, smiling at him. 'That's yours,' he said, 'for private analysis, if you like. Sorry it took so long. But what can you do?'

Slovak said nothing. He took the can and went out without a backward glance. He picked up a cab in the street and told him to drive him out onto the highway where the car was parked. It was only when he had paid off the driver and had got into the car and started it that it struck him as odd that they should have allowed him to return to his car and drive it home. If he were unfit to drive when they picked him up, why had they let him return to his car now? Would that simple fact not prick the whole bubble of their hoax and make it plain to anyone that their purpose had not been serious in the first place? But then, they would find no alcohol in his blood anyway, so how could they proceed? Clearly, they had no intention of doing so. Were they, then, not at all concerned that *he* might take action against them? It struck him, then,

73

that were he to do so, they would simply deny that he had ever been there. And how could he prove that he ever had?

It had been an odd experience and he wasn't sure of what to make of it. When he returned to the house he called Bellis. Bellis said, 'Where were you? O'Malley called me. You never showed up!'

'I was picked up on the highway and breathalysed.'

There was a pause at the other end and then a short laugh. 'Jesus, *you*?'

'Yes,' Slovak replied, drily.

'Had you been drinking?'

'No.'

'Why did they pick you up then?'

'I'm not sure. Maybe it was just a couple of jokers.'

'Maybe. Or . . .'

'Or what?'

'Do they know you're here?'

'They may or they may not.'

'What does that mean?'

'I had a run in with the Chief of Police's car the other day.'

'Groczek's?'

'Yes.'

'Jesus Christ, how did that happen?'

'It's not important. It could be though, that either he or one of the others knew me.'

'It's not likely, is it?'

'No. But then what do you make of what I just told you?'

There was a short pause. Then Bellis said, 'Well, it could mean nothing at all. They're pretty hot on drunken driving in this county. It's been one of Groczek's little crusades. It hasn't won him many friends either. Maybe the cops just wanted to show him what eager beavers they were?'

'You're forgetting I hadn't had a drink in twenty-four hours. I blew into the bag, the crystals didn't even blink.'

'You think, then,' Bellis said, slowly, 'they maybe just wanted you to know they know you're here?'

'Maybe.'

'What if that's right?'

'What if it is?'

'Will it change things?'

'Why should it? If they know I'm here, I know they know. All we've done is confided in each other a little.'

'What about O'Malley?'

'Fix another meeting. I'll call you to confirm.'

He hung up and sat there thinking. The afternoon had darkened into dusk but he remained sitting there, without turning on the light. He had told Bellis that if Groczek knew he was there, and was letting him know that, it was of small consequence. But was it? How much did Groczek know about him? And if he knew enough, how did that change the situation?

Groczek arrived home with the file on Slovak in his case. It had arrived earlier in the day and Fallon had gone down to the airport to pick it up. Groczek had put it aside, not wanting to read it then, but preferring to wait until he was in the quiet of his own study. After all, he told himself, there was nothing urgent about it, nothing that would justify taking off time from his more pressing duties in the office. The man might, after all, and despite what he had said so confidently to Rosetti, be down here simply on a vacation. Yet he could not deny that he felt a certain impatience and several times his eyes strayed in the direction of the file. However, he resisted the impulse.

He had a drink before dinner and glanced through the paper. There were follow-up stories on the press conference reporting reactions from different sources. He hadn't the patience to read them. His wife, Mary, came in. He poured her a drink and she sat there, sipping it. She was a somewhat faded lady, faded earlier than she should, by rights, have been, since she had had no children and as far as Groczek could see, had no cares of any consequence to produce that look of fractured complaint she perpetually carried with her. Relations between them, however, were not antagonistic. The one scarcely impinged on the consciousness of the other. They remained together by old habit and inertia. Neither had the energy to contemplate a break and start afresh in other directions. Groczek's energies were all directed and used up elsewhere and hers produced nothing more than an occasional bout of spring cleaning. They were not so much content with their situation as indifferent to the possibility of others.

After dinner he excused himself and went into his study. It was a large, comfortable room in which he spent much of his time when at home. On the wall behind the desk hung mementos of his days in Vietnam – a helmet, his military policeman's armband, his service revolver, a Viet Cong flag and one or two other things. Those had been good days, he remembered, where the issues had all seemed clear before they had become muddied over by chanting teenagers.

He put the file on his desk in front of him and sat down and opened it. He was immediately confronted by an inside cover on which various photographs and snapshots had been fixed. In the centre was an enlarged head and shoulders of Slovak. The face stared up at him. It was unmistakable. It was an interesting face, the eyes especially even in the photograph were large and intelligent and with a burning intensity emerging from behind them.

He looked at the other photographs around it. There were snaps of Slovak getting into his car, in a restaurant with two men, on a beach lying alone and leaving a nightclub with a girl. He recognised the girl as the one in the car at the time of the collision. He didn't know who she was and made a mental note to find out. However, turning the snapshot over, he saw that her name had been written on the back – Margaret Phillips – followed by the comment, 'See notes'. He took the large photograph of Slovak out and laid it beside him. He then turned to the text which, according to the names on the front, had been compiled by Rosetti and two others. He began reading.

'For some years there had been rumours in the underworld of a "mind" at work behind some of the most daring robberies of the past two decades – a single mind. For a long time these rumours were regarded as typical underworld gossip, another illustration of the way in which small-time crooks are apt to romanticise their profession. This view is no longer held.

'We first became conscious of the possibility that there may be some truth in these rumours by virtue of their sheer persistence stretching over a decade. It is in the nature of rumours to be insubstantial and in the nature of hardened, experienced police officers to deal mainly in facts. We mention this merely by way of explaining why it has taken so long for this department to act. It is not our intention to offer it as an excuse.

'When it was finally realised that these rumours may have a kernel of truth in them, certain crimes were looked at again with a view to establishing whether, from a professional point of view, crimes that appeared to have no special connection were, or could have been, the work of a single mind.

'The rumours, as far as we could gather, seemed to attach themselves most definitely to three major robberies. They attached themselves to others, but in a looser sort of way, and we did not feel justified, at that stage, in linking them all together. There was a fourth, the train robbery outside of Detroit in 1975 in which $8,000,000 worth of platinum was lifted. We shall refer to this later in a special context.

'The three major robberies were the payroll robbery at A.C. Chemicals in Chicago in 1962 – close to $2,000,000; the gold bullion robbery at Kennedy Airport in 1966 – close to $5,000,000; the safe deposit boxes at Bank of America in 1970, also in Chicago – over $6,000,000 in jewellery, notes and bonds.

77

'All these robberies, to some extent, hit the public imagination. There have been others, but they did not, at that stage, have sufficiently strong connections with those mentioned to justify looking at in the same way. However, it cannot be ruled out that a connection may be found later.

'When these robberies were put side by side and all the evidence and information examined in the light of how they had been carried out, it became clear fairly quickly that they exhibited certain features very much in common. Firstly, in each case security had been so tight and so constantly reviewed that it was considered virtually impossible for a robbery to be successful. In the event, a single weak spot had been discovered in each situation that rendered that judgement invalid, and the weakness discovered in such a way as to indicate not merely the most meticulous research which had gone into the investigation that exposed it, but an exceptionally brilliant notion of how that weakness might be exploited. In the case of the gold bullion robbery, for example, it involved no more than a certain door being jammed for no more than three minutes which prevented the handlers returning to the bullion.

Secondly, the manner in which the robberies were carried out all required a chain of events to take place with precision timing. Transport had to be assembled, doors unlocked, alarm systems disengaged, people placed in the right positions, all to a routine that had to function like clockwork. Although this is also a feature of many other robberies, it was the elaborateness of the preparations in these cases that, frankly, we observed with some admiration as the details unfolded to us. For example, in the case of the train robbery, if one examines the line, there is only one place that the train could be effectively stopped which, at the same time, offered an escape route with a minimum chance of discovery for the longest possible time. That spot was at a level-crossing that was in full view of an army camp situated only a few hundred yards away. No trains ever stopped there, and strange men loading goods from a train into waiting trucks would certainly have aroused interest. In the event, *army* trucks were used which, though noticed, aroused no interest at all. It may be added that the train was then driven on along nearly the whole length of its route, keeping to its schedule.

'Thirdly, the efficiency of the distribution network after the robbery has also been remarkable in each case. As every policeman knows, much of the success of police work is based upon weaknesses in the disposal of stolen property after the robbery. In all these cases, no traces of the property have ever been found and it must be concluded that their hot value has been realised in countries adjacent to our own, which suggests, certainly in the case of the platinum, a highly organised and most efficient disposal system. It is not beyond the bounds of possibility that in this case certain foreign governments or their front agencies may be involved.'

Groczek paused for a moment from his reading and looked at the photograph of Slovak lying beside him on the desk. His initial scepticism at the deference in the tone of the text was beginning to disappear and its place taken by a certain nagging doubt. Was this man really as good as this or was this all some fanciful notion in the minds of three impressionable cops in New York, seeking to justify their pay and positions by creating the possibility of superminds at work? He wasn't sure. He turned back to the text and read on.

'Lastly, in each case, where some of those involved in the robberies have been caught, all have been somewhat vague as to who planned and organised the one in question. In each case there have, unquestionably, been leaders, some known to us, but after considerable interrogation a strong doubt has been revealed as to how the whole operation was conceived and by whom. This is normally the kind of information that is eventually revealed by long and close questioning of those arrested, since it is also the kind of information most desperately wanted by the police after a robbery. However, in each of these four cases, those who have been identified to the police as among the leaders of that particular escapade do not, in our opinion, possess the kind of intelligence and imagination required to conceive and plan such robberies. For example, Carl Serpi, who was eventually arrested and charged with robbery of the Bank of America, has been known to us for some time and does not, from all we know of him, possess the required mental resources. Yet it was he who apparently led that operation.

'When the information concerning these four robberies was placed side by side and examined in depth over a long period, the conclusion was drawn that the rumours referred to at the beginning could no longer be ignored and that, in fact, there was a single mind at work behind all of them. It became, then, the problem of identifying that mind. This was obviously going to be difficult.

'At first we floundered about since we had no notion where to look. We studied in detail all the evidence involved in each of the cases, especially the reports of the interrogations by interviewing officers. These seemed to tell us nothing that we did not know already, but we went over them so many times that finally one thing in the interrogation of Serpi kept returning to us as unexplained. Serpi stated that the sum of money that had been put up for his bail, and which was very large, had been found by a man who had been present in his lawyer's office one day before the trial and who had been introduced to him as a stockbroker friend of his lawyer. The man's name was never mentioned and he never saw him again. This remark in the statement passed unnoticed, presumably because it was considered irrelevant where Serpi's bail money had come from and because Serpi either did not know the name or was unwilling to divulge it. We interviewed Serpi in prison.

He said that he had never known the name of the man and we believe that statement to be true. He did, however, give us a fairly full physical description of him, though he seemed genuinely puzzled as to why we should want it.

'A physical description was not, of course, much use to us and we filed it away. Then we had a piece of luck, the kind that investigations of this sort often depend upon for their success. Some three years after this interview with Serpi, Serpi's lawyer, Feldt, was indicted on a fraud charge. He was never convicted but his books were seized and investigated. He had received a number of cheques, very large, from a property company in Ohio. He claimed these were monies collected on behalf of clients whose properties were managed by that company. This did not add up in the books, however, and the company was quietly investigated. It appeared that the major stockholder in that company was a Mr. Frank Slovak who took very little active interest in its affairs. Nothing could be found out about him and he could not be contacted because he was away travelling to South America. All queries were satisfactorily answered by the company's manager and eventually the case against Feldt collapsed. Feldt left the country shortly afterwards and settled in Panama.

'Feldt, however, came under the surveillance of the Panama police, suspected of trafficking in stolen bonds. Since nothing was known of him, they took a photo of him and sent it to us, asking if we had any information on him that would be useful to them and giving us what they knew of him. On the photo was another man talking to Feldt. The Panama police were at pains to point out that this man was not in any way involved. He was merely staying at the same hotel as Feldt and at the time the photograph was taken had fallen into conversation with him. The Panama police had taken the trouble to check him out. He was a businessman on his way through to Brazil. His name was Frank Slovak.'

Despite himself, Groczek began to feel the same excitement, the same thrill of the chase that Rosetti must have felt as the connections began to be made. He read on.

'The face of Slovak was not clear in the photograph, since the photograph had been taken of Feldt. It became necessary, therefore, to find a good photograph of Slovak. This was done at the passport office. Serpi's description of the man in Feldt's office fitted pretty well, both as to features, colouring and build, it being possible to measure the latter against Feldt in the photo. It was not conclusive, but it was worth pursuing.

'We then circulated his photograph and passport number to all immigration points and awaited Slovak's return to this country. He returned a month later. We then began a very discreet watch on him, keeping him under fairly close observation, at the same time that we began a quiet investigation into his background. In fact, *we watched him plan the train robbery outside of Detroit.*'

Groczek felt his heart beat a tiny bit faster as he read this last passage. What were they saying – that they watched him plan a robbery and couldn't stop him? What nonsense was this? What were they talking about? He found himself perspiring a little. He dabbed his forehead with his handkerchief and read on.

'We say that we watched him. It should be remembered that while we watched him, the robbery had not yet taken place; we had no idea that he was planning one or anything at all, and his movements seemed normal and explicable in terms perfectly acceptable to us. It was only *afterwards*, when the news of the robbery had *broken*, that we looked at each other and looked again at Slovak and saw that we may have been had, that it was possible to interpret his actions in a totally different light and in such a way as to become convinced that he had, in fact, planned the robbery. We stress that it was possible. We believe he did it, but it was all interpretation which, applied to the movements of numerous men,

82

could have yielded the same conclusion. All these movements and activities in the period concerned are listed in minute detail at the back of this report.

'The effect on us was twofold. First, we had witnessed what seemed to us, afterwards, an extraordinary conjuring trick. Before our very eyes and under our very noses, he had accomplished what he had wanted to accomplish while seeming to accomplish something else or, if you like, nothing at all. Secondly, and to be honest, we acquired a profound admiration for the man. We accept that it is not our business to do so. We merely state what happened.'

Groczek rose, very agitated, and began to pace up and down the room furiously. Who were these policemen who stood back and admired, who stood by and watched? Where were their brains? A robbery is carried out under their noses by a man they know to be a criminal and they do nothing, nothing! What was the country coming to? And Rosetti, of all people, an experienced cop! He paused and thought for a moment. Yes, but a college graduate, too. Always the emphasis on theory, the fascination with ideas. Theory was invading every corner of life, paralysing the will to act. They had, in effect, stood gaping at a man juggling balls in the air, while his henchmen had picked their pockets. And they confessed it in this report, without shame or embarrassment. Not only confessed it, but confessed their admiration for the way it was done and doubtless expected applause for their honesty and their objectivity, for the scientific way they recorded the injury done to themselves. Could they not see that the injury had been done to the whole force, to the idea of law and order?

He sat down again, angrily, at his desk. There was more and more but he would not read it. He would not be party to this shameful dereliction of duty by reading it. He was sick and tired of reading how clever they had been in doing nothing at all; of reading their true confessions, of how sporting they were and how well they had accepted their defeat. Above all, he was sick of reading how clever this man was, how unique. No one was that clever, certainly no one man pitted against the remorseless forces of the law in motion.

He turned over pages and pages. He was looking for a report on the man himself. What had these buffoons found out about him, about the real man, the flesh and blood man? Had they found out anything at all? He stopped turning pages as he came to it and saw the heading – Frank Slovak.

'Frank Slovak was born in 1930 in the Greenpoint area of Brooklyn. His mother, born in 1905, was of Irish stock and also born in Brooklyn. Little is known of when the family entered the country but in all probability it was in the 1880s. There is nothing to distinguish the family from hundreds of others. They were hard working and respectable. None of the family had any police record. In 1928 his mother married Oscar Slovak, a Pole who entered this country in 1919. On his entry papers his profession was given as mathematics teacher, but he worked for most of his life in New York as a store book-keeper.

'Frank Slovak went to PS19, Brooklyn. He was an exceptional student by all accounts. Records at the school, still preserved, show that in test after test of mental ability he consistently scored marks that placed him in the so-called "genius" category, that is, exceeding 145. Considerable efforts were made to persuade him to take scholarships, but he refused.

'He was quiet and well behaved, giving little trouble to his teachers. He did not mix easily and had no known close friends. Although exceptionally gifted he was often lazy and would do no work, sometimes for a whole term. These periods of inactivity were often followed by periods that were described by one old teacher who remembered him as "mental explosions", in which he would work at a pace and with a fury that no one could live with, not even the teachers. He left school at sixteen.

'For a while after he left school he worked in an engineering factory, making a differential gear. He then disappeared for three years and it is thought that he may have gone abroad because a passport was issued, about that date, to a Frank Slovak, though of a different address. According to neighbours of whom discreet enquiries were made, he turned up again in the 1950s, seemingly quite well off for one still in his early twenties. After 1958 nothing more in any detail is known of him until he came under observation from our department, and it is only fair to add that very little has been gleaned about him even during this time.

'Prior to the train robbery, in 1975, he was seen in New York in the company of a girl, Margaret Phillips, whose photo is in the file. This was unusual since he had, until that time, no known regular companions of either sex. Enquiries elicited no background information on Margaret Phillips, except that she was not a native of New York and was obviously of an upper-middle-class family. Despite this, she worked as a hostess in a nightclub called The Golden Spade, not exactly the sort of place she might expect to run into her family, if she has any and if they ever visited the city. None of the girls she worked with was very forthcoming about Phillips, which is not unusual with girls of that sort.

'Phillips and Slovak eventually took an apartment together. They shared it for about a year. Then Phillips disappeared. At first it was thought that she had merely gone home or away on vacation, but she never returned. Slovak remained in the apartment for about six months and then he, too, disappeared. All track of him was lost, until he showed up once again a few months ago.

'This is all that is now known for certain about this man. It should be remembered that, if the information is somewhat

85

sketchy, this is partly due to the fact that very little of concrete importance has emerged to enable us to justify the continuing use of manpower and resources in filling in the blanks about him. Every day makes more and more pressing claims upon these resources and we have to admit that Slovak, far from becoming better known to us as we studied him, seemed to fade away before our eyes. It was almost as if the more we knew about him the less substantial he became. There were times when we thought he was rapidly turning into the invisible man. Nevertheless, we cannot emphasise enough that this man is no ordinary criminal. His power is considerable and his connections extensive. Even certain leading Mafiosi speak of him with awe, or rather do *not* speak of him, which brings us to the last, strange little anecdote to end this curious dossier, a story which came to us out of the blue recently and which best illustrates how formidable this man is.

'Dino Scapelli, the most respected figure in the Mafia, and who was so sensationally gunned down three months ago, had put out a contract on Slovak. That is hard line news from areas we have learned to trust. No one knows why and maybe no one ever will. Even more important, no one in these areas had ever heard of Slovak. "Who is Slovak, man?" was the common, if quietly muttered, greeting around town three months ago. Everybody asked, nobody knew. But it may be said with some certainty that that was the most his name has ever been mentioned out loud.'

Groczek closed the file and sat very still. In a way, he wished he had not read it. Far from putting Slovak in the right perspective, it had put him in the wrong. It had turned him into some kind of shadowy figure of greatness, all powerful, all knowing, a figure beyond the reach of any man, a law unto himself. It was a portrait not of a man but of a superman, calculated to put any policeman who read it at an immediate disadvantage. Any policeman, that is, except Groczek. All it had succeeded in doing for him was to arouse in him a determination to show Slovak that here, at least, in this city, he had met his match.

He picked up the photo once more and stared at it. The face was a living face, even on the photograph. It seemed to float up off the surface at him and to take up a position of its own. And as he looked at it he had the strangest of impressions which he felt with an intensity that momentarily unnerved him. It was that Slovak had entered the room and was observing him and that, further, his presence there, in some way, had put the two of them into direct communication with each other.

Chapter Six

It was two whole days before Bellis was able to arrange another meeting with O'Malley. During these two days Slovak never went out of the house. For the most part, he sat in a chair and stared out of the window at the countryside. But his mind was not still. It was in a fever of excitement, more highly geared than he had ever known it at the outset of an operation.

Neither was he totally inactive. He had made certain calls, spoken to certain people. The response had been, as he would have expected, gratifying. There was interest, much interest. They were free and available. No, he would not discuss the operation in detail nor the commodity involved. He merely quoted its value. It was enough. His name was enough. Wheels were set in motion, parts began to move. They would hear from him again soon.

When the hour came for him to leave for his meeting, he drove the car to the edge of the city, parked it, and took a cab. His blue Ferrari was too noticeable. Not that it would worry him greatly if the police were watching him. They had watched him in New York once, and he had performed in full view of them and they had been none the wiser. However, this was an occasion he had to be careful. He had no wish for any witnesses to his meeting with O'Malley. And besides, this time he really must see him.

It was lunchtime and the traffic was heavy. The cab inched its way forward, stopped, and moved again. The traffic was solid in front and behind. He sat in the back of the cab and patiently waited. He would be a little late but there was nothing he could do. He turned and looked through the rear window to check once more that he was not being followed and saw the red Plymouth he had noticed a few days earlier on his return to the house from the hotel. He was puzzled. He couldn't quite see how they had picked him up again. And further, it puzzled him that they should be quite so obvious about it, as if they didn't care if he spotted them or not. Well, perhaps they didn't. Perhaps it was another confirmation of the view that they simply wanted him to know that they knew he was here, in the city. He would have to change cabs. It was a nuisance but there was nothing else he could do about it.

The cab had driven forward fifty yards and stopped at the lights. The road was clear in front. When the lights changed again its passage would be unobstructed for a while. He leaned forward, told the driver he had changed his mind, paid him and got out of the cab. He shut the door, wove his way through the waiting traffic and stood on the kerb.

The Plymouth was now virtually opposite him. He stared at the driver. The driver was staring straight in front of him, yet Slovak knew that he had seen him get out of the cab. Idly, as though bored and not knowing where else to look to relieve the monotony, the driver turned and looked in Slovak's direction. For a moment, their gaze met and he saw the look in the driver's eyes acknowledge the stalemate. He saw him, in fact, sigh as he turned away and stared once again at the traffic up ahead of him. There was nothing he could do. He could not get out of his car and leave it there, neither could he wait, however innocently, for Slovak to resume his journey. The lights changed. The traffic moved off and with it the Plymouth, resignedly. Slovak smiled to himself.

He waited until the car had disappeared from sight, then looked round for another cab. He found one within a few minutes and directed him to the Botanical Gardens. He paid off the driver and walked in. He found the hot house of rare plants he was looking for and went inside. A party of school-children were being conducted round by a teacher who was explaining in a low, monotonous voice the origin of the plants and their characteristics.

At the far end, a man was standing, gazing out of the windows onto the park outside and taking no interest in the plants. As Slovak approached him, the man turned and looked at him enquiringly. 'Mr. O'Malley?' Slovak asked, quietly. The man nodded. Slovak looked round and saw a seat unoccupied. 'Let's sit down,' he said.

They walked to the seat and sat down. Slovak detected instantly a certain sullenness in the man's attitude, as if he were there against his will. Slovak ignored it. It was equally possible that it was irritation that the first meeting had been abortive and that he had been required to come again. Or, perhaps, it was merely nervousness.

'You're late,' O'Malley said, looking round, edgily. 'I'd begun to think you weren't going to show again.'

'The traffic was heavy,' Slovak replied. 'And I had to change cabs.'

'You weren't followed?' O'Malley asked, turning quickly.

'Yes, I was,' Slovak answered, 'that's why I changed cabs. But I shook them off.' He looked at O'Malley for a moment. 'I say I was followed,' he went on, slowly, 'but I can't be certain. I just have the feeling that I was. Do you *know* if I'm being followed?'

O'Malley looked away. 'They know you're here,' he said, finally.

'But do you *know* that I'm being followed?'

89

O'Malley nodded. 'Groczek knows about you. He's keeping tabs on you. He's put Schuster on it. Schuster's job is to follow you around.'

Slovak thought for a moment. 'Well,' he said, 'provided it stays at that, it doesn't bother me. They can watch all they like, they won't see much.'

'Bellis said they picked you up on the highway when you were on your way here.'

'Do you know anything about that?'

'Nothing.'

'How would you explain it then? I mean, you being a cop?'

O'Malley shook his head. 'You could just have been unlucky.'

Slovak nodded. He looked at O'Malley. The man was obviously on edge. He must try to put him more at his ease. 'First of all,' he began, 'I must thank you for meeting me.'

'I told Bellis I didn't do this sort of thing anymore.'

'Well, then,' Slovak smiled, 'that's even more reason for me to thank you.'

'I gave it up. We were all on the take at one time, before Groczek took over. He threw a lot of us out.'

'But he overlooked you?' Slovak smiled again.

O'Malley looked at him and looked away. 'I was lucky, but I didn't push my luck. I got clean and I stayed clean.'

There was a short pause. Then Slovak said, 'No one gets clean. No one. The dirt clings. You can't touch pitch without rolling in it.' He looked at him. 'I don't believe in redemption, O'Malley. Not in this world.'

'I'm telling you, I made a fresh start.'

Slovak shook his head slowly. 'The only fresh start you get is when you come out head first.'

'I think different,' O'Malley answered, sullenly.

'Then you think wrong. And I'm here to prove it.'

There was a short silence. A hardened note had crept into Slovak's voice that heralded the end, as far as he was con-

90

cerned, of all further philosophical dispute. O'Malley recognised it. He looked at Slovak. 'I'd never heard of you, least not till a couple of days ago. Bellis said you were big, very big.'

Slovak nodded. 'Big enough.'

'What do you want?'

'I want information. You'll be well paid.'

'I don't want the money.'

'Then give it to your favourite charity.'

The voice had suddenly gone ice-cold. It sent a shiver through O'Malley and he was silent for a moment. Then he asked, 'What do you want to know?'

'The junk that was picked up by the police – where is it being held?'

O'Malley stared at him incredulously and then started to laugh. 'You're not seriously thinking of . . .?' He stopped. The idea was so outrageous he could scarcely put it into words. He shook his head. 'You'll never get away with it.'

'You're a two hundred a week cop. Save your breath to cool your feet with. Where is it being held?'

'In a vault in the basement of the Roundhouse, Police Headquarters.' He paused a moment, and then added, 'You'll need to mount a military operation to get in there.'

'I'm paying for information, not advice,' Slovak answered coldly.

O'Malley turned away. Slovak was silent for a while. Then he said, 'I want a diagram of the layout of the building. Show all doors and walls and their measurements, alarms, waterpipes and gaspipes and electric circuits. I want a copy of the duty rosta.' He thought again for a moment. 'Where do architects file the building plans?'

'At City Hall. It's a department of the land registry.'

'I want a photostat copy of the plans of the building and any structural alteration that may have been made since it was built, you understand?'

O'Malley nodded. 'Is that all?'

'No,' Slovak answered.

'What else do you want?'

'What about a smile?'

O'Malley turned and looked at him. Slovak's cold gaze seemed to penetrate the inmost depths of his soul. If he harboured secret thoughts, he would do well to get rid of them.

'You worry me,' Slovak added, quietly.

O'Malley looked away. 'You don't have to worry,' he answered.

'No,' Slovak said, 'I don't have to.' There was another pause and then he said, 'We'll meet again in two days. I'll let you know where and when.'

O'Malley nodded and Slovak, after a pause, rose and walked away.

O'Malley met him again two days later. He brought with him a carefully drawn diagram of the police headquarters building and photostat copies of the building plans lodged by the architects when the building had been erected. Slovak looked them over carefully and then put them away. O'Malley also gave him a copy of the duty rosta. This would tell him how many men were likely to be in the building at any given time .

O'Malley's attitude was slightly less sullen this time and rather more co-operative. He had clearly seen or heard something which impressed him, and he was eager to communicate his information to Slovak. 'They've got a file on you, did you know that?'

'A file?' Slovak prompted.

O'Malley nodded. 'Groczek had it sent down from New York. I don't know what's in it, but I saw it lying on his desk and heard him talking to Fallon about it.'

'What did you hear?'

'Not much, but Groczek is obviously worried about you, about being here, I mean. He's convinced you came down here to pull something off, but he doesn't know what.' Slovak nodded. It wasn't news to him. 'What if he gets the hang of it? I mean, what if he catches on?'

'He won't. That's the last thing he'll think of. There are plenty of rich pickings in this city. He'll bust a gut trying to figure out which one it is, but he won't think of the junk. He's got that. He's just lifted that from someone else. That's safe. That's over and done with. He's not going to think in a million years that someone's going to lift it from *him*. Would you, in his place?' Slovak shook his head. 'No. He'll be looking everywhere except in his own pocket.'

O'Malley looked at him with grudging admiration. The man was right, and his reading of Groczek was right. And it was clever. He shook his head, wonderingly. 'I don't know what it says in that file about you, but it's sure got Groczek worried. I never heard him so mad. He was talking to Fallon. "Slovak, Slovak," that's all I heard all morning. He bawled out the New York department, too, calling them incompetents. At one point I heard him say he'd run you out of town, if need be.'

Slovak smiled. 'He knows better than that. What else did you hear?'

'They're making enquiries about a girl.'

'A girl?'

'Margaret Phillips? Was she in the car with you when you had the run in with Groczek?' Slovak nodded slowly. 'Well, they've found out where she lives and they're digging up what they can about her.'

'What have they found?'

'I don't know, but they've found something. I heard Fallon telling someone to pull her in.'

Slovak sat very still and was silent. He felt deeply disturbed. This was something new, it was something he hadn't thought of. What did it mean? Was it nothing more than a routine police enquiry or was it an attempt to get at Slovak through her? He found the latter hard to believe. It would amount to

93

harassment and he doubted if even Groczek would go so far on so little evidence. Whatever was in that file was either too little to alarm him or, if he were alarmed, as O'Malley had suggested, then it would have made clear to Groczek that he, Slovak, was not a man to be provoked, not without putting himself in the very gravest of danger. *That* would be in the file. The clear implication of any picture they had built of him in that file must be that Slovak was a man to be handled at a distance. He expected to be handled at a distance. He did not expect them, in the circumstances, to ignore his presence entirely. That would not be according to the rules. But anything more would be intolerable and he was inclined to believe that Groczek would not enter into it. Groczek would prefer to wait and to watch and to see. He would hope to see one false move but, of course, that wouldn't come. No, on the whole, he was inclined to believe that their interest in Maggie was no more than normal police routine.

He dismissed it from his mind and turned to O'Malley. 'Have they set a date for the trial?' he asked.

'The fourteenth of next month.'

Slovak nodded. That gave him a clear month in which to operate, to make his plans. It was more than enough. 'By the way,' O'Malley added, 'they're not destroying the junk. They're pumping it back into Health and Welfare. They're using it for registered addicts on maintenance.'

Slovak stared at him. This was something new. 'Are you sure?' he asked.

"It's certain. The D.A.'s office got clearance from Washington. It came in a letter this morning.'

'That means the stuff will have to be processed. Will it be done here?'

'No,' O'Malley replied, 'there are no facilities here. It'll be sent to Boston and done in the labs there.'

Slovak thought for a while. This would make a difference. The drugs would have to be moved. Movement would make them vulnerable, however they were transported. The whole operation was suddenly thrown into a new light. He looked at O'Malley. 'You'll keep me informed of any plans to move the drugs before or after the trial.'

O'Malley nodded. Slovak stood up and O'Malley stood up with him. Slovak turned to go but O'Malley stopped him nervously. 'Look,' he said, 'I know you don't think much of me, but – robbing the police?' He shook his head. 'They'll never let you get away with it. You'll make them the butt of every joke in the country. Groczek won't rest till he gets that junk back and gets *you*. You've got to see that. It's different. It's just a different sort of thing. It's never been done before, Jesus, they'll take you apart!'

Slovak said, 'You just supply me with that information. Don't concern yourself about anything else.' He turned and walked swiftly away.

He took a cab back to where he had left his car and drove slowly home. His mind was racing. He was in a high state of excitement. This was going to be easier than he had thought. The drugs would have to go by road, rail or air. Whichever way they went, they would be exposed. And when, suddenly, he saw how it could be done, whichever way they chose to move them, he laughed out loud. No idea had ever seemed more beautiful to him.

He turned off the highway onto the road that led up to the house. It was dark, and as he approached he saw lights gleaming through the trees. He was puzzled. He had left in daylight, surely, and there was no reason for him to have turned on the lights. Perhaps Maggie had returned. His heart leapt a little.

The moment he turned into the drive he could see that the house was ablaze with light. Every room was lit up and light flooded from the house onto the garden. He brought his car to a halt. Three police cars stood in the drive. The door into the house was wide open. He got out of his car and closed the door. He walked towards the house. He glimpsed men inside moving this way and that. He went into the hall and entered the main living room.

The room was in a state of total disarray. Furniture had been turned over, drawers turned out and carpets pulled up violently where they had been nailed down. Men were swarming all over it, looking in every nook and cranny. He stared at them, not sure at first if what he was seeing was actually real. 'What are you doing here?' he asked, sharply.

His voice struck the room like the single tolling of a bell. It sounded false to him. Every movement in the room suddenly ceased, each action half caught in the act of completing it. Then every head turned and looked in his direction, fixing him, almost as an intruder who had no right to be there. A man detached himself from the others and walked slowly over to him. 'Mr. Slovak?' he asked.

'Who are you?' Slovak said, 'What are you doing here?'

'I'm Deputy Chief Fallon,' the man replied.

'What are you looking for? What right have you got to come in here?'

Fallon took a warrant from his jacket and handed it to him. Slovak looked at it and saw the items named in the warrant. 'Junk,' he asked, 'what makes you think you'll find junk here?'

'We have our reasons. I don't have to explain them to you. They were enough to get the warrant issued.' The man stared at Slovak for a while, as if he were taking this first opportunity to take a good look at him. There was an amused look in his eye whose source was that of a sudden, new-found pleasure that had been offered him, an unexpected diversion from a dull routine. The look toyed with Slovak and Slovak felt the muscles in his jaw twitch. 'You're from out of town, I believe,' the man went on. Slovak didn't answer. 'New York?'

'Have you finished in here?' Slovak asked coldly.

'Not quite.' The man smiled and continued to regard him steadily. Then he turned and looked casually round. 'I believe this house belongs to Margaret Phillips?' he said, finally.

Slovak nodded. 'That's right,' he answered.

'Have you known her long?'

'What's that to you?' Slovak asked.

There was a short silence. The man frowned. Clearly he was not used to being spoken to in this fashion. His eyes narrowed and he said to Slovak, 'Turn your pockets out.'

'What?' Slovak asked quietly.

'Turn your pockets out. Then pull the linings inside out.'

Slovak hesitated. He couldn't understand why this was happening to him. Were they genuine in their belief that there was junk hidden in the house or was this another attempt to provoke him? The idea of turning out his pockets, like some common criminal, outraged him. He looked past the man at the police officers standing in different parts of the room. They were all quite still and staring stonily at him. He decided it would be even more undignified if he were to resist and place himself in the position of being forcibly searched.

Slowly, he began to empty out his pockets, placing the contents on the desk beside him. They all waited patiently for him to complete the operation, as if no amount of time taken by him could put them out in any way. When he had finished, they still waited, making no move towards him and he saw they were waiting for something else. One by one he pulled the linings of all his pockets out and the man nodded, satisfied.

Then he said, 'Take off your clothes.'

The silence into which the words were dropped seemed to shatter it, though they were spoken quietly. Slovak felt the room begin to throb with a new and deeper tension. He turned pale and located the source of the throbbing in his heart, which had begun to beat very fast. The air in the room seemed to become all at once heavier, exerting an immense pressure upon his head, so that the throbbing increased in frequency, until it became a drumming noise in his ears. He shook his head, slowly. 'No,' he said.

'The law allows,' the man replied, softly, 'in search of junk, the law allows.'

Slovak stared at him and saw that he intended to have his

way. He felt the strength suddenly return to his legs and he moved swiftly towards the still open door but just as swiftly one of the police officers kicked it shut and Slovak stopped dead. It was like a trap closing. Every nerve in his body began to scream and he fought to keep down a wildly rising tide of hysteria.

'Take them off,' the man repeated, slowly. And when he didn't move, but continued to stand there, rigidly, added, 'or shall we do it?'

The threat made him shake. The thought of those hands upon him, violating him, raping his privacy so frightened him, that he shook visibly and he saw the man notice it and the corners of his mouth twitch up in a smile.

The momentary paralysis of his will had turned his arms into great weights which he found he could move only slowly and with a supreme effort. His limbs were heavy, as limbs become in a dream, and his hands could scarcely lift off the jacket which also seemed to have increased enormously in weight.

He got it off, however, and handed it to the man, who took it and without glancing round tossed it unceremoniously to one of the policemen standing by who proceeded to search it. The man then waited impassively for the next item of clothing. Piece by piece, Slovak took off his clothes and each piece was tossed carelessly to a different policeman who then went solemnly through the motions of searching it. Finally, Slovak removed his underpants and stood before them all stark naked.

He saw from the corners of his eyes, or perhaps only felt the smirks that appeared on the faces of the men around him. No one moved. Fallon stood there, appraising him in his nakedness as if wanting to keep him in that state for the longest possible time before declaring the ordeal over. The silence dragged on for so long and became so unnatural that finally one of the men broke into a nervous guffaw, which was silenced at once by a frowning look from his chief.

'Well,' Slovak asked, at last, unable to bear the situation any longer, 'did you find anything?'

'Not yet,' the man replied. He paused a moment, then stepped forward and stood very close to him. 'Open your mouth.'

They could do nothing to humiliate him more than they had already done. He opened his mouth and Fallon looked inside, peering this way and that like a dentist. He nodded, satisfied. Slovak closed his mouth. Without removing his eyes from Slovak, Fallon held his hand out to a policeman standing near. 'Wexler,' he said.

Wexler put his hand in his pocket and drew out a small, sealed envelope which he placed on the palm of Fallon's hand. Fallon took it. His eyes remained fixed on Slovak's face as if anxious not to miss any emotion that might flicker across it and with a quick movement he ripped the envelope across the top, put his fingers inside and withdrew from it a rubber finger-stall. With elaborate movements, far larger than were needed, he drew the stall on to his middle finger.

Slovak's whole frame went utterly rigid. Perspiration poured out of him, standing out on every square inch of his naked frame, so that he looked as if he had just emerged from a shower. He saw what the intention was and knew that he could not allow it. Surely, he would die first?

'Bend over,' Fallon said.

He could not move. Try as he might, every muscle and joint in his body was frozen into a paroxysm of terror. He trembled and shook with the effort to comply that vied with the rage in him to resist. He felt the gaze of these men running through him, dismantling the machinery of his inner self and creating an immense confusion in him.

He heard Fallon say again, 'Bend over,' and, when again he found himself unable to move, he heard him add, slowly, 'All bodily orifices – the law allows in search of junk.'

It seemed to him, then, that it was not they who were seek-

99

ing this humiliation of himself but that *he* was seeking it, that in some strange way, some dark and unaccountable way he had brought it all on himself. *He* was to blame and no one else. He could have avoided this situation. He could have refused to enter the house. When he saw that the lights were blazing and that strangers were moving all over the house, he could have stayed outside in the dark and merely watched until they went away. There had been no compulsion on him to enter. Why had he done so? Was it from an old arrogance that he was untouchable? Was it that he had nothing but contempt for these people and was, in his own way, challenging them to bring about this humiliation, not believing they would dare to do it? Or was it that he wanted them to do it?

He could not make up his mind what reason there was for his deliberate courting of this situation, this toying with a desire to be subjected to this outrage. He only knew that the moment he understood that it was not they who had brought about this situation but that it was he, himself, whether consciously or unconsciously who had contrived it, all his resistance seemed to vanish. It seemed to him that he had no cause, any longer, to refuse to comply with their request and that, deeply repugnant as it was to him to do so, he had no choice but to submit.

He bent over, almost touching his toes. Pride would not allow him to bend his knees. He let his head hang. He closed his eyes. He felt Fallon step up to him and pause. He shook. The agony of waiting was unendurable. Then, just as he felt that he could bear the position no longer, he felt a hand part his buttocks and the finger was thrust violently and deep into his rectum. For a moment, it remained there, a bewildering mixture of pain and pleasure. Then, it was swiftly withdrawn.

He heard the snap of the rubber as Fallon ripped the finger-stall off. He saw it drop in the waste basket beside him. He heard the voice, brisk and clear say, 'Right! This man is clean! Nothing on his person! Let's go!'

He heard the noise of passing feet as the men walked out of the room. Still he did not move. He heard the front door slam. Car doors were opened and closed in quick succession. Engines burst into life, one after the other, and the cars screeched away up the drive and out onto the road leading down to the highway. It was only when the last murmur of the car engines had receded to nothing, that he leant against the desk and then slowly slid down it onto the floor in a state of almost complete collapse.

Fallon knocked on Groczek's door, opened it, and then stood back to allow Maggie to pass in front of him. Groczek looked up from his desk, nodded and indicated a chair for her to sit down in. She sat down on the chair facing him and crossed her legs. Fallon went out and shut the door.

Groczek looked at her, appraisingly. She was, certainly, a very beautiful woman, cool but capable, he felt, of great depth of feeling. He got up from his chair, came round towards her and sat on the edge of his desk, looking at her. 'It was good of you to come,' he said, smiling.

'I was picked up,' Maggie replied, 'and bundled into a car. That's why I'm here.'

Groczek clucked his tongue deprecatingly. 'They were told to ask you,' he said, 'if you'd mind coming and talking to me. They get over-zealous, you know. They try too hard to please.' He smiled winningly at her. 'You don't mind, do you?'

'Yes, I do mind,' Maggie said, 'and unless you're holding me for something, I'd really like to go.'

'Well, but you're here, now,' Groczek coaxed, 'and after all, there's no reason why a decent, law-abiding citizen shouldn't help the police. I only want to ask a few questions. You're not going to demand to see lawyers or quote the fifth amendment at me?'

He sat there, smiling at her, utterly reasonable.

'If you think I'm a perfectly respectable citizen,' Maggie

said finally, 'then you should treat me like one. Decent people aren't bundled into cars.'

'Will you accept my apologies,' he asked, 'and let's start all over again?' He paused a moment, and then went on, 'You're a friend of Frank Slovak. Well, you were in the car with him when we had our little collision. How long have you known him?'

'A few years.'

'Where did you first meet him?'

'In New York. I worked there for a while.'

'What was he doing?'

'I don't know.'

'You must have known. You lived with him for a while, didn't you?'

'I never asked him.'

'Well, didn't he go out every day?'

'No.'

'Didn't that strike you as odd? I mean, a man has to make a living.'

'It was none of my business.'

There was a pause for a moment and Groczek studied her. Then he said, 'What made you go to New York?'

Maggie shrugged. 'What makes anyone go to New York? I wanted a change.'

'To get away from home?' She didn't answer. 'Your family's quite wealthy, I believe, sober citizens. Weren't they worried about you?'

'They knew where I was.'

'Did they know what you were doing there?'

'What was I doing?'

'Working in a nightclub, weren't you?'

'If you say so. You seem to be asking me a lot of questions you already know the answers to.'

'I just want to test how co-operative you are. What was the name of the nightclub?' She didn't answer. 'The Golden

102

Spade?' Again she said nothing. He smiled. 'Not too co-operative, are you? The Golden Spade isn't exactly a very savoury spot. What were you doing – slumming?'

She stared at him steadily for a moment. What right had he to ask her all these questions? What right had he to treat her with such obvious contempt? She checked, momentarily, the tide of anger rising up inside her but when he said, 'I asked you a question,' in a low and menacing voice, she said responding on the level he had been treating her, 'Fuck off.'

He slapped her hard across the face, knocking her head sideways. She made no response, but simply sat there, staring at him. Then he said, 'I wouldn't take that from anyone,' and then was silent once more. He got up from his desk and went and stood by the window, staring out of it across the city. 'A girl from a background like yours,' he went on, finally, shaking his head, 'where do you learn such language?'

He turned from the window and looked at her. 'Once upon a time us "cops" could rely on people like you and your class. You were our natural allies. Now, you're no better than the rest of the junk-ridden hippies and dead beats and drop-outs. I don't know what the world is coming to – the pus oozes out of every corner.'

He left the window and came and sat down once more behind his desk. He looked at her, his face dark and angry. 'Don't you speak to me again like that, ever, or I'll knock your teeth out, woman or no woman.' He glared at her as if he had a mind to strike her again, but all he did was to sit quite still for a while. Then, he said, 'Now, you listen to me. You lived with Slovak for a while and you never knew what he did. Amazing. Well, now, pin back your ears and hear me. He's a criminal. He's what they call an "engineer". He plans very big jobs – only the biggest. I know, because I've got a file on him. The New York police have been watching him for quite some time. And that's how I know all about you.'

'Did you bring me here to tell me that?'

'No. I want to know something that I think you're more likely to know than anyone. What is he down here for?'

'He came down to see me.'

'No.' Groczek shook his head slowly and certainly. 'He came down here for something else.'

'Are you charging me with anything?'

'I'll tell you when I'm charging you with something.' He pointed a finger at her. 'Right now, you're just helping me with an investigation.'

'Investigation into what?'

'A robbery.'

'What robbery?'

'Ah, well, that's just it – it hasn't taken place yet. But it will. That's what he's down here for. Now, I want to know what it is.'

'Do you think he'd tell me?'

'Yes. Strangely enough, I think he would.' He paused for a moment. 'That's your house he's in, isn't it?'

She nodded. 'I've lent it to him.'

'How long is he staying?'

'I don't know.'

'You didn't ask him?'

'No.'

He stared at her a while, thinking. Then he said, 'I could make it very hard for you, you know? I could make it hard for anyone in this city. I could make it hard for him, too, do you understand?'

'What am I supposed to do about it?'

'I want you to tell him that. I want you to make it clear to him that I know he's down here to do a job. I don't know yet what it is, but that's not as important as knowing why he's here – you tell him that. And tell him this, too. There's no way he can pull a caper in this city without my knowing he's behind it. There's no way he can pull it and get away with it, I'll see to that. Tell him. And tell him while he's here he'll

104

never be out of my thoughts, just as I know damned well I'm never out of his – and that's how we understand each other.'

There was a short pause. Then Maggie said, 'Can I go now?'

'You can go. But see that he gets that message, and let him understand that until he does – understand, I mean – I'll pull you in whenever I think fit.'

There was another short silence. It was her turn and he waited. But she said nothing. She got up, without a word, and walked out. He sat there staring after her, a smile of immense satisfaction on his face.

Chapter Seven

As she put her key into the lock and opened the door, he came out of the shadows where he had been waiting for her and pushed her inside. She gasped with fright at first, not knowing who it was, and then, when she saw him, she flushed angrily. 'What are you doing?' she asked, 'what's the matter with you?'

He shut the door and stared at her with such intensity that she grew afraid again. 'Frank,' she said, 'Frank, what is it?'

'Why didn't you tell me?' he asked.

She looked at him, bewildered. 'Tell you? Tell you what?'

Suddenly, all restraint seemed to leave him. He grabbed her and shook her till her teeth rattled and she screamed at him, 'Frank! Frank!'

'Why didn't you tell me?' he shouted. 'You bitch! Why didn't you tell me? You're taking dope or pushing it, which is it?'

'Leave me alone!' She screamed at him, trying to tear herself away from him, but he held on to her, slamming her back against the wall, like a man demented till all the breath was

105

gone from her body and she felt her back was about to break.

'They know about you,' he said, 'the cops *know* about you! You let me take that house and you never told me!'

'Frank, stop it, stop it! Oh, God, please stop it – Frank!' Her last, long piercing scream seemed to get through to him and he let go of her. She fell back against the wall sobbing.

But he wasn't finished with her yet, and his sudden calm only added to her fear of him. He reached out and took a handful of her hair, forcing her head back and exposing her neck in a tight, white arc. 'I ought to cut your throat,' he said to her.

'I don't know what you're talking about,' she sobbed, 'please let me go, please!'

'Why didn't you tell me?' he asked again. 'You *know* how I work, you know I do nothing that leads them to me, nothing!'

'Oh, Frank, will you please tell me what I've done,' she cried, 'I don't know what you're talking about.'

'The cops were at the house tonight. They turned it over. They turned *me* over!' She screamed again as he wrenched her head back even farther, but he seemed not to hear her. 'They were looking for junk,' he went on, grimly, 'junk! They had a warrant. Now, why would they do that, Maggie? Why – if they had no connections with you? What have they got on you? You've been picked up before, haven't you? You've been pulled in. You've been on the dope, you bitch, and you never told me! You could've ruined everything, everything!'

With one last, violent effort he flung her across the room and she collapsed onto a sofa. He stood there, watching her, his face quivering with rage and anger. She pulled herself up and turned and faced him, wiping the tears off her cheeks with the palms of her hands. She could see that the violence was leaving him and that he was already beginning to hate himself for having hurt her. She said quietly, 'Did you see any needle marks, Frank?'

The question jolted him. It was true, he had had her lying naked beside him and he hadn't seen any marks on her. Surely he would have noticed? 'Maybe they healed,' he said, though he already knew she was telling the truth, 'maybe you kicked the habit, but not before the cops knew about it. Why else would they turn your house over?'

She sat wearily down on the sofa, leaned back and closed her eyes, as if she wanted to shut him out for good, as if she had suddenly lost all interest in him. But he couldn't let go. 'Well?' he asked, insistently.

'Go away, Frank, leave me alone. I didn't ask you to come here. I didn't ask you to live in my house. Just go away and leave me alone.'

'They were looking for junk, Maggie,' he repeated, though there was no longer any conviction in his voice, 'they were looking for junk. They turned everything over. They turned *me* over. They stripped me and searched me.'

'They weren't looking for junk, Frank, they were looking for you,' she said, tiredly. Then she turned and looked at him and laughed when she saw the look on his face. 'You're incredible. It would never enter your head that might happen to you. You're too big, too important, so there has to be some other reason. It has to be me.' She shook her head and looked away again. Then she went on, 'It's you they want, Frank, not me. They know about you and they want you out.'

'Out?' He couldn't understand her. What was she saying? 'What do you mean, out?'

She laughed again. 'Out,' she repeated, 'out of this city, out of this county. They're not going to leave you alone. Don't you understand? They're going to make life so uncomfortable for you, you'll just pull up and get out.' She paused a moment and then added, 'and I wish you would.'

He stood there, staring at her, puzzled. He couldn't quite take in what she was saying to him. 'Me,' he asked, 'they're harassing me? Like some cheap pickpocket?' She laughed again, a high, slightly hysterical note in it, for his manner suddenly appeared comic to her but he didn't hear it. What had finally penetrated was that what she was saying was true. The idea that had been forming itself within his mind and which he had resisted giving expression to, *she* had stated quite simply and clearly. They were harassing him, like some down and out, some public petty nuisance they wanted out of the territory and for whom no laws could be found that effectively applied. It was unbelievable and yet he knew it was true.

It was, of course, Groczek. He should have known. He had under-estimated him – not his ability, no, but his nerve, or was it his desperation? He would have to deal with him, put him in his place. He had stepped out of line. This small mind had failed to understand the rules of the game. Instead of making proper moves, he had merely blundered into the board and imagined he'd won when he saw all the pieces on the floor. That was typical of the man. He had misjudged him, under-estimated not his size but his smallness, not his strength of mind but his weakness. That was an error, too, an error he should not have made. He should have seen it coming earlier. It disturbed him to think he had made such errors, small though they were. He must put them right at once, set the scales to balance so that they both knew where they were and could start again.

'It's Groczek, isn't it,' he said, quietly, 'Groczek. I should've known.' He thought again for a while and nodded to himself. Yes, and pulling her in, that was part of the harassment, too, getting at him through her. It upset him to think he had brought this on her, and even more that he had thought for a while that she had betrayed him. She was lighting a cigarette and her hand was trembling. He came over and sat down beside her. 'Maggie,' he said, softly, 'I'm sorry. I should've known better.' She didn't answer, just sat there pulling hard on the cigarette. 'I'll make it up to you.'

'Just go away, Frank,' she replied, 'that's all the making-up I want you to do.'

The idea flickered briefly in his mind and he stared at it. 'Would you come away with me if I did?'

'Come away with you? Where? To start something else all over again? You don't seem to understand, Frank, I hate what you are. It's not just that it frightens me, I hate it. It's wrong! And most people know it's wrong! I know you don't see that or you don't feel it, but it is! Dear God, it's unbelievable, I should have to sit here and explain to you that what you do is wrong, but I do believe you don't see it the way everyone else sees it. Some damned,' – she searched for the word but couldn't find the right one – '*connection* in you is gone, or maybe it was never there in the first place, I don't know, but you don't think or feel like anyone else. Most people have a sense of right and wrong, Frank, *you* don't! I don't say you don't have it with other things, but in *this* you don't, and it frightens me and I hate it, can't you see that?'

He could see it and yet he couldn't, or couldn't see that it *mattered*. It was a fine distinction but it was the only one he could make. He knew what she was saying and knew she meant it, but why was it so important to her? Why couldn't she just accept him the way he was?

All this was now, however, beside the point. He knew what he had to do. If he were to accomplish what he had come here to do, he must first go to see Groczek. He must set up the board again between them, replace the pieces. It would never do to let him think that in some way he had altered the position to the balance of his own advantage. Groczek must be put back in his place and then things could proceed again and then they could be finished. And only when they were finished could he make any progress with Maggie.

Without another word he got up and left the apartment, closing the door quietly behind him. He got into his car and drove to the western end of the city. It was late but it never occurred to him that Groczek would be either in bed or out. He found the house, which was part of a small group of middingly expensive dwellings, built on a rise in the ground where it ran out of the city. He parked the car. There was a light over the door. He approached it and rang the bell.

A woman's voice answered on the speaker system. 'What do you want?' she asked.

'I've come to see Chief Groczek,' he said.

'It's very late. Is he expecting you?'

'He's expecting me. Tell him it's Frank Slovak.'

There was a pause, a long pause, and then he heard footsteps approach the front door and the door was opened. A woman stood there, a faded woman in a housecoat. 'He'll see you,' she said, quietly, 'he's in the study.'

She closed the door and led the way through the hall to the rear of the house which was quiet and dark, as if most of the lights had been put out just prior to the occupants retiring to bed. She paused outside a heavy door and knocked. Groczek's voice said, 'Come in.'

She opened the door and stood aside. Groczek was working at his desk. A single light shone on his papers, plunging the rest of the room, which was large, into shadows. From where he stood, just inside the doorway, Slovak saw Groczek lift his head and stare across the room at him. Their eyes met briefly and again Slovak felt oddly unnerved, as he had done in the car after the collision. It was again the sense of his own self-scrutiny having separated from him entirely and having taken up its position in the spot where Groczek sat. But the feeling was momentary and it passed. Groczek said, quietly, 'All right, Mary.'

She looked at Slovak and he passed in front of her without giving her a look and stood on the carpet staring across the desk at Groczek. He heard the door close quietly behind him. This was only the second time he had seen Groczek face to face and yet he felt he knew already, everything he needed to know about the man, but that there was also part of him that was unfamiliar, dark, hidden, so to speak, in shadow and it was the perception of that darker side which, he saw, had unnerved him at first. He could not quite make out why this had happened but he felt that by the end of the evening he would know.

Groczek did not move from his desk but merely indicated the black leather chair in front of it and said, 'Sit down.' Slovak sat down, his eyes never leaving Groczek's face. He sank slowly back into the soft leather, withdrawing into the partial shadow in which the back of the chair was swathed, feeling almost a sense of relief, as if someone had shaded his eyes from a glare.

Groczek studied him a moment, his head nodding on his shoulders as though making notes for himself and ticking them off one by one. Then, his head came up slightly, and he said, in a sharp, commanding voice, 'Well, what do you want?'

Slovak said, quietly, 'I'm being harassed.'

'Harassed?'

Slovak nodded. 'Harassed,' he repeated, 'and I don't like it.'

Groczek smiled at him and tilted his head sideways. 'Never happened to you before?'

'No,' said Slovak, in an even tone, 'never. And, as I say, I don't like it. I know that you're behind it. They wouldn't do it unless you told them to. And so I've come to you.'

'Do you want to make a complaint?'

The voice was thin, amused. Slovak shook his head. 'No, I don't make complaints. I never have cause, as I see it.'

'Don't make complaints?' Groczek smiled. 'Well, that's a pity. We have a whole procedure for investigating complaints. It's very thorough, very efficient and very fair.'

The man was playing with him. It was the breathalyser all over again, the house search, the body search. It was a refusal to take him seriously. He leaned forward so that his face was

111

partially caught in the light from the desk and said, 'Listen to me, for your own good. You're a little fish and you've swum into a big pond. But big ponds don't make big fish. They stay just the size they were when they swam into it. So keep your distance. If you snap at me again, I'll swallow you whole.'

'Got a lot of power, have you?' Groczek asked, archly, 'a lot of connections?'

'More than you ever dreamed of,' Slovak replied, quietly, 'or that you could ever dream of. Now, take my advice. Swim about a bit. Enjoy yourself, play among the rushes. It's a big pond – maybe I won't even know you're around.'

There was a long pause. Slovak waited to see if his words had gone home and then, when Groczek didn't reply, he rose from his chair and without another word, walked to the door. He felt Groczek's eyes watching him all the way and as he put his hand on the door knob, Groczek said, 'I've been reading about you.'

He stopped. He turned, slowly, and looked at him. Groczek grinned and nodded at him. 'Reading about you. Fascinating.' He picked up the file and held it in the air for him to see, letting it fall back upon the desk from a height, making a sharp, flat report that reverberated through the room. Slovak didn't move. 'Did you know we'd got a file on you?' Groczek asked. 'Very impressive. Only needs a touch of colour to make it look like a travel agent's brochure.'

He got up from behind his desk and came round to the front. He sat on the edge of it, one leg dangling, utterly relaxed, and in no sense impatient for the interview to end. He laughed. 'Quote. "This five star crook offers a welcome challenge to the tired cop, looking for a little excitement away from his normal routine. He comes equipped with a great brain and powerful connections. He is not to be under-estimated. Can be relied upon to be one step ahead all the time and give anyone a great run for his money. He will never be

112

caught, of course, but the exhilaration of the chase is as reviving as a month in the mountain air." Unquote.' He laughed again. 'Are you really that good?'

There was a short silence. Then Slovak said, 'You'll find out.' He turned the handle of the door and opened it.

Groczek said coldly, 'You're not going anywhere. Who are you kidding?'

Slovak paused, his back to Groczek and staring out through the open door into the dimly lit hall. He could feel Groczek's eyes upon him and his words, flung from the desk across the room were like a knife quivering in his back. He wanted to go and yet felt an immense compulsion to stay. Quietly, he closed the door again and turned once more to Groczek.

Groczek smiled at him. 'Bright boy, aren't you?' he said. 'Won a scholarship to college, no doubt, but couldn't afford to go – just like me.'

'Didn't choose to,' Slovak corrected, softly.

'Well, well, it all comes to the same,' Groczek replied, 'let's not quibble.'

'Is that all you've got to say?' Slovak asked after a pause.

'I've got a lot more to say, you know that. That's why you've stopped there. That's why you didn't go through that door, because you sensed I've got a lot to say and you want to hear it.' He paused a moment, and then went on, 'There's something between you and me, isn't there? You know it and I know it and that's what you want to find out.'

He sat there, grinning at him, confident, sure of his position and his authority. Slovak stared at him. At that moment, he had absolutely nothing to say, only an immense urge to listen, as if he must, above all else, know this man.

'Yes, it's an impressive file,' Groczek said, glancing down at it. 'Told me quite a lot. Not that I really needed any New York cop to tell me about you. I know all about you, already.' And he added, after a pause, 'Just as you know all about me.'

He waited for some response, but when none came he went on, 'We're the same, you and I, haven't you noticed? We even look alike.'

And there was a sense in which they did. Slovak had already registered that at the back of his mind but not commented on it. It wasn't that they were identical, or could be mistaken for each other, but there was a physical likeness as to shape, bulk and colouring which was almost as powerful in its effect as an identity between them.

'You know,' Groczek continued, 'I've got a theory – that there are only about a dozen physical types in the whole world, black, brown, yellow and white, endlessly repeating themselves. You can predict people's behaviour from the way they look, did you know that?'

'You ought to write a book about it.'

'Well, I don't suppose you'd read it,' Groczek answered, expansively, not at all put out, 'and anyway, it's all up there.' He tapped his forehead and smiled. 'But it's not surprising, is it, that all those tiny genes that make us look alike on the outside should make us look alike on the in? It's just physiology. People don't study it enough. Ask any cop who draws up an identikit picture – he knows.'

He got off the desk and came towards him, standing in front of him grinning, obviously enjoying himself. 'We're like two sides of the same coin, you and me. We're like the north and south poles, identical but opposite.'

'So?'

'So that's why I know you didn't come here tonight, just to complain. You came for something else. Sit down and I'll tell you.'

Slovak didn't move. Groczek waited, standing only a few inches in front of him, smiling invitingly. Then, when he could see that Slovak had no intention of moving, he shrugged and walked back to his desk, sitting on the edge again and looking at him with a sideways tilt of the head.

114

'You came down here to pull a job, didn't you? Oh, come on, you can admit it. There's no one here, no bugs or anything. Isn't that what you came for?'

'That's for you to find out.'

'Oh, I *know* – I don't have to find out. What I don't know is *what*? What you came to pull. But I'll find that out too, I promise you. There's no way you can operate in *my* city without my knowing about it, you understand? *That* you can do in New York, but not here.'

He was silent for a moment, studying Slovak who still stood by the door as if half his mind were tugging at him to go and the other half urging him to stay just a moment longer. Groczek could see the conflict going on inside him and he was amused. 'I see you're still stuck by that door, and I'll tell you why. Because you haven't yet heard what it was you came to hear. You're still waiting. Well, you mustn't deny me my little bit of fun. You see, although we know each other very well, there's also a sense in which we don't know each other at all. That's the sense in which we don't really know ourselves and so there's always the possibility of surprise. That's what keeps us alive. That's what's keeping you there at this very moment. There's something that I can tell you about yourself that no one else can.'

He laughed again and waved his hand in the air in a self-deprecating gesture of acknowledgement to the silent laughter of angels who had come to watch his performance and, in truth, Slovak had to acknowledge that the man had uncanny insights. He seemed to know him remarkably well.

'For instance, you didn't come down here just to pull a job, did you?' Groczek continued. 'No, I'll tell you why you came down. You came down here because of me. You'd heard about *me*, hadn't you? You'd heard that I was the best, and you had to test it. You couldn't leave it alone. You just had to know. You couldn't rest. You couldn't sleep or eat until that little enigma was solved. And solved it shall be, I promise you.'

115

Groczek laughed, and shook his head. 'But that's not what you really came down for either, is it? Not entirely. I can read you like a book. And you know why, don't you? I've explained that to you.' He paused for a while and then got off the desk and came over to Slovak. He pointed at a swing mirror standing on a small cabinet by the wall. 'Look in there,' he said.

Slowly, reluctantly, Slovak raised his eyes and stared into the mirror. He saw Groczek and himself reflected in it. 'We're peas from the same pod, you and I,' Groczek said, 'I could have been you, you could have been me – but for the Grace of God, as they say.' He laughed out loud again as a thought suddenly struck him. 'Well, it proves it, doesn't it – we both ended up in crime.'

The joke amused him and his laughter brayed out across the room. Slovak, however, was unamused. He stood quite still, staring into the mirror at the reflection of himself and Groczek. Groczek looked at Slovak in the mirror and then looked at Slovak himself.

'Do you know why I'm a cop?' he asked. 'Because I like to hunt. It's as simple as that and as crude. I enjoy it. Naturally, I don't tell anyone that, the public wouldn't like it. A cop's not supposed to get pleasure out of his work. Still, I'm all for blood sports, I really believe the deer enjoys it, don't you?'

Slovak didn't answer. He had turned from the mirror and was looking straight at Groczek. Groczek was studying him, tilting his head this way and that as if making a very profound assessment. Finally, he shook his head and said, 'You're not just in crime for the money. You're in it for the excitement, the challenge. That's your protein and it's mine.'

'You talk a lot, don't you?' Slovak said.

'Sometimes.' Groczek was silent for a while, then he turned to the mirror and pointed. 'Look in there, again,' and when Slovak didn't respond, he said, 'Go on, look. What are you afraid of?'

There was a pause. Then, slowly, Slovak turned and looked once more in the mirror, staring at the reflection of them both in it.

'We make a pair, don't we?' Groczek went on, 'we balance each other – a natural balance, like in nature. Ecology they call it now, don't they? That's how we need each other. Look.'

He stepped aside, removing his image from the mirror, his eyes fixed on Slovak, watching his every reaction. 'You feel strange, don't you?' Groczek asked, 'unbalanced, incomplete? The ecology of things has been disturbed. Who are you? You're not sure anymore. You're even beginning to doubt if you exist at all.'

And it was true, though Groczek could not have known this, for his eyes were riveted on Slovak's face, watching for every change in expression, and so never saw that as he moved away from the mirror, Slovak's reflection disappeared too, or seemed to Slovak to disappear. It was an odd sensation that he had had before and couldn't fully explain, how, now and then, his reflection seemed to come and go in a glass as if he couldn't hold it there no matter how he tried to fix it with his eyes.

Groczek, however, was unaware of this, intent only on making his own point. He stepped up again beside Slovak and pointed into the mirror once more. 'See,' he said, as his reflection took its place again beside that of Slovak, 'now it's all right. A proper balance.' And, indeed, the two of them, side by side, restored a symmetry that was, in some way, pleasing, that made, as Groczek said, a proper balance.

'Who are you?' Groczek asked, 'isn't that what you came here to find out? Really find out? Wasn't that the real object of your journey here, as much as anything else? Isn't that the true nature of this whole enterprise?'

The room had gone so quiet that Slovak could almost feel the silence throbbing. Again, he felt an immense urge to leave. Groczek's presence was becoming unbearable to him, imposing a great strain on him. Each word he spoke was like the thin

117

blade of a knife inserted into the fine cracks of his mind, scraping out the loose mortar and widening the gaps.

'You despise yourself, don't you,' Groczek continued, 'you act out this play about yourself being a big shot but really, deep inside, you despise yourself.' He nodded understandingly. 'I know that feeling. It's that other face we put up to show the world that finally turns round and looks at *us*. It's a penetrating stare, isn't it? Cuts right through you. First, it's sort of sympathetic and friendly. It likes you, approves of you as a person, approves of what you do and how you look to the world. Then, the look kind of goes sour and doesn't much like what it sees, doesn't much like itself, I suppose, seeing that it's not really anything at all – just an impersonation.'

Slovak could stand it no more. He felt the blade of Groczek's knife finally break through to the other side. It was as though a whole brick had now been removed and that Groczek had thrust his hands inside him and was taking the pieces apart, bit by bit, and that if he didn't get out of the room he would collapse inwardly, he would *implode*. He took a step towards the door and his hand was on the door knob again when Groczek said, with a short laugh, 'You want approval, don't you, recognition?'

'I've had all I need,' Slovak said, without turning.

'Oh, yes,' Groczek replied, contemptuously, 'from the morons, maybe, who inhabit that tiny, twilight world you live in. But that's not enough. You want more than that, much more. You need it, or you'll just vanish. People don't know who you are. All those jobs you've pulled, brilliant jobs, weren't they? Set the public on their ears. All those headlines in the press, those news flashes on radio and television – but no mention of you, nothing. You've worked in the dark for so long you don't know if you've been dreaming it or living it. You're even beginning to doubt if you exist at all – like I said.'

Groczek had touched now, on the naked truth of it. It was clever of him to have done so, but it wouldn't get him far.

118

Slovak turned round, slowly, and looked at Groczek, letting his hand fall away from the handle of the door.

'But you don't have any doubts, I suppose?' he said.

'Oh, no,' Groczek replied, shaking his head, slowly, and smiling confidently at him, 'and I'll tell you something else. Neither will you, when I've finished with you. When I send you up for thirty years, you'll know you're no different from the rest. And that's really what you want, isn't it? You really want to be like all the rest, one of the crowd. You've been separated from the herd too long. It's lonely out there. Oh, it has its advantages. You live better than the rest and it satisfies a certain vanity. But it's a strain too, isn't it. It's that old struggle between the desire for freedom and the fear of it, the need to be part of the herd and the desire to break away. Everybody has it, but you've got it, mister, in spades, as they say. You cut the cord clean through, you broke the connection and you're never going to find your way back – not alone, anyway. You need help and I'm going to provide it. Yes, me,' he went on, smiling, 'little old me. I'm going to bring you in, put you back in the herd again. And you'll never leave it.'

For a long while, Slovak stared at him. Then, he shook his head slowly. 'No,' he said, 'you're not big enough, nowhere near.'

'You forget.' Groczek grinned. 'I have the help of a brilliant mind.'

'Whose?'

'Why, yours,' said Groczek, 'whose do you think?' and he put a hand on the mirror and spun it, so that it turned rapidly on its stand and walked away back to his desk. A point of light, caught in the mirror, flickered on Slovak's face, seeming to hold him there. It was an absurd, flamboyant gesture, a cheap trick and he could easily have put out his hand and stopped the mirror turning, but instead he stood there watching it get slower and slower until at last it stopped turning altogether. Only then did he turn and look at Groczek.

119

Groczek had seated himself behind the desk again and was leaning back in his chair, regarding him steadily, waiting for him to respond.

'Mine,' Slovak asked, finally, 'why mine?'

'Well,' Groczek answered, 'I'll try and explain.' The room seemed to become even stiller than it was before and the silence more heavy. Slovak waited. Groczek had taken out a cigar and cut the end off it while he was choosing the words he wanted to use, but having cut off the end he didn't light it but merely left it dangling between his fingers.

He looked up at Slovak and then said, 'I'll put it this way. There's a certain kind of bright boy who carries with him, like a parrot on his back, his own Angel of Death, his own destroyer. Why?' Groczek shrugged. 'Who knows. Maybe it's the guilt, maybe he finally gets just plain tired of his own cleverness. It becomes a burden to him, a crushing weight. It's like a great weariness that comes from knowing he can never be caught. And so he begins to want to, want to be caught, I mean. It's a strange, mysterious and perverse process, but it's real, it happens, and it proceeds from his desire to be normal again, to feel that he can make a mistake and get caught like anyone else.'

Slovak recognised a partial truth in what Groczek was saying. It was familiar to him. Groczek had, in fact, put it into words better than he could have done himself. It was true, the weariness had touched him, he had felt it blow over him and he had trapped that same thought in his mind like a seed that had blown his way and settled. But it was not the whole truth. It was no more than the fleeting desire one had sometimes, to put one's hand in a flame, out of cussedness, out of perversity. Or was it more? Was Groczek perhaps more right than he thought? Was it, for instance, from a desire to feel pain and in feeling pain to be reassured that one actually felt at all?

'Why?' he asked, and for the first time leading the conversation on, 'why doesn't he just give himself up?'

120

Groczek shook his head and looked at Slovak with some disappointment. It was almost as if he had expected something better. 'He can't,' he said, 'just give himself up.'

'Why not?'

'It's too easy. It lacks form, excitement. He prefers to get careless, risk more, and look for someone who'll be bright enough to take the burden off him.'

'And that's you?'

Groczek nodded slowly. 'Yes,' he said, 'that's me.'

'And you think it'll happen?'

'Oh, yes,' Groczek answered, 'it'll happen. That's certain. You see, it's a sort of game he plays and the game has already begun. By taking ever increasing risks, he tries to tempt a sort of divine retribution. If the retribution doesn't come, well, he feels momentarily absolved, as if he's had a sign of approval. He can honestly say, "Look, I gave you your chance, you didn't take it. I didn't hide. I didn't skulk." And the burden of guilt lifts for a while, because he took the chance, deliberately exposed himself. But it doesn't lift for long. He has to start all over again, increasing the risks, lengthening the odds against himself. And, of course, when the retribution does come, well, that, in a way, is what he's been looking for.'

There was a long pause. Groczek never moved. His eyes were fixed on Slovak, confident and assured. Slovak said to him, 'You think you know me pretty well, don't you?'

Groczek nodded. 'Like I said, we're the same, inside and out.'

'Yes, the same,' Slovak repeated. He was silent for a moment and then he walked slowly over to Groczek and, leaning down, put his face close to his so that their eyes were no more than inches away from each other's. 'You've forgotten something then,' he said.

'Have I?' Groczek seemed amused. 'What's that?'

'There's a parrot on your back, too.' Slovak turned, walked swiftly to the door and opened it. He glanced back once.

121

Groczek was sitting exactly where he had left him, utterly transfixed, Slovak's words seeming to have pierced him like an arrow. Slovak went out, closing the door behind him.

He drove the car back fast to the house. His mind was utterly clear. He knew what he had to do, knew now what he had come there to do. Not only must he seize the heroin – and that was already planned in his mind, the labour and the equipment spoken for – he must also and in the process destroy Groczek utterly.

Chapter Eight

After Slovak had gone his words continued to ring in Groczek's head. He continued to sit there, in the semi-darkness, long after he heard the front door close. He was shaking. His nerve had gone. One phrase had destroyed it, had sent the rising tower of his confidence crashing to the ground. It was absurd, yet it had happened, absurd because his position was in no way weakened by the confrontation – he was still Groczek, Chief of Police, with all the power and resources at his command that went with the post – yet he knew, beyond doubt, that it had happened. He felt his confidence draining out of him like a great internal haemorrhage. As he continued to sit there, he had, for a while, the distinct impression that he was bleeding to death, literally, which was not, after all, so fanciful when one remembered the role that confidence played in the life of a man. Slovak's blow had inflicted a large, gaping wound in that confidence and yet was it not the last, despairing blow of a man himself mortally wounded? Groczek was not sure.

The wound, however, healed, or seemed to. Perhaps it was due to the fact that Slovak disappeared from the scene and, inevitably, Groczek began to wonder if he had not been more successful than he realised. Perhaps, after all, he had frightened him off. Though, in the following days, he found his mind constantly returning to Slovak and pondering his whereabouts; still, as time passed he found himself thinking less and less about him until at last he, too, began to wonder if his presence there had not been a dream after all, nothing more than a scene, powerfully enacted in his mind in the quiet of his own study.

The wound healed and his confidence began slowly to return. Fallon noticed it and became more cheerful. He had been puzzled by Groczek's brooding manner over these few days. It was unlike his chief. He knew that it had something to do with Slovak but had found Groczek's obsession with the man unhealthy and not at all fitting with the Groczek he had known. He had tried to provoke him on the subject several times but Groczek had remained non-committal. All he would say was that he knew Slovak was there to pull a job, despite what Rosetti might think, and that a man with a reputation of that sort could not simply be left to go his own way when he entered your territory. He, therefore, wanted him kept constantly under observation.

Fallon had shrugged mentally. Observation was one thing, obsession was another. There were, after all, other things happening in the territory that required Groczek's attention more urgently than the mere arrival of a man with a reputation. Slovak had done nothing since he arrived that in anyone else would have excited comment let alone suspicion. To produce in Groczek such a mood of preoccupation seemed, to Fallon, little short of self-indulgence. He began to wonder if he were not witnessing the first signs of Groczek cracking under the strain of his commitments. He had seen it happen before with others. It began with obsessions with trivia, the blowing-up of minor incidents into events of major importance so that all perspective was lost. He had seen it turn into paranoia, into

123

E

the belief that the world was conspiring against one. Small and harmless conversations on the other side of the room were suddenly seen as conspiracies, carried on in whispers, and directed against oneself. He had seen the signs of strain before in others and wondered if he were not seeing them again in Groczek.

As the day of the trial approached, Groczek became more and more absorbed in it. He spent long hours in the D.A.'s office, preparing the case, going over the evidence. The expiry of the warrant was not considered by any means a powerful obstacle to conviction. Doubtless the judge would take it into account but it was not likely to prove a high hurdle.

On the third day of the trial he went into the box to give evidence. He was relaxed and good-humoured. The trial had been going well, and if he had been in any doubt of this, his doubts would have instantly vanished when he looked at the faces of the defendants sitting with their counsels. They knew they were in trouble. They were the faces of men around whom a net was being drawn and who knew it and could not stop it. When he took his seat in the witness box, he smiled at them and was pleased to see them scowl and turn away.

The D.A. led him through their carefully rehearsed evidence. He answered briefly and to the point. He described the manner in which the activities of the ring had first come to his notice, the painstaking detective work that had closely followed its activities, the case that had been built up against it, the information that had led them to the huge consignment arriving in the ship and that had enabled them to follow its progress to the restaurant in which the consignment was to be broken up, sold and redistributed throughout the country. He left nothing out except his sources of information which he claimed, as always, the right to protect. It made an impressive case and he saw that the jury were impressed by it.

The D.A. sat down and Young's defence counsel, Hearst, rose to his feet to cross examine. He was an elderly, grey-haired man. He had considerable experience and Groczek had met him many times before. They did not like each other. Groczek did not approve of the hectoring manner that Hearst assumed in court or the implications he always managed to implant in a jury that the police were more interested in convictions than in the truth of the matter.

Groczek, however, was not worried. He sat there, at ease with himself and the world, staring round the courtroom, while Hearst studied the notes he had made on the pad in front of him, his thick glasses slipping down to the end of his nose. The courtroom was fairly full, the case having attracted considerable attention and only a few places were unoccupied.

Hearst began by taking him back over the evidence he had submitted under examination by the D.A. Step by step he tried to show that there was another interpretation to be placed upon this evidence, namely, that if, in fact – and it was yet to be proved – his client's premises were being used as the headquarters of a drug ring in the city, it was perfectly possible that his client knew nothing about it.

Groczek defended himself and his account easily and confidently. Twist and turn as Hearst would, shaping and reshaping his questions, Groczek would admit no other possible interpretation to the facts he had given. His answers, sometimes sharp, sometimes amused, gave Hearst no respite, left him no openings to leap through. His patience wore thinner and thinner and his exasperation began to show.

'You say,' Hearst said to him, finally, 'that Mr. Young's connection with this alleged drug ring has been known to you for some time?'

Groczek nodded. 'That's right.'

'Known to you as a result of information whose source you apparently cannot disclose?'

'That is correct.'

'Why not?'

'That's obvious, isn't it?'

'You're suggesting,' Hearst continued, 'that there would be some kind of threat to your source if his identity were known?'

'I am.'

'Well, that's very dramatic, Chief Groczek, and very convenient, of course, for the police, but do you expect a court to take such evidence seriously?'

'Why not? It led us to the biggest haul of drugs ever made in this country and to your client being arrested, charged and tried.'

'But not yet,' Hearst returned, drily, 'convicted.'

'As you say,' Groczek answered with equal emphasis, 'not yet,' and he looked across at Young, leaving him in no doubt that that happy event would not be long delayed. 'The fact is,' Groczek went on, 'we are not relying on the evidence of this source to convict. If that were so, we'd have brought him or her into court naturally. We have other evidence we are relying on.'

'I haven't heard it, yet,' Hearst replied, sourly, staring down at his notes and trying to find a new line of approach.

'Everyone else has,' Groczek answered mildly.

'I was talking of evidence,' Hearst said, 'I doubt if the jury has yet heard anything in this court that could be remotely described as evidence.'

Groczek smiled. 'That's for them to decide, isn't it?' he asked, with a sideways look at the jury.

Hearst scowled again and once more studied the papers in front of him. He knew he was at the end with this witness and that the best thing was simply to let him go. The longer he stayed in the box the worse it was, he felt, for his client. But he had to make one more attempt to leave a more favourable impression.

'I suggest to you, Chief Groczek, that you have no real evidence that my client was aware his premises were being used for the purpose of storing illicit drugs?' He waited for a moment for an answer and then, when none came, he looked

126

up from his notes on which his eyes had been fixed while he asked the question and said, 'Well, have you?'

Groczek was not looking at him. Within the few moments that Hearst had dropped his eyes, asked his question and raised them again, Groczek had been transformed. The smile had faded from his face and the blood drained from it. He was no longer looking at Hearst. Instead, he was staring into the back of the court, at the door at the far end, through which a man had slipped and was now passing along a row of people to take an empty seat. It was Slovak.

The sight of him shocked Groczek and his mouth went suddenly dry. He heard Hearst speaking to him but it seemed a long way off. Slovak sat towards the rear of the court staring at him. So far had Slovak been from Groczek's mind at that moment that he could only stare stupidly in his direction unable, for a moment, to locate the man in any sort of time or place. He heard Hearst call his name sharply, but still it seemed a long way off. Slovak's eyes held his own as firmly as if they were magnetised and it took an immense effort of will to pull them away and return them once more to Hearst. 'I'm – sorry,' he said, and found his voice hoarse and strange.

'Well, have you?' Hearst asked, impatiently.

'Have I,' Groczek repeated, staring at Hearst as if he were a stranger whose presence he had noted for the first time. 'Have I?' he said again, puzzled.

'Any evidence,' Hearst reiterated, grittily, feeling that Groczek was trying to make a fool of him.

Groczek stared at Hearst, lost, disorientated. Try as he would, his mind would not sift and sort the question into its proper compartment. The words made sense and he had a vague notion that its related matter floated somewhere in his mind but he could not bring the two together. Once again his eyes turned and looked at Slovak. What was he doing there? Why had he come? Where had he been? The man's eyes were fixed on him and there was a slight smile on his

127

face as if he saw that his sudden appearance in the court had thrown Groczek utterly and that the reaction had been expected, planned almost. Groczek felt a sudden surge of fury with himself at being deflected so easily. He heard again Hearst's impatient voice, 'Chief Groczek, I must ask you to reply to the question,' and he turned and shouted at him as the question finally related itself to the matter. 'They were delivered to his premises!'

The voice was pitched so high and so unnaturally in the context that it produced, for a moment, a stunned silence. Hearst stared at him, puzzled. The judge raised an eyebrow, but said nothing. A quietness had fallen over the court and every jury head was turned in his direction. 'They were delivered to his premises,' Groczek repeated quietly.

'They could have been delivered to yours . . .'

'I don't think so.'

'. . . if you'd been running a restaurant.' Groczek didn't answer. 'Thank you, that's all,' Hearst said.

Groczek stepped down from the box and walked towards his seat in the court. He felt, as he did so, all the while Slovak's eyes upon him. He paused in the aisle opposite the row where his seat was and turned and looked at Slovak. Slovak was sitting some few rows behind him and watching him. He seemed amused. Groczek's eyes fell away from Slovak's. He could not, at that moment, meet the man's gaze. He eased his way along the row to his own seat and sat down.

A trolley was being wheeled into court bearing the cardboard boxes of tin cans containing the heroin. The D.A. was on his feet. 'We're entering these as exhibit 13, Your Honour.'

'This, I take it,' said the judge, 'is the "junk".' He pronounced the word with a slight emphasis to let the court know that his education had not so far removed him from the world that he was unfamiliar with its current slang.

'It is, Your Honour,' the D.A. replied.

'You intend to prove it's junk, I suppose?' the judge asked.

'My next witness is an expert, Your Honour. Call Dr. Goldfine.'

Dr. Goldfine's name was called. He walked into court, a brisk young man, very sure of himself and his facts. He took his seat in the box and was sworn in. The D.A. began establishing his identity and the extent of his reputation.

Groczek heard and yet did not hear. His mind was totally preoccupied with the image of Slovak he could see before him and the felt presence of the man behind him. He knew that Slovak's eyes were fixed on his back and he felt an enormous urge to turn round and look at him again. At the same time, he knew that it would, in some way, be an admission of defeat for him if he did. And, after all, what was there to look at? What was this man to him in this situation? The court was a public court. Anyone could come in. What did it signify that Slovak had chosen to enter the courtroom at that moment? He forced his attention back to the court and the interchange that was going on between the D.A. and the sprightly Goldfine.

'And what conclusion did you come to after you had examined it?'

'It's diacetylmorphine, no question about it.'

'What on earth is diacetylmorphine?' the judge asked, irritably. 'I suppose you're going to explain it, so that normal people can understand what goes on in these courts?'

'It's heroin, Your Honour,' the D.A. offered, helpfully.

'Well, why couldn't he have said "heroin"?' the judge replied, 'you know my preference for plain language.'

The D.A. sighed. 'I apologise, Your Honour.' He turned once again to Dr. Goldfine. 'Is it pure heroin?'

'Oh, yes,' Goldfine answered, 'the illicit stuff's usually diluted but this isn't.'

Groczek sat there listening to the exchange, an immense weariness with the whole case suddenly overtaking him. It all seemed now, irrelevant. He wasn't interested. His mind refused to focus any more upon it and he knew why. He was fighting what he now recognised to be a losing battle to defeat an all-consuming desire to turn and look again at Slovak. He was beginning to feel he had to. There was a taste of defeat in his mouth that was unpleasant to him, the defeat of someone whose eyes had looked away before they should, who had been challenged by a stare and retreated from it. It was absurd, he knew, a child's game, and yet he could not overcome the feeling that he had failed to measure up. The shock of seeing Slovak so unexpectedly in the court had deprived him, momentarily, of his resources. He knew he had been found wanting and he felt the need to put it right. He must let Slovak know that things were as they had been between them and that though a moment's advantage may have been gaind by surprise, it was now recovered. He turned with a savage resolve and looked.

The seat on which Slovak sat was empty. Such had been the effort of will required by Groczek to turn and look once again into those piercing eyes that when his gaze fell onto the empty seat he had the sensation of falling into space, tumbling headlong over and over, and he needed another moment to recover. He stared round the court. Slovak was nowhere to be seen. Every head was turned in the direction of Goldfine and the D.A. and the people on either side of the empty seat seemed as unaware of Slovak's absence as they had been of his presence.

Slowly Groczek turned round again to face the court. Inevitably, he began to wonder if indeed he had actually seen Slovak in the court at all, but cursed himself for a fool to begin doubting the evidence of his own senses. He had *seen* the man. The man had slipped into the court and out again deliberately. He had wanted to show Groczek that he was back, that he had not gone away for good and that the contest – for such it was, in Slovak's mind, anyway – was on again. His appearance in the court, so quick, so cool, had been deliberately calculated to unnerve him and, up to a point, it had succeeded. Groczek

130

smiled. Yes, it had. One had to admire the man, admire his form. He had wanted to show him that he could come and go at will, but had chosen the most impudent moment to do it, in court, at the scene of Groczek's own, personal triumph. Groczek laughed.

He brought his mind back to the evidence being given in court. He felt better. He felt able to relax once again and take a proper interest in what was going on. The D.A. was saying to Goldfine, 'You examined all the cans?'

'All of them,' Goldfine replied.

'Did they all contain heroin?'

'Yes.'

'Not – water chestnuts?' The D.A.'s tone was playful.

'Oh, no,' Goldfine replied, confidently, 'diacetylmorphine, like I said. You wouldn't get much in the way of lunch out of that lot.'

Groczek turned and stared idly at the cans on the trolley. He had seen them a dozen times. There was nothing new about them. Yet the more he stared at them, the more he felt his brow contracting, as if to contain within his head the seed of a thought that was slowly germinating there and yet which threatened, at any moment, to be blown away. What was it? He could not identify it, yet it came, unaccountably, accompanied by a feeling of disaster. The thought, unexpressed, was generating a feeling, like a cloud approaching him that would shortly envelop him entirely. The feeling he recognised instantly but the thought he could not identify. It stayed, tantalisingly, beneath the surface. He turned slowly once more and looked at Goldfine.

'How much would you say was there?' the D.A. asked.

'About a 100 kilogrammes.'

The judge said, predictably, 'Must we use these European expressions?'

'About 200 pounds, if you like, Your Honour,' Goldfine blandly conceded.

131

The D.A. nodded. 'How much would it be worth?'

'You mean on the black market? About $10,000,000. That's a hell of a lot of heroin.'

'Thank you, Dr. Goldfine.'

'No questions,' Hearst said.

Goldfine got down and walked out of the court. Groczek's eyes followed him all the way until he disappeared. His brow contracted further. Something was bothering him. Something was wrong and it frightened him. The thought that was trying to germinate in his mind had now actually begun to throb, as if with the effort of breaking through to the surface. What was it? Try as he would, he could not formulate it, yet it was there and with it the feeling that something was wrong, terribly wrong. But what?

He felt tiny beads of perspiration begin to break out on his forehead, whether from the effort his mind was making or from the unnamed fear, he could not make out. He looked around the court. Another witness was being sworn in. He half heard the exchange of dialogue but it meant nothing to him. He forced his mind back to Goldfine. Why had he been the focus of his attention just then? Why had his eyes followed him out of court, as if hoping to find something meaningful there upon his person? No, it wasn't Goldfine, it was something to do with Goldfine, something he had come into court to deal with; yes, the cans of heroin on the trolley.

An excitement was building up in him now, but he knew he wasn't there yet. He turned to look at the trolley but the trolley had been wheeled out of court. He had seen it go. There was nothing odd about that – he would expect that. Then why was his head now beginning to throb with the excitement and the portent of an immense but undefinable danger? He turned and looked once more behind him at the seat in which Slovak had sat. It was empty. Well, it had been empty ten minutes ago when he had looked. Why, then, did he look now? What was he looking for?

He stared at the empty seat. His gaze was imprisoned by it. The answer lay there, in its emptiness. He sat quite still. He sensed that the struggle was nearly over. He felt in his mind, as if two inert masses were being moved slowly, and with great effort by a third towards each other, and when they had moved into a proper relationship, one to the other, everything would become clear and he would see it, see what his mind had been straining towards. And they came, those two masses, came at last into their alignment – the absence of Slovak and the absence of the trolley. His head sang with the effort and his mind reeled as the connection was finally made. 'My God,' he said out loud.

He had made the connection and he couldn't move. He knew now what it was that Slovak had come there to do. The audacity stunned him. The unthinkable nature of it left him, at the instant, bereft of strength either of mind or limb. He just sat there, empty, staring at the seat where Slovak had been, unable to focus upon anything except the shattering revelation that had just been made to him – that Slovak's intention was *nothing less than to effect a robbery of the police.* So paralysing was that thought, that he could do nothing but sit there and contemplate it. And then, as the paralysis slowly left him, the danger flooded back in once more and he said, once again, 'My God,' and leapt from his seat.

He fell and stumbled over the feet of those sitting next to him in his haste to get out. Everything in court stopped and everyone looked at him. Such was his panic, such the frenzy that had seized him to get out of the door, that it needed but the mention of the word 'fire' to have created a stampede. But no one moved, only stared at him, puzzled. He rushed from the courtroom, through the doors and into the hall outside. 'Sergeant,' he roared! 'Wexler! Spivack!'

They came running in all directions. He set off at a run down the corridor, the others following. He knew where he was going – room 4B, the storage room, the room where the evidence was kept before being brought into court. He had to get there, had to get there fast. It was two flights up and no time to wait for elevators. He raced up the stairs with Wexler, Spivack and the sergeant close behind him. Pray God, he thought, he was not too late.

He came to a halt outside the room. He seized the handle. The door was locked. He pounded on it but got no reply. 'Who's in charge here?' Groczek asked, turning to the sergeant.

'The clerk should be in there, sir,' the sergeant said, bewildered, 'I don't understand it.'

'Break it down,' Groczek said.

'Break it down, sir?'

'Break it down, you fool,' Groczek roared at him, 'do as you're told!'

Without another word, the three policemen hurled themselves at the door. It was of solid oak and yielded not even a groan. 'Get an axe,' Groczek shouted, 'there's a fire axe down the corridor!'

Wexler turned and ran down the corridor. In his rage and frustration Groczek kicked at the door. Spivack and the sergeant looked at him then looked at each other. A court official came running up breathlessly, a small, neat, fussy man, staring at them aghast. 'What are you doing, what are you doing?' he asked.

'Where's the clerk?' Groczek shouted at him.

'Clerk? Isn't he there?'

'No, he's *not* there,' Groczek snarled, 'do you think I'd be breaking down the door if he was!'

The official looked flustered. 'Well, maybe . . .'

'Is there a window in that room?' Groczek cut across him savagely.

'Yes, yes, of course.'

'Where does it look on to?'

'Juniper Street.'

Groczek looked at Spivack. 'Get down there! Pick up any-body who looks suspicious and hold them! Old ladies, nuns, anyone!'

Spivack turned and sped off down the corridor as Wexler came running back with the axe. 'Give it to me,' Groczek said, snatching the axe.

'You can't,' screamed the official, 'you can't break that door!'

'Stand aside,' Groczek answered, grimly, pushing him away. He swung the axe back over his shoulder, but paused, as an old man came hurrying along.

'Now, now, what's this?' the old man shouted. 'What are you doing with my door?'

'Are you the clerk?' Groczek asked furiously.

'Sure I am.'

'What do you mean leaving that room, when there's valu-able evidence in there?'

'I went to the john,' the clerk said indignantly, 'I went to the john!'

'Give me the key!'

'I'm allowed to go to the john, aren't I?' the clerk asked, turning to the official in amazement.

'You crazy old fool,' Groczek shouted at him, 'there's $10,000,000 worth of drugs in there! At least there was!'

He snatched the key from the old man and pushed it into the lock. The blood was pounding in his head. He *had* to get into that room. He had the most terrible foreboding. He struggled with the key in the lock. Beside him the old man fretted and fumed. 'I've been here thirty-five years! We've had jewellery and cash and gold bars and everything in there! *Nothing's* ever been lost!'

Groczek turned on him, something snapping in his head. 'IT'S THE WRONG KEY! WILL YOU OPEN THIS DOOR!'

'It's not the wrong key,' the old man answered, snatching it from him, 'you have to turn it twice! I'm going to complain about this!'

He turned the handle. Groczek burst into the room past him, knocking him sideways as he did so, and stopped dead, looking at the trolley in the centre of the room. The cardboard boxes with the cans of heroin were all neatly stacked on top of it. Relief poured over him. His head spun with it. He felt, had he opened his mouth to speak at that moment, he might have sobbed. He strode across the room and looked out of the window onto the alleyway below. Spivack was down there looking up at him. Spivack shrugged in the direction of his chief, indicating he had seen nothing to cause alarm. Groczek beckoned him back up.

Behind Groczek, the old man quivered with rage and indignation. 'I told you it was all right,' he said, 'I told you.'

Groczek turned to Wexler. 'Get this stuff into the van and back into the vaults,' he said. Then he turned to the old man. 'And I'll see the Chief Clerk of the court about the security of this building! It's a disgrace! It should have been looked into years ago!' He strode out of the room.

The old man looked at Wexler. His lips were quivering with emotion and his eyes were watering. 'We've had millions of dollars worth of stuff through here. What's the matter with him? Is he always like that?'

Wexler sighed and shook his head. He had certainly never seen Groczek in such a panic. He patted the old man on the back and wheeled the trolley out into the corridor. The sergeant and Spivack joined him outside the room and walked it to the elevator.

Groczek was waiting on the sidewalk outside. He watched the junk put into the van and the doors locked. He got into his own car and followed the van back to police headquarters. Wexler, Spivack and the sergeant carried the boxes downstairs to the huge iron vault that stood in the basement among the filing cabinets. Groczek opened the combination, which he changed every day, pulled open the heavy door and loaded the boxes into the safe. He closed the safe and locked it. Then he went back up to his office.

Only then did he realise how much he was shaking. He went to his cabinet and poured himself a stiff drink. He had been scared more than he remembered having been for a very long time.

Yet now he began to wonder if he had not exaggerated the whole thing. In the quiet and calm of his office, free of the charged atmosphere of the court, he wondered if he had not imagined it all, if, in fact, the presence of Slovak in the court had not simply precipitated him into losing all control. Had he not, to a certain extent, been brainwashed? Had not Slovak, judging the exact balance of his mind at that moment, simply stretched out a finger and tilted the balance in the wrong direction? But why? For the fun of it? For the sheer devilment of it? Or was that too clever? Was the panic, the sudden surge of fright as he saw the possibility, saw what he thought was the set-up, nothing more than the product of his own fevered imagination?

He paced the room with the drink in his hand. He could not make up his mind. It was true that, to a degree, he had been conditioned, perhaps programmed to act in the way that he had. Rosetti's awed tones when he spoke to him about Slovak on the telephone, the file with its carefully built picture of the man creating a superhuman image that spelt disaster for anyone tangling with him. Was he really that big, that powerful? Was he really responsible for the rubbing out of Dino Scappelli as the file suggested? And then, the meeting with the man himself in his study that had suddenly at the end, unnerved him. He hadn't expected that.

Had all these things conspired to create in him such an admiration for the man that, despite the persuasion of his own commonsense he had come to believe Slovak capable of anything? Even – and he phrased it carefully in his mind – of robbing the police? He couldn't believe it. Here, in the calm and security of his own office, the proposition seemed to him fantastic. No one could pull that off. Slovak's appearance in the court had been nothing more than a game, a desire to upset him at a moment when he least expected it. He was, in effect, and in his own way, merely setting up the pieces again. He had merely chosen the scene of the courtroom to do it in.

The moment he said it to himself, he knew that he didn't believe it. Slovak's appearance in that court had something to do with the heroin. The man made gestures, but they were not empty ones. He had come into court to announce his intentions and Groczek cursed himself for a fool for not having seen before why Slovak had come here in the first place. But it had never occurred to him. There were a dozen things he might have come to the city for – but for that? To lift a haul of junk that he, Groczek, had seized after months of preparation and which was now safely in his hands? No wonder he hadn't seen it. His mind had careered in all directions, in its endeavour to solve the mystery of Slovak's appearance in the city, but it had never gone in that one, not till today, not till Slovak himself had prodded it.

It was typical of the man that he would do it that way. It was not enough for Slovak merely to plan any longer. It had all become too tame, too easy. He was bored with his own cleverness. He wanted to lengthen the odds against himself, to perform, as it were, in full view and before Groczek's very eyes.

Groczek nodded to himself. He understood it, now. His panic, though misjudged, had not been without foundation. Slovak had been drawn to the city by more than a scent of wonderful pickings to be had there. He had, in a strange and perverse way, recreated Groczek in the image of his own executioner. The man was hell bent on self-destruction.

There was a knock on the door and Fallon came in. Groczek turned and looked at him. 'What happened?' Fallon asked.

'Nothing,' Groczek said, and went to the cabinet to refill his glass.

'I heard there was a panic in the court.'

'A small one.'

'Over the junk?'

Groczek didn't answer at once. He poured another drink and handed it to Fallon. He lifted the glass and drank. Then he said, 'I know what Slovak's here for. He came for the drugs. I should have seen it before.'

'The drugs?' Fallon sounded incredulous. '*Our* drugs? The stuff we've got in the safe?'

Groczek nodded. 'That's right.'

'He can't be serious?'

'He's serious. I just don't understand why it took me so long to figure it out. But that's what he's here for.'

There was a pause. Then Fallon laughed. 'Well, he won't get them.'

'No, he won't get them,' Groczek answered after a pause, and then was silent for a moment more. Then he said, 'But if he does, I'll be the laughing stock of the country.'

Chapter Nine

Groczek's preoccupation with the safety of the drugs did not lessen in the days that followed. It grew. Having secured clearance on his suggestion of making proper use of the illicit heroin, he now had the problem of moving it. He was beginning to regret that bright idea. It complicated matters unnecessarily. He knew that whatever way he chose to move them, the drugs would become vulnerable the moment they were in transit. They were, of course, vulnerable even in the police vaults; though Fallon scoffed at the idea, Groczek knew

139

better. Slovak had master-minded more difficult robberies than that of a vault in the basement of police headquarters. It was merely the novelty of the idea that prevented Fallon from seeing it. Still, moving them obviously exposed them even more.

He was, however, in no position to alter his mind about them. He could not now say to those authorities who had commended him for his suggestion that he did not, on reflection, consider himself capable of delivering the heroin to its destination. He would not so much lose face as simply not be believed. He would be offering as evidence for his change of heart nothing more substantial than his belief that Slovak intended to lift them. On examination, what would such a belief turn out to be but the product of a highly charged imagination and irrational fears that a police chief ought not to have? To test the steps by which he had arrived at his conclusion would be to invite serious doubts as to his continued competence, to say nothing of the state of his mental health. If Slovak were considered a threat, then Slovak should be watched and, if necessary, neutralised. That was normal police procedure. What was the problem? The trouble was they did not know Slovak as he, Groczek, had come to know him.

Groczek could see that, on the face of it, he was making altogether too much of it, yet he also knew that the face of things was not always all there was to the truth of things. He felt like a man who had the ability to hit the ball right, but kept hitting it wrong. There were simply occasions when sheer physical ability and experience were not everything. Some mechanism in the mind also had to be switched on and when it had switched itself off it was not always easy to find it and switch it back on again.

Groczek knew exactly what it was that had been switched off in his case. It was confidence, certainly, the belief that things would go right because he made them go right. And he

140

knew, too, what had switched this mechanism off. It was fear, the fear of being made to look ridiculous. Let no one make a mistake about it, any police chief who could not guard his own property would be an object of such ridicule in the eyes of the world that he might just as well put a gun to his head and pull the trigger. To have accomplished, with such diffi- culty, the feat of having seized the drugs in the first place and then so easily to have lost them again would provoke such gales of laughter throughout the country that he could not help but be blown away by them. It was that fear, sneaking though it may be, that lodged in the back of his mind.

His only comfort lay in the thought that Slovak, too, must have his problems and his doubts. This was more than just another robbery to him. It meant more for all the reasons that Groczek had, himself, divined and the consciousness of the special occasion would also serve to impair Slovak's ability. Slovak, himself, would not necessarily be functioning at the top of his form and that, to a certain extent, restored the balance.

Slovak had disappeared again. Since the day he had ap- peared in court nothing had been seen of him and since that day, unaccountably, the trial had not been going so well. It was as if he had appeared at the trial merely to put a curse on it and Groczek was not now so sure of the result as he had been when it started. This, however, did not weigh so heavily with him as it might otherwise have done, but for his pre- occupation with Slovak and the drugs. Great as was his desire to see a conviction, it was as nothing to his desire to be rid of the stuff in the vaults and to have seen Slovak try and ignomi- niously fail. Yet even that was mixed with the fear that he might actually succeed.

Groczek's mind had never been so divided. It was divided between admiration for the man and hatred for him. It was divided between a fear that Slovak might give up, might not actually try, and a fear that he actually would and, if he did,

141

between a belief that his whole preposterous scheme would fail and a belief that Groczek could do nothing to stop him succeeding. Never had he been so ambivalent about anything – which was symptomatic of his state of mind. He veered, from day to day, from one direction to its opposite. It affected everything he did. He became more uncertain, his decisions, usually so quick and clear, became increasingly hedged with qualifications. His temper became shorter and even Fallon found it, at times, difficult to approach him.

Fallon did not understand his anxiety, but then Fallon, like the others, did not fully appreciate the problem. Fallon was a good officer and an excellent deputy, but he lacked imagination. He found himself less and less able to talk to Fallon about it because he sensed that Fallon was impatient with him, felt that Groczek was making altogether too much of it. But Groczek trusted his instincts in these matters, trusted, in fact, his fear.

In the event, the trial did not go as he had expected. The sentences were light, almost minimal and, of course, an appeal was immediately lodged. Young, himself, was found 'Not Guilty', it being considered there was insufficient evidence to convict. The expired warrant had played a larger part in the trial than anyone had thought it would, while the judge had gradually grown more hostile to the prosecution. While Groczek felt, in some way, that the outcome was a rebuff to him and his force, he was not as depressed by it as he might otherwise have been. His mind was now almost exclusively occupied with Slovak and the problem of moving the drugs. This had to be done fairly soon. He did not feel safe with them even in the vaults.

When he returned home on the evening the trial was completed, he found his wife watching the report of it on television. He stood, for a moment, watching the pictures of the defendants emerge from the court, released on bail pending appeal and saw himself emerge behind them. The reporters had

142

crowded round him asking for comment but he had waved them away and got into his own car and driven off.

He poured himself a drink and poured one for his wife and handed it to her. 'They got off lightly, didn't they?' she said.

He nodded. 'Yes,' he said, 'lightly.'

'I don't know why you work so hard.'

It was an old complaint. There was some justice in it. If he allowed himself, he could feel very bitter about the courts. The public didn't understand. When you had been clever on their behalf, painstaking, patient and vigilant, and when all your efforts had resulted in arrest, a verdict that favoured the criminal was like a slap in the face, a public reproof. It wasn't simply that one lost a case and, like some lawyer, could shrug and go on to the next one. In its own way such a verdict was saying, 'We believe them and not you, we believe our enemies and not our servants. They appeared to us, in court, more deserving of our trust.' Well, one had to learn to live with it. That was the sort of ball game it was.

'Do you want to eat?' she asked.

'No, I'm not hungry.' He hovered for a moment, feeling that he ought to stay and talk for a while, but he wanted to get away into his study, to be by himself and to think, to think about Slovak and to think about the drugs. He could not leave it alone and he could not share his anxiety with her.

'I've got some work to do,' he said, 'do you mind?'

She shook her head and went on watching the television. He turned to go. 'That man who came here that night,' she asked, 'that strange man, who called here so late. Did he have anything to do with the case?'

'Why do you ask?'

'I just wondered. I've been thinking about him.'

He smiled. 'Why have you been thinking about him?'

'I don't know. He keeps coming back into my head. You never mentioned him at breakfast in the morning and you seemed upset. Did he upset you?'

143

He stared at her for a moment and then said, 'No, of course not.' He turned and went out.

He closed the door of his study and sat down at his desk. Even his wife was noticing that he was not quite as he should be and had, intuitively, linked the observation with Slovak.

He opened the file on Slovak, as he had done so often in the past few weeks, and stared down again at the enlarged centre photograph of him. His own eyes went straight to Slovak's as they always did. There was something riveting about the man's face and, looking down at it, he had once again the overwhelming impression that Slovak was in the room with him.

He closed the file irritably. For the time being, he must put Slovak out of his mind and concentrate on the problem of moving the drugs. He felt he must do this soon. Whenever he thought about them, he felt a small quiver of anxiety run through him. The security in a police building was oddly in many ways not as great as it was at a bank, and though there were always people on duty there, this did not constitute any guarantee of safety. Even army barracks had been attacked in the past and Groczek could hardly mount a large-scale security operation for any length of time outside and inside the building. Apart from the difficulty, he would plainly make himself look foolish to the public.

The big problem was leaks. Although he had cleared the force out when he took it over, he was under no illusions about the trustworthiness of the force as a whole. There were rotten apples in every barrel and one could contaminate many. It was like a continuously growing mould. What made him most uncertain was that he knew, in a case of this kind, there was virtually no way of being sure that whichever route he decided to go with the drugs, the information would not be leaked by someone. It was immensely difficult, in view of the preparations required, to keep the movement entirely secret until the last moment. Slovak was certain to have found some-

144

one inside the force ready to sell that information. With a commodity as valuable as heroin, money was no object and could buy almost anything and anyone. Even Fallon, in the end, could not be excluded from the possibility of corruption.

At the thought that it might even be Fallon, he tossed his head impatiently and yet it was odd how the thought would not be completely dismissed, despite the reproof he administered to himself for having thought of it. Higher officials than Fallon had been corrupted in the past for less than was at stake here.

The lingering doubt about Fallon, foolish as it seemed, revived his own agitation all over again. Could he then trust no one? The drugs had to be moved by road, rail or plane. Was he saying, in effect, that whichever way he chose, Slovak would be in possession of that information almost as soon as he was himself? It seemed absurd, yet he felt that it was true. He therefore must proceed on the assumption that an attempt would certainly be made on the drugs once they were in transit. Which way then should he choose?

The idea of sending them by road did not commend itself at all. Policemen in a car or in even two or three were particularly vulnerable. It would be by plane or train. Either way they would have to be transported to the airport or the station and he had relatively little faith in the security of airports. Apart from which, it was a longer drive to the airport than to the station. On balance, he was beginning to favour sending them, under guard, by rail.

Yet immediately he thought of it, he saw the dangers there too. Slovak had already stopped a train. The description of the incident was in the file and there was no reason to suppose he might not pull a similar caper with this one. The more he thought about it, the less was he able to come down firmly on one side or the other and the more his agitation grew. He simply could not make up his mind. Was he vastly over-exaggerating the whole problem and the ability of Slovak to intervene at will? And if he were, how had he been brought to this pitiful state? By what psychological pressures had he been reduced from a man of decision and iron resolve to a man who could only waver indecisively between one course of action and another? It astonished him.

His train of thought was interrupted by Fallon who had called in on his way home. 'I thought you'd like to know,' he said, 'that Slovak is back at the house.'

'When did he get back?'

'Tonight – about an hour ago. I heard just as I was leaving the office.'

There was a pause. Groczek took out a cigar and lit it, blowing the smoke out in a steady, reflective stream. Then he said, 'He's going to make an attempt on those drugs.'

'Let him. I hope, in a way, he does.'

Groczek studied him for a moment. 'Why don't we pull him in?'

'What?'

'Hold him until after the stuff's been moved.'

'On what charge?'

'We'll find one. That shouldn't be too difficult.'

Fallon stared at him, and Groczek saw that he had fallen a notch in Fallon's estimation. 'You think I'm making too much of this, don't you?'

'Frankly, yes.'

'I think you're not making enough.' He paused for a moment, and then said, 'Have you read this file?'

Fallon shrugged, 'Not properly.'

'You don't think it worth your time?'

'The fact is,' Fallon replied, 'you've had it in the house since it arrived.'

Groczek turned away. It was true, he'd kept the file at home. It hadn't been deliberate and yet he had come back to it almost every evening. Had he, unconsciously, wanted to keep it for himself? Had he so personalised his conflict with Slovak

146

that, without realising it, he had kept the file to himself? 'It makes interesting reading,' he said.

'It's one cop's view,' Fallon shrugged, with a touch of disinterest.

Groczek nodded. 'I felt like that when I first read it. I felt, "That's Rosetti justifying himself and his unit spending a lot of money and time and coming up with little else but imagination". Well, I no longer feel quite the same. This man is no ordinary criminal.'

'I didn't say he was. Still . . .'

'Did you know he was responsible for rubbing out Dino Scapelli?'

'I suppose,' Fallon said, coolly, 'if we had proof of that we could pick him up.'

'No, there's no proof,' Groczek conceded, aware of the scarcely veiled sarcasm in his deputy's voice, 'but Scapelli had a contract out on Slovak. Rosetti discovered that. No one knows why and perhaps it's not important. But when that old man puts out a contract, it's usually completed.'

'Except in this case?'

Groczek nodded. 'Scapelli was gunned down last year. The hint is that Slovak retaliated, surely and swiftly. If it's true, I know of no other man capable of pulling that off and surviving.'

There was a long pause. Then Fallon said, 'Look, we have a simple problem. We have to transport the junk 400 miles. It can go by road, rail or plane. Personally, I think it should go by rail, but either way, we can take all necessary precautions. More we cannot do.'

'Suppose he finds out which way it's going?'

'He won't. We'll keep it top-level security.'

'But suppose he does?'

'He's not Superman.' Fallon's voice had a note of contempt in it that did not go unnoticed.

'If he succeeds in lifting those drugs,' Groczek said grimly,

147

'do you know how that will look? I'll be the butt of every joker in the country.'

'For Christ's sake,' Fallon growled impatiently, 'are you saying we can't protect our own property?'

'Perhaps,' Groczek answered after a pause, 'perhaps that's what I am saying.'

'Then destroy it.'

There was an even longer pause. Then Groczek shook his head. 'I can't do that. Not now. And, hell, I won't do it, either!'

'That's better,' Fallon grinned. 'Look, I'll get a bullion car laid on with security guards. He won't break into that.'

Groczek nodded and sighed. 'You're right. I'm making too much of it. I don't know why. He's got me jumping. I feel it's like he can see every move I make.'

'Why don't you take a holiday – I mean, three or four months? Everyone knows you deserve it. You haven't had a proper rest since you took over here. That kind of pressure can get on top of us all.'

'When this is over – maybe. You're right, I've had too much of it. But not till this is over.'

'You could leave it to me, you know?'

Groczek looked at him. He was tempted. It would solve a lot of problems. He'd have an excuse, too, if things went wrong. He wouldn't be so directly involved. And yet, he knew that he couldn't. It was odd, but he didn't entirely trust Fallon any more, not since that thought had entered his head. Oh, it wasn't just Fallon. He felt he could trust no one, in the circumstances, not entirely. And then, too, if he accepted Fallon's offer, wouldn't he be running out? If he did that, would he ever be able to face himself again? Would he not be conceding the field to Slovak without a shot being fired? He knew that he couldn't do that. He knew that what was between him and Slovak could not be resolved in that way. He knew that somewhere on the road ahead the two must collide. The collision was, in some way, predestined.

Unless, of course, Slovak died suddenly. A heart attack might pluck him out of Groczek's life, out of life itself. Or a car crash. No one could predict that and so it could not be considered part of the whole scheme, unless . . . and here, Groczek paused for a moment, for the thought fluttered wildly at the back of his mind and he could not quite make it settle. And when in the stillness of the room and suddenly aware of Fallon's eyes upon him, it settled and he saw what it was, he felt his heart flutter as fast as the thought itself had done. Unless – he had been on the verge of formulating it – unless he, Groczek, should kill him. That would dispose of this problem and who could say, once the thought had actually entered his head, that it had not become part of the very web of things he had been considering and would not take its place along with the others in determining their pace and direction and inevitable end? The idea fascinated him.

But only for a moment. Beyond that there was Fallon gazing at him, waiting patiently for a response to his offer, the world of the normal, of the practical routine that had a place for every event and an approved method of dealing with it. Fallon was dependable. It had been absurd to mistrust him for a moment and the mistrust was an indication of the wayward paths that imagination could lead a policeman into. There had been too much imagination of late, too little reliance on the reality of experience. He could not understand how all this had come about. It was not like him. When he looked back over his time since Slovak had arrived, it had the quality, sometimes, of a dream. Yes, that expressed it best. He felt himself, at times, the prisoner of a dream.

'You could leave it to me, you know,' Fallon had said to him and Groczek now nodded.

'Yes, I know I could. I rely on you, you know, more than

149

you think. But I can't leave it to you. Not this one. I'll stay with it. We'll do it your way. When it's over, I'll take a rest.'

Fallon shrugged, graciously, without resentment and said, 'Well, goodnight.'

'Goodnight,' Groczek answered, but again was swept by a last moment of indecision and said, as Fallon opened the door, 'You really don't think we should pull him in? I mean – really?' and felt a wave of shame run through him as Fallon stood there, staring at him, not deigning to reply, as if the question were not worthy of him. Groczek nodded and waved him away with a gesture that invited him to take no notice and to forget that he ever asked. Fallon went out and closed the door behind him.

Fallon did, indeed, take it all in hand. He arranged with Levin, the head security man on the railroad, to provide a bullion car on the day set for the transfer of the drugs. This was no problem. There were at least three in the area. The city had large marshalling yards connected with the docks and the postal authorities and even the military had, from time to time, made use of them.

He went, however, further than this. He was careful not to explain to Levin what it was that was being moved. This was according to Groczek's strict instructions. But he asked him to report anything at all that struck him as odd or unusual over the next few days. Levin had asked him, 'Like what?' but Fallon had been vague since he was unsure himself. He stressed only that Levin should ask railroad security to be especially alert to anything and that he, Fallon, would not object to being troubled by the reporting of even the most trivial of incidents. And Fallon gave Wexler and O'Malley the job of working with Levin and keeping in close touch.

Fallon explained all this to Groczek and Groczek was satisfied. Having finally committed himself to a decision, having put the machinery into operation, Groczek began to feel better. The meeting with Fallon had helped. When Fallon had departed that night, Groczek had felt a deep sense of shame that he had presented so vacillating and indecisive an image. Before Fallon's calm and precise assessment of the facts, he must have looked like a man in the first grip of a neurosis. It had made him angry with himself, and the anger had helped.

He changed the combination of the lock on the safe in the vaults every day and checked that the contents were still intact. He confided the combination to no one, not even Fallon. Slovak's house was kept under constant surveillance but Slovak appeared to go nowhere and receive no visitors. Groczek would have liked to have tapped his telephone but felt unable to ask for the authority to do so. There was no case he could have made out that would have sounded in any way convincing, so he did not try. Having decided to treat the situation as in no way out of the ordinary, he left Fallon to get on with the arrangements and himself attended to matters that he had somewhat neglected. The next three or four days saw Groczek's mind so restored to normal that he even spent a day with his wife at the country club, relaxing.

So it was that he felt a cold shiver run through him, when he heard Fallon's voice on the telephone asking him if he would come down to the railroad yards. No, he would prefer, for security reasons, not to discuss it on the telephone, but it was something he, Fallon, felt he ought to know about. With a deep sense of foreboding, Groczek got into his car and drove down to the yards.

He saw Fallon at the open end of the repair sheds talking to Levin. The noise of hammering and drilling was considerable and they walked away from the sheds towards him when they saw his car draw up, in order to talk more easily.

Groczek got out of his car and came towards them. He shook hands with Levin, whom he knew slightly and looked at Fallon. 'Well?' he asked.

Fallon looked at Levin. 'You tell him, Tom,' he said.

Levin looked at Groczek and shrugged, slightly embarrassed.

'Hell,' he said, 'it could be nothing at all and I may be just wasting your time, Chief.'

'What is it?' Groczek asked quietly.

'Well,' Levin said, 'I was asked to report anything that might strike me as odd, over the next few days – no matter how small it might seem.'

'I asked him,' Fallon nodded.

Groczek looked at Levin again. Levin said, 'We have three bullion cars in use here. Three days ago, I was looking through the dockets that come in from the repair sheds. Work cards, really. They report work being done and the labour time being spent. Anyway, I saw that one of the bullion cars had developed a crack on the front axle and had come in for repair. Naturally, I didn't think much of it. It can happen to a coach anytime and, anyway, I knew we had another two. I came down this morning just to look over the one I'd earmarked for the trip and found it being literally taken apart by a repair crew. Apparently, it had developed a lean and it wasn't considered safe. It would be out of action for at least two weeks.'

He paused. Groczek stared at him. He knew what was coming, but he wanted to hear it from Levin. Levin went on, 'That just left the third. It was out in a siding so I went and had a look at it. It's a very old one, one we've been meaning to scrap for years, but you know how it is. The railroads don't make a profit and, well, anyway – what I'm saying is, it's not up to the standard of the other two. I mean, it's not what I'd call one hundred per cent secure. It's O.K. for some purposes but . . .' He paused and looked again at Fallon who nodded encouragingly, and Levin went on, 'Well, I don't know what it is you're moving, but I get the feeling it's pretty important. So, like I said, I just thought I'd mention it. It could be nothing at all and, I mean, the coach is O.K. for most purposes.'

He trailed off a little lamely, as if now he had said it all he felt he was, perhaps, overdoing it. Fallon looked at Groczek. 'What do you think – coincidence?'

Groczek stared at him. 'I'll tell you what I think,' he said, and his voice was hoarse and trembled a little. 'I think he's getting information on every move we make. I think he's just picked the car he *wants* us to use. That's what I think.'

Fallon sighed and nodded. 'I think you're right.' There was an accusing look in Groczek's eye and Fallon felt that he had let his chief down. He shrugged. 'Well, what do we do? Do we transport it today, as arranged, or what?'

All the old uncertainty returned to Groczek. He felt he was back to where he had been before and, in a curious way, he was also pleased. It gratified him to be right. His assessment had been right and Fallon's wrong. He had not overestimated the man. Fallon had underestimated him. Slovak had discovered they were transporting the heroin by train and had reached out into the repair sheds. Someone, maybe more than one, working in the yards had been bought. The security cars had been tampered with. It was a set-up. The odds against two of them dropping out of action in so short a time and in the circumstances were too great to admit of coincidence. Slovak was choosing the car for Groczek to use. Only Levin's alertness had prevented him from falling for it.

Groczek felt an odd sense of satisfaction as he contemplated the situation. The man was, at least, living up to his reputation. He was not disappointing. Well, that was all to the good. At least he now knew where he stood. All the indecisiveness that had characterised his actions over Slovak and the heroin suddenly vanished. His mind was clear and calm. He had been right and his confidence suddenly came flooding back to him, and with it the solution for his dilemma. It was simple, so simple that he wondered that he had not seen it before.

Groczek had walked away from them while this was going through his mind, paused and thought about it. Now, he turned and walked back to them and stopped in front of them.

153

He nodded. 'All right,' he said, 'he thinks he's got it all sewn up. Let him. We'll use the coach *he's* picked out for us – but I want it reinforced. Once it's locked, nothing gets in there, nothing, you understand?'

Levin said, 'I'll see to it. It'll take a few days to do it properly.'

'It doesn't matter,' Groczek answered, 'just see that it's done properly.' He turned and walked back to his car. He got in and slammed the door. He said to the driver, 'Stop off at Mostyn's.'

'Mostyn's, sir? The department store?'

'Yes,' Groczek said, 'I want to pick something up for my wife.'

He settled back in the seat. He felt elated, and a growing sense of impatience to be on with it and done. The car stopped at Mostyn's. He got out and went inside. In about fifteen minutes he came back out, clutching a parcel. The car drove on to the office. When he returned home, he gave the parcel to his wife. Her eyebrows went up when he handed it to her. He was not a man to give unexpected presents. 'Open it,' he said, smiling.

She opened it, tearing off the paper. She took out a most beautiful handbag. 'What have you been doing?' she asked, glancing at him.

'Doing?' he replied, with an air of injured innocence.

'Are you making amends for something?'

'Now, now, Mary,' he said, 'what a thing to say. Can't I bring you a present?'

'Well, you don't usually.'

'Well, that's true, that's true,' he said, contritely, 'but I've been very down, lately, and giving you a hard time.'

'I had noticed,' she said.

'Well, there you are. Anyway, I had to go and see Green-berg, the managing director of Mostyn's about something. I saw this on the counter and thought you'd like it.'

'It's lovely,' she answered, placing it on her hip and looking down admiringly at it, 'thank you.' She looked up at him. 'Are you all right, now?'

'Fine. It was nothing. Something preying on my mind.' He shook his head, dismissing it. 'It's over.'

'Not a woman?'

He laughed out loud, heard himself laugh and realised that it was the first time he had laughed genuinely for some time. He put his hands on her shoulders, brought her towards him and kissed her lightly on the cheek. 'No way,' he said, 'and why don't we eat out tonight?'

Three nights later he drove down to the repair sheds to examine the work being done on the car. Levin was there with Fallon, and O'Malley stood by looking on. Levin had arranged two shifts to work on the coach and special lights had been rigged up to enable the work to continue till midnight each night. The noise was shattering. Men swarmed all over the coach, cutting in vents and windows, hammering, sawing and chiselling.

Fallon came to meet him as he approached and they stood for a moment, watching the men work. 'Will it be finished tonight?' Groczek asked.

Fallon nodded. 'Yes,' he said.

Groczek walked forward and peered inside. A steel wire lining was being fitted all round the inside of the car. It looked impressive. Fallon said, 'Even if they stop the train, it would take so long to break through that they'd give up, I swear it. We'd have cops swarming all around before they got inside.'

Groczek nodded, satisfied. Fallon had done a good job. 'All right,' he said, 'then we'll move the stuff tomorrow morning sharp at ten.'

He turned and walked back to the car. Fallon walked with him, leaving Levin and O'Malley still watching the progress of the work. Groczek opened the car door and looked at Fallon and smiled. It was his turn, now, he felt, to reassure Fallon.

F

'You'll see,' he said, 'how we'll throw a monkey wrench into that billion dollar brain. I'll have it fusing in so many parts it'll look like the fourth of July.'

It was extraordinary how he could see it all in his mind's eye but, then, wasn't that the fruit of long experience and careful planning in these things? Slovak nodded to himself. He was sitting in the main room of the house watching the daylight fade on the gentle slopes outside and thinking of Groczek. And he smiled to himself as he thought of him.

He smiled as he recalled the look on Groczek's face when he had seen Slovak in the court for the first time. He had the look of a man who had seen Death beckoning him in a crowd. Groczek's brain had frozen, momentarily, and Slovak knew that it would. It was extraordinary how one could predict the outcome of certain planned events, given the right knowledge and the right insights. Of course, one needed to know one's man and he knew Groczek. And besides, Groczek was not in a position to make the running. He was like a man at the start of a race who was never sure which foot to lead off with. He was a man who must constantly be caught on the hop.

It was very satisfying. He felt at the very peak of his powers. He felt he could accomplish anything. Everything was prepared, with his usual attention to minute detail. He had written the script and cast it with his usual care, having by now and by virtue of his immense reputation the pick of the most skilled actors in the country. It only remained for the play to be staged and when it was, as it shortly would be, he had no doubts as to it being a success. Why should he? He could not remember a failure. Success had accompanied him through life like a good companion. It would hardly desert him now.

At first, Groczek had seemed to have the advantage. He had caught Slovak off balance, unaccountably off balance and there had been a moment when Slovak had been shaken to the core. But he had recovered quickly. It was wonderful how he had swung his adversary round and seen him, then, retreat, puzzled, hurt.

Sitting there, in the quiet of the house and the stillness of the countryside around him, Slovak could feel Groczek's agonising state of indecision. Groczek knew, must know, that whichever way he chose to transport the drugs, Slovak would be in receipt of that information almost as soon as Groczek had decided it. There was no way that Groczek could shut it down. And further, he knew that the moment they were moved, they would be exposed at every stage of the journey. There was no way he could avoid it, and knowing it would make him less competent not more. Anxiety would dilute his capacity.

The more he thought of it, the more satisfied Slovak felt. It would soon be over, and Groczek would be destroyed utterly in the process. He saw that now, as the prime object of the whole venture. In destroying Groczek he would be, in a way, liberating himself, separating himself, once and for all, from that gaze that threatened him and that had become identified in his mind with Groczek. He was fully aware that this simple identification was, to some extent, an illusion. He did not confuse the two in his mind, mistake them for one and the same thing. This gaze of his, or rather of that other self that he had so laboriously created over the years to present to others, this gaze of that other self which had so often turned itself inward to scrutinise the source from which it had emerged, had finally separated itself and become independent but he did not confuse it with Groczek. It was simply that they had, in a way, become allies, as if both were bent on his destruction. It was as though part of himself was aiding and abetting Groczek in his plan. Groczek had seen that. 'You forget,' he had said to him, 'I have the help of a brilliant mind,' and when Slovak had asked, 'Whose?' Groczek had replied, 'Why, yours, of course – who else?'

157

That expressed it entirely. Groczek had been clever to see that, had been clever to discern that element of self-destruction in Slovak, but then, there was that in every man, to some extent, and most of all it was in Groczek, too. It was precisely that that Groczek, in his manic surge, had failed to see. Slovak, in his own way, thus had his strongest ally in Groczek, and in destroying Groczek he felt, intuitively, and as he had said to himself a moment ago, he would be going a long way towards liberating himself and that he would never, afterwards, be quite the same again.

Chapter Ten

Groczek drove the security van himself through the city streets, weaving in and out of the traffic, towards the police head-quarters building. He would not deny that he felt agitated. He was committed. There was no further excuse for procras-tination. The drugs would be moved today and that would be an end to it. He had made all his preparations, taken all the precautions that he felt able to take. He had tried to fore-see all that might go wrong. He had taxed his imagination and his experience to the limit. He could not see how he could fail. He felt satisfied – but agitated.

He brought the security van to a halt outside the police station and jumped down. Fallon was waiting for him on the sidewalk. Fallon couldn't understand why Groczek had insisted on bringing another security van from another division or why he had insisted on driving it himself, but Groczek was in an uncommunicative mood and Fallon, was, already, to some extent, disinterested. He, himself, had no doubts about the safety of the drugs, but he had expressed himself on the sub-ject of Groczek's exaggerated fears before and was not prepared to do so again. Slovak's interference with the security cars in the railroad had become, for Fallon, not so much an indication of Slovak's cleverness as his lack of it. They had, after all, forestalled him.

Groczek and Fallon walked down the steps that led to the basement and entered the room in which stood the large iron safe. A group of police officers stood about, talking quietly among themselves. They broke off as Groczek and Fallon entered. Groczek nodded to them 'Good morning' and went to the safe. He turned the combination lock this way and that, grasped the huge, iron handles and swung the door open. He stood back and pointed to the cardboard boxes containing the cans of heroin that lay inside. 'Bring them out,' he said, 'we're moving them out this morning.'

Wexler and Spivack stepped forward. They leant inside and pulled the boxes out, piling them on the floor. Groczek and Fallon watched them. Wexler and Spivack closed the safe and stepped back. Groczek stepped up to the safe and once more turned the lock to its right combination, locking it. Then he turned and looked at the detectives waiting there. His eyes roamed across each face. He knew them all, some better than others, but all of them he knew well. And yet, in a sense, he didn't know them. He knew that information was being leaked, and any one of them, despite his alert and attentive air, might be the one Slovak had already got at. Up to a point, he trusted none of them. Yet that mattered little now. He had kept everything to himself, he had confided in no one, not even Fallon. Whatever information he was now about to put to them they would be too late to make use of. He had seen that this was the only way to proceed with any security at all.

'Now hear me,' he said to them, 'and hear me good. There's around $10,000,000 worth of junk in those cans, and we're shipping them out to the labs in Boston. I believe that the moment we start, a serious and well-organised attempt will be made to heist the lot somewhere on its journey.'

159

The detectives glanced at each other in mild surprise and scepticism. A heist? From them? From the police? Well, that was new. They'd never heard that one before, and slight smiles began to appear around the corners of their mouths. Groczek noted it and nodded grimly. 'You needn't look so goddamned pleased with yourselves,' he said, 'at least, till it's over. Now, I don't know when or where it's going to happen. It may be on the road to the station or it may be on the train itself. But my information is that it's going to happen, so get this and get it straight – from the moment we step outside this building, those drugs – and our reputations – are at grave risk. I need hardly tell you,' he went on grimly, 'just how comical it will appear to the gentlemen of the press if we lose them.'

The thought seemed to sober them. It was hard to credit and yet, if Groczek felt the drugs were at serious risk, there must be something in it and certainly, if a successful heist were pulled they would all look pretty sick. There was a moment's heavy silence while Groczek stared at each and every face, conveying to each a sombre warning of what might happen to him if anything went wrong. Then he nodded to Wexler and Spivack and a couple of others. 'All right,' he said, 'pick them up.'

The detectives stooped and picked up the boxes. Groczek turned and led the way out, followed by Fallon. They climbed the stairs from the basement to the sidewalk outside. Groczek went to the rear of the security van, unlocked the door and stood aside. 'Put them in,' he said, 'just over there.' He pointed to the side of the van near the door and one by one the detectives deposited their load on the floor of the van and stepped back.

All this while, Groczek's eyes had surveyed the busy street outside the headquarters building. It was a fine day and people were going about their business in the normal way. He noted nothing odd or unusual anywhere that might arouse his sus-

160

picions. It had crossed his mind to have armed guards standing outside the building to watch the loading into the van, but he had decided against it. It would have been making altogether too much of it, he felt, and drawing unnecessary attention to the operation.

Two police cars had drawn in on either side of the van. Groczek turned to Fallon. 'I'll ride inside. Put two men up front. You take the lead car. I want one car in front and one behind, and tell them whatever happens, they're not to get separated. All right.'

Fallon nodded. He had, on Groczek's instructions, issued each officer with a gas mask. He was in no position to question Groczek's elaborate precautions yet he could not dispel the air of melodrama that overhung the whole scene. Groczek climbed into the van and Fallon slammed it shut. He detailed two officers to the front of the van and split the rest into two groups, taking a car each. He, himself, took the lead car. The cars and the van moved off in convoy through the busy streets.

Groczek sat on the bench in the van staring out through the small, barred window onto the passing scene outside. He was tense, but he felt better now that he was on the move. The next most vulnerable point would undoubtedly be the moment when they transferred the junk from the van to the security car at the station. He was under no illusions about Slovak. The man was subtle, but it would not prevent him mounting, if he thought fit, a military-style operation at the station, which was why Groczek had not even excluded the use of gas.

He stared down at the boxes at his feet. He would never have believed they would have caused him more anxiety *after* he had seized them than they had before. It was the last thing he might have expected. It was odd how the roles had been so swiftly reversed, how for months he had patiently watched and waited and pounced at the right moment and now, having secured his prize, someone else had arrived on the scene

161

to watch *him*, to wait patiently for the moment to pounce on *him* and dispossess him of the very thing he had worked so hard to secure.

He felt the van slow a little and then come to a halt at traffic lights. He turned once more and gazed out of the window. Two cars, one black and one green, which he had noticed fall in behind them as the convoy moved off were still there, drawing up now, slightly alongside. He told himself that it was inevitable that, in a city heavy with traffic, one shared a route for a while with vehicles that had no more connection with one's own than that they happened to be going in the same direction, yet in the circumstances they took on a suspicious air. The black car, slightly in front, had six men in it. They huddled down in their seats, staring straight in front of them. It was irrational and yet a car with six men in it appeared more sinister than a car with only three or perhaps even with two men and a woman. There was something about the heavy masculinity of it, the way they all sat cramped inside and staring stolidly ahead of them that seemed to give it a grimmer purpose than it, in all probability, had. Doubtless, endless films with cars filled with gangsters had something to do with the air of 'not being quite right' that the car conveyed and, probably too, it was all in his imagination.

The van moved off as the lights changed and the black car drew a little more abreast of the van. Groczek stared out of the window at the men in the car. He recognised none of them and they appeared uninterested in the van – too uninterested? The man on the nearest side turned, idly, and stared at the van alongside him, his eyes holding it disinterestedly for a moment before turning away. For all Groczek knew, they were six men on their way to the station to catch a train for a business meeting in the next town.

In the lead car, Fallon, too, had noticed the black car and the green one had been with them for some time but, unlike Groczek, had not viewed them with any deep suspicion. He

162

had noted them, as a policeman notes these things, out of old habit, his senses all working for him, but he had filed the image away somewhere at the back of his mind and turned his attention to other things. When he next noticed the black car it had passed the security van in the rear and was drawing just abreast of Fallon's car. Fallon turned round further to get a clearer view of it and was flung violently forward as his driver stepped on the brake and the car came to an abrupt halt. Almost at once, Fallon felt himself flung forward again as the security van struck his own car in the rear. A moment later, he saw the cause of the sudden halt. A large truck had emerged from a side street, attempting to enter the main road and had stopped right across the front of Fallon's car.

Every nerve in Fallon's body came alight, glowed, as if an electric charge had been suddenly shot through it. Out of the corner of his eye he saw the doors of the black car alongside him opening and men getting out. 'Get the masks on,' he shouted, pushing open his own door. He leapt out of his car grabbing his own mask, and flung himself towards the truck driver who had opened his cabin door and was on his way down. 'Stay where you are,' Fallon shouted.

Something in Fallon's tone froze the driver and he stopped, one hand on the open door, a foot dangling towards the ground. At the same time, police were pouring out of the two cars, pulling on their masks and with guns already in their hands. Fallon turned on the men who had got out of the black car and were advancing towards the truck driver. 'Freeze,' he shouted. The men froze, staring round in some bewilderment at the sudden superfluity of men all around them, their faces grotesquely hidden in the masks.

Fallon ran to the rear of the truck, tearing open the canvas flaps. There was nothing inside. He came back to the front of the truck. 'What the hell do you think you're doing?' the truck driver shouted at him.

'Shut up,' Fallon yelled, furiously, 'where's your licence?'

163

The truck driver stared at him. 'Your driver's licence!' Fallon shouted again. The driver reached inside his cabin and came out with his licence. Fallon snatched it and looked at it. It all seemed in order. Furiously, he handed the licence back.

'And what about yours?' the truck driver said, aggressively, 'what about some identification?'

'We're police,' Fallon replied grittily, 'and back this crumby truck up!'

'How do I know that?' the driver asked. 'You could be anyone.'

'BACK IT UP!' Fallon yelled.

'You ought to put lights there,' the driver growled, 'nobody can get out of that goddamned turning.'

Grumbling to himself, the truck driver got back into his seat. Fallon turned and faced the men who had got out of the black car. 'Where were you going?' he asked menacingly.

The men looked at each other, lamely. Then one of them said, 'We were just going to have a quiet word with that driver, sir.'

'I've had a quiet word with him,' Fallon snarled, 'get back into your car.'

From inside the security van, Groczek watched the men from the car that had engaged his attention earlier get back inside. Somehow they looked neither sinister nor threatening anymore. He gazed out of the window, his attention wandering to the street. Crowds of people were standing about, watching. Everything looked innocent enough and yet? He crossed the floor of the van and looked out the other side, his gaze raking the street along its length in both directions. There was nothing to arouse his suspicions. When the van had come to an abrupt halt he had been flung onto the floor of the security car and he had known, or thought he had known, that this was the moment he had been expecting. But nothing was happening. Some fool of a truck driver who hadn't the

164

patience to wait had decided to barge his way into the road, bringing everything to a halt.

He returned to the other window and looked out again. All the cars behind the truck were backing up and making, as usual, a mess of it. The truck driver was leaning out of his window, waving them back. The detectives had ripped off their masks and were climbing back into their cars again. They all looked a little sheepish. Well, Groczek thought, better look a fool than be one.

The convoy moved off once again. Groczek sat quite still. They were not far now from the station. Despite the false alarm, despite the fact that everyone had over-reacted, he was well aware that they all, at this very moment, might be being watched by Slovak or by the people he employed. He was under no illusions about that.

The convoy turned into the station grounds and swung round towards the freight yards. From the window Groczek could see in the distance the security car, in effect a large container on which the men had worked reinforcing it in every way. It was hanging in mid-air, held by a crane, and was slowly being set down upon the platform of the rail truck. He could see Levin and O'Malley standing by watching the men guide it down square. As the convoy drew up the crane was unhooked and the men swarmed all over the container, locking it down securely onto the platform.

The convoy came to a halt and Groczek unlocked the door from the inside and jumped down as Fallon came round to him. 'Damn fool truck driver,' he said to Groczek, shaking his head, 'I thought something was about to break.'

'So did I,' Groczek replied, 'you did right. Better to be safe, though, than sorry.'

Fallon nodded. He was still annoyed with himself and was partly, in his mind, blaming Groczek for the panic. Groczek's certainty that an attempt would be made on the junk had

165

infected him too. He would never have reacted in that way normally. Even now, his chief was paying him no attention, but was gazing round the great station yard, his eyes probing every corner and every face, tense and alert for the slightest sign of trouble but there was nothing that could give him the smallest cause for alarm.

'Do you think we're being watched?' Fallon asked.

'I don't know. What do you think?'

Fallon shrugged. 'Let's get the stuff in the container,' he said. His patience was beginning to wear thin.

Groczek nodded. He turned back to the security van and jerked his head at the waiting detectives. 'O.K.,' he said, 'bring it out.'

Wexler, Spivack and two others leaned inside and picked the boxes up in their arms. Groczek led the way over to the container whose rear doors now stood open. On either side stood two armed railroad guards. 'You'll be met at Boston,' he said, 'by a police escort. It's all been arranged. The radio will keep you in touch with local police all along the route. That's been arranged, too.' He handed one of the guards an envelope. 'Inside is a code word. When you get to Boston, you won't open the door of the container until that code is given you over the radio, O.K.?'

The guards nodded, turned and went inside. The doors of the container slammed shut and were bolted from the inside. Groczek and Fallon stood back. The train was ready to go. 'Satisfied?' Fallon asked, with a grin at Groczek.

Groczek both nodded and shrugged. 'Almost,' he said, enigmatically, and stood there without saying anything more, waiting for the train to pull out. It seemed to take an interminable amount of time. What was it that kept everything waiting so long in railroads? Everything seemed ready, what was holding it up? Levin had assured him the train would pull out as soon as the junk was loaded. Groczek began to grow impatient. What had gone wrong? He turned to Levin.

166

'What's the matter?' he asked him, 'why doesn't it pull out?'

Levin shrugged. 'I don't know, sir,' he said, 'I'll go and find out, though.'

He walked down the length of the platform towards the engine. It was a long walk. Groczek could see, in the distance, the driver's head leaning out of the cabin and looking back in his direction, as if waiting for someone to give him the signal to move. But no one did.

Once again Groczek turned his gaze to the yards all around. His impatience was once again turning into anxiety, a sense that things might yet go wrong. He could not put his finger on it, only that he had the vaguest sense of being watched, of Slovak's presence somewhere within the complex. It was absurd, but he couldn't shake the feeling off. He saw Levin walking back down the platform towards him. He had spoken to the driver and seemed to have had a small argument with him. Groczek waited until Levin got within earshot and then could contain his impatience no longer. 'Well?' he asked.

Levin lifted his shoulders helplessly. 'He's waiting for his sandwiches,' he said, 'he left them in the locker room. Some-one's gone back to pick them up.' Groczek looked back down the platform. Another man, in no hurry was walking towards the engine, a parcel in one hand. Groczek saw him hand it up to the driver. The driver waved and disappeared inside the cabin. Another moment, and the train jerked, and jerked again and then began to roll out of the station.

For a moment Groczek and Fallon stood watching the train as it began gathering speed along the track. 'Well,' Fallon said, looking at Groczek, 'so far so good.'

'You think so?' Groczek replied. 'Come here.'

Groczek turned and walked back towards the security van in which he had come, followed by Fallon. He opened the van door and got up into the van. He looked back at Fallon. 'Come on up,' he said.

Fallon climbed up after him. Groczek was at the rear of

167

the van. On the floor, Fallon saw a bundle of things covered with sacking. He looked down at it curiously. Groczek pulled away the sacking, revealing a number of cardboard boxes, all bearing the stamp of the Oriental Spice Company. The tops had been opened and Fallon saw inside the cans of water chestnuts identical to those they had just put on the train. Groczek pointed to them. 'That's the heroin,' he said, 'the stuff that went on the train is chalk – powdered chalk.'

Fallon's mouth fell open. He stared from the heroin back up to Groczek who was looking at him, more than satisfied with the effect he had produced. 'What's the idea?' Fallon asked.

'You'll see,' Groczek said. 'I told you I'd throw a monkey wrench into that billion-dollar brain and now you'll see how it's done. Come on.'

He got down from the van and Fallon followed him. 'Call the men around,' Groczek said. Fallon called the detectives back to the van. They stood around waiting for Groczek to address them. Groczek pointed inside the van. 'That's the heroin,' he said, 'the stuff you took out of the safe. What you just put on the train were cans of powdered chalk. This stuff's going a different route. Get back into your cars and follow me. Wexler, Spivack, you drive the van. And don't get separated.'

The detectives turned and piled back into their cars. Wexler and Spivack climbed up into the front seats of the security van. Groczek and Fallon got into the lead car. 'Mostyn's,' Groczek said to the driver.

The driver started the engine, put the car into gear and pulled away. Groczek turned and looked behind him. The security van pulled away a second later and fell in behind. Fallon turned and looked at Groczek. 'Mostyn's?' he asked.

Groczek nodded. 'I decided to send the stuff by helicopter. I've made all arrangements with young Greenberg. They have a regular run for their executives. They'll take the stuff for us.'

'Couldn't you have used one of our own choppers?' Fallon asked.

'No, I couldn't,' Groczek replied, 'there's no way I could have put that into use without everyone knowing about it. There's too much paper work. It would have been leaked. For all we know, the train journey's been leaked.'

'We've kept it pretty tight,' Fallon said.

Groczek shook his head. 'Maybe. But there's too many people involved. There's Levin, there's O'Malley, there's you. There's the driver – he's towing an extra car and has to be told. There are clerks in the office who do the paper work. And Slovak knew what we were doing to that container, you can bet your life.'

'All the same,' Fallon said, feeling slightly irritated at having been left out, 'it seems a hell of a lot of trouble to go to just to shift a load of chalk onto a train.'

'You don't understand,' Grczek replied patiently, 'or you just don't appreciate that there was probably nothing decided in that office that Slovak didn't get to know about. You still think I exaggerate that?'

'No,' Fallon conceded, reluctantly.

'You saw what happened in the repair yards. Anyway, *I* saw, and that was good enough for me. So I thought, "Well, if I can't plug a leak, I'll float the information out on it that I want him to have". I *had* to go that route by train. That was my blind. Mostyn's is my cover. I tell you, Slovak'll rue the day he ever chose my patch to piss on.'

They drove on in silence for a moment. Fallon didn't know whether he was impressed or not. It seemed, as he had said, a lot of trouble to go to. He, himself, didn't think that even Slovak, if he stopped the train, would be able to cut his way into that container before the police, summoned by the guards on the radio, could arrive on the scene. He said so to Groczek.

Groczek nodded. 'Maybe,' he said, 'but I'm taking no chances. I've looked at that route. There are one or two

169

patches along there where the local police could take anything up to twenty minutes to half an hour to get to it. If I've looked at it, so has Slovak. Maybe he could cut his way in, maybe he couldn't, but like I said, I'm taking no chances.'

'Well,' said Fallon, after a pause, 'I have to admit it's a good idea – to cover yourself like that, I mean.' Groczek nodded, satisfied and looked back again to check the security van was still behind them. Fallon gazed out of the window. A thought was nagging at his mind. He felt slightly embarrassed to put it into words and yet, before he could stop himself, it was out. 'I just wonder, though,' he said, 'if Slovak really is as clever as all that . . .'

'He is,' Groczek said in a tone that brooked no contradiction.

'Well, then, I wonder,' Fallon continued, 'if he hasn't thought to cover *himself*.'

There was a long silence. Groczek continued to stare out of the window at the passing street. He felt a cold hand move inside his stomach, a wave of unease pass over him. Was it possible? He knew it was possible the moment Fallon said it. But he wanted to hear it from Fallon. He turned to him. 'How?' he asked, and his voice caught in the back of his throat as he said the word.

Fallon shrugged. 'Well, he certainly could have had us under observation from the moment we left headquarters. We haven't exactly been invisible.'

'But he's seen us put the stuff on the train,' Groczek said.

Fallon nodded. 'Sure, and right now we ought to be going back to H.Q. but we're going in a totally different direction.' There was a moment's pause. Groczek knew this to be true and found himself gazing uneasily out of the window at the traffic all around them. But then, it seemed unlikely. 'Add to that,' Fallon went on, 'you visited the Oriental Spice Company yourself.'

'I had to,' Groczek answered, in a low voice, and looked a

shade contritely at Fallon. 'I couldn't tell you, you know that.'

'Oh, sure,' Fallon said with an easy laugh, 'I'm not blaming you. Hell, no! But, well, we've been watching *him*. What makes you so sure he hasn't been watching you?'

Groczek wasn't sure. Suddenly he wasn't sure of anything. What Fallon said was true. And he seemed, for all he covered it up, to take a small delight in saying it. Groczek shrugged that off. He could understand Fallon's sense of pique at being excluded. Still the fact was that Slovak could quite easily have had him watched. It was the last thing a policeman would think of, that someone was actually watching *him*. And if he had been watching him, Slovak would know of his visit to the Oriental Spice Company and would put two and two together. That wouldn't be hard. Why else would Groczek have gone at this stage?

'Well, then,' Groczek said, finally, 'if you're right, and he *has* covered himself, he'll have to seize the stuff between here and Mostyn's. Once it's on that chopper, that's it.'

'That's right,' Fallon said, 'if he doesn't get it between here and Mostyn's, then he won't get it at all.' He smiled at Groczek. 'And that makes this part of the journey just about the most dangerous of all.'

Groczek said nothing. He recognised the truth of what Fallon was saying. Whether he was right or not only time would tell, but there was no doubt in his mind now, that what he thought would be the easiest part of the journey had turned out to be, potentially at any rate, the most dangerous. If Slovak were not to be tricked quite so easily, if he had, as Fallon suggested, covered *him*self, then he would have to move sometime between now and putting the drugs on the helicopter. And, suddenly, he remembered, too, that the cop who had driven him to Mostyn's that day was also the cop who had driven him to the Oriental Spice Company when he had asked to see its vice-president. True, he had waited outside

171

both times, but supposing it was he who was peddling information to Slovak? Slovak would not have been slow to spot the way Groczek's mind was moving.

They were pulling up now, in front of Mostyn's. They had to carry the stuff from the security van to the top floor of the store where Greenberg would be waiting, ready to conduct them up to the roof and to the waiting helicopter. It was not the sort of trip Greenberg's chopper would normally make, but he had been happy to accommodate Groczek. The service elevator, which they would take, would be held ready for them on the ground floor.

Groczek sat in the car for a moment after it had come to a halt, staring out along both sides of the street. The store took up a whole block and the sidewalk outside was crowded with shoppers and people going about their business. Traffic in the street was heavy but there was nothing Groczek could see that aroused his suspicions.

He got out of the car and Fallon got out the other side and joined him on the sidewalk in front of the store. The security van with the other car following had pulled up behind them. Groczek looked around; nothing gave cause for alarm. He nodded to the security van, got down and went round to the back. The detectives from the other cars piled out and surrounded the rear of the van as Wexler and Spivack, aided by two others, leant inside and took up an armful of the boxes each.

Seeing the heroin again, carried so casually, looking so vulnerable to a snatch there and then, gave Groczek a moment of extreme and shuddering anxiety. He suddenly felt they were all exposed, unnecessarily so, and began to wonder if he might not have been better off taking his chances on the train. But it was too late for that now. He took a firm grip of himself and led the way inside the store, followed by the detectives carrying the heroin and the rest bringing up a watchful rear.

The store was crowded. People were milling about every-

172

where, the press of shoppers all around them doing nothing to ease Groczek's anxiety. But this was how he had wanted it, no special arrangements, everything normal. Groczek led the way across the store. 'We're taking the service elevator,' he said to Fallon, 'it should be ready and waiting for us.'

The elevator, however, was not there. Groczek came to a halt in front of the shiny, metal doors and looked up at the indicator clock. The elevator was on the tenth floor. Groczek shook his head. 'Why can't people do what they say they'll do?' he asked.

Irritably, he pressed the button, but nothing moved. He pressed it again and again. 'Come on, come on,' he muttered. He looked at Fallon. Fallon lifted his shoulders helplessly. What could one do? If an elevator was stuck with its gate open on the tenth floor, no amount of button pressing would bring it down again. Clearly, someone had jammed open the gates. That seemed, after all, perfectly normal in a service elevator. Storeworkers were constantly bringing things up and down.

Groczek, however, didn't like it. Perhaps it had no significance but Greenberg had said he would see to it that it was waiting for them and it wasn't. The elevator was stuck on the tenth floor. Was it an oversight or had it been planned? He turned and looked back at the store. Everything looked normal and yet his own agitation was beginning to affect what he saw. He knew that. He knew that in his situation it was simple for the mind to transform the normal into the suspicious, yet he could not shake off the feeling that all was not right. The line dividing illusion and reality was beginning to crumble.

Fallon stretched out a finger and pressed the button. The elevator began to descend at once. Groczek did not look at him, for he was sure Fallon would have seen the look of irritation on his face and been mildly amused by it. He stood there, facing the doors, and staring stonily up at the indicator as the

173

elevator descended lower and lower. It came finally to rest and the doors opened. Two store workers emerged, staring at the waiting group curiously. Groczek watched them until they had passed out of sight, then jerked his head at the detectives. One by one they passed inside. Groczek nodded to Fallon and Fallon pressed the button. The elevator began to ascend.

The elevator rose silently and smoothly but, it seemed to Groczek, terribly slowly. He stood facing the doors, his face expressionless. Fallon and the rest of the detectives stood around him silently; perhaps beginning to wonder where this was all to end, if perhaps when the boxes they were carrying had been safely placed on board the helicopter, Groczek might not dramatically reveal yet another consignment to go by yet another route. Groczek was not unaware of the thoughts likely to be passing through their minds, but he was not put out by them. He had one objective in his mind, to see the heroin safely stowed on the helicopter and safely arrived at the labs. All other considerations melted away in the heat of that obsession. He may seem to them to have been unnecessarily elaborate in his precautions but all that would be justified in the end.

Abruptly and unexpectedly the elevator slowed to a halt. Groczek froze and even Fallon and the others stiffened perceptibly. Groczek put his hand involuntarily on the handle of his gun and felt himself begin to tug at it and then pause as he was overtaken by a sense of foolishness, as if something inside him was warning him not to over-react once again, that this could once more be a false alarm like the others, an event of no significance, twisted and tortured out of shape by his obsessional fears into the long awaited attack upon his enterprise.

He gripped the gun but found himself unable to draw it. They all stared fixedly at the doors of the elevator, waiting for them to open. They began, silently and smoothly, to pull back. Groczek stood there, watching them, waiting to see what they

174

would reveal, forcing himself to remain utterly still and not to be precipitated yet again into a moment of panic, but he saw, before the others, the sub-machine gun thrust low inside as the door opened a foot, felt a sense of utter paralysis as he stared down at the black nozzle, felt his mouth open to cry a warning but heard no sound come out, saw, in a daze, flame leap from the muzzle of the gun and the chatter fill his ears in one long raking round of fire.

The door bumped back upon its hinge and rested. No one moved. Groczek and Fallon and the others stared at the space revealed opposite them, stared stonily into the faces of two store workers, loaded with toys, smiles on their faces frozen as they stared at a group of strangers in their service elevator they had clearly not expected to see. There was a long silence. No one spoke. Then Fallon stretched out a finger and pressed the button again. Once more the elevator doors slowly closed, blocking out the store workers, their frozen smiles and their bundles of toys. The elevator rose again to the top floor.

It came to a halt and the doors opened onto the top floor. Groczek stepped out, followed by the others. In a tight group they crossed the heavily carpeted floor towards the door that led up to the roof. They were in the credit department and clerks sat behind rows of desks, watching their progress. Groczek put his hand on the handle of the small door, turned it and found it locked.

It was curious. After having mentally kicked himself in the elevator, having told himself that nothing now could go wrong, he felt again, at this small obstacle, at something being not quite as he had expected it, an irrational sense of panic. But the panic came from a different source. Whereas his panic before had stemmed from the constant expectation that something was about to happen, he now recognised that it welled up, perversely, because he had, after that foolish incident in the elevator, switched himself off deliberately. His senses were refusing any longer to respond to danger signals, refusing at the request of a more pressing inner voice that told him his real danger was in beginning to look absurd.

Yet with his hand upon the unexpectedly locked door, another part of him was suddenly recognising that that low tuning of his fears was the greatest danger to him of all, and that that diminished responsiveness could, unless he exerted himself immensely at this last stage of his journey, result in his total ruination. Of *course* it was here, *here*, at the very last moment, when all his fears were allayed, when he saw himself home and dry, that he was at his most vulnerable. They all were. Slovak would know that. He would know better than anyone for he, more than most, had planned stages for himself and been hyper-aware of the dangers of falling at the last fence. Groczek felt the blood rush to his head and the thrust of blood acted like an injection of high octane fuel. He whirled round at the clerks, snarling, 'Where's the key to this door?'

No one moved. A row of faces stared at him. He couldn't quite make them out. No one responded. Was each waiting for someone else to answer or were they waiting for something else? 'Where's the key to this door?' he shouted once again.

From behind a glass partition, a large, bull-necked man appeared and stood for a moment, looking at him. Then, slowly, ponderously, he moved towards Groczek. 'Stay were you are,' Groczek said to him. The man seemed not to hear him. He continued to advance towards him and as he did so, two or three of the clerks rose in their desks. Somewhere inside his head, Groczek felt an old alarm bell going off. He couldn't make it all out. These were clerks in the credit department of a store, yet grouped as they were, and staring at him as they were, they did not look like clerks. There was something odd about them all, something threatening. He felt his hand tugging at his revolver, felt it come out in his hand and saw the man approaching him stop and stare at him, puzzled. Behind him, he heard the door leading up to the roof open from the outside. He swung round and saw young Greenberg coming towards him, smiling.

'There you are,' Greenberg said, 'we're waiting to leave.' He paused as he saw the gun in Groczek's hand. 'Is something wrong?' he asked.

Groczek stared at Greenberg, then looked at the man and the clerks behind the desks and the thought flashed through his mind that they might have wondered if this were not some sort of stick-up, in the same way that he had wondered if they were not there to lift the drugs from him. He shook his head at Greenberg and said, 'Nothing's wrong. I just thought you'd be waiting at the door, that's all. When I found it locked . . .'

'I just stepped up to tell the pilot something,' Greenberg said, 'we always keep the door locked as a safety precaution. Could we hurry? My chief merchandising man and accountant have to be picked up in Boston. We've got a board meeting back here at four.'

Groczek nodded, his lips pursed in a thin line. He followed Greenberg to the door and up the flight of steps. Fallon and the detectives carrying the boxes followed them up onto the roof. Mostyn's helicopter stood there waiting to take off with the pilot already on board. The detectives loaded the boxes onto the plane. Wexler and Spivack stepped back but Groczek said to them, 'Get in. You're going with them.' They shrugged and got inside the helicopter.

Greenberg stepped up to the pilot and shouted above the noise of the motor, 'All right, Stephen? The labs first, then pick up Ryan and Silverstein at the airport.' The pilot nodded. Greenberg turned back to Groczek. 'We'll go below,' he said, 'there's a lot of wind when he takes off.' Groczek nodded. They followed Greenberg back down the stairs and Greenberg closed and locked the door. He was a young, attractive man, the nephew of the original owner of the store, who had built branches all over the country. 'There it goes,' he said, glancing out of the window as the helicopter rose high over the city,

177

'you've no idea how much time that little machine saves us. Come down to my office and have a drink.'

Groczek shook his head. 'I'll take a rain-check on it. But, thanks, anyway, and for your co-operation.'

'Forget it,' Greenberg said, smiling, 'you know we're always glad to help the police. Any time.'

Groczek shook hands and he and Fallon and the others walked away to the elevator while Greenberg went on to his own office. They waited for the elevator to arrive. No one spoke. There seemed nothing more to say. They got into the elevator, descended to the ground floor, walked through the crowds of shoppers and got into the cars. It was strange how normal and unsuspicious everything now appeared.

They drove back to the headquarters building and Fallon came into Groczek's office with him. He flopped down into a chair and stretched out his legs. Groczek went to the cabinet and poured each of them a drink. 'Well,' Fallon said, as he took it, 'are you satisfied now?'

Groczek nodded. Yes, he was satisfied. He had panicked, it was true, panicked perhaps more than he should have done, but the circumstances were exceptional and he felt unable to blame himself for that. He had accomplished what he set out to do. However many false alarms he had responded to, the drugs were safely on their way and he was rightly satisfied. Greenberg's helicopter would be met by a police escort as it landed on the lawns in front of the labs and the contents conducted from there under guard, into the buildings. Nothing, now, could go wrong. What, he found himself wondering now, was – what would Slovak's next move be?

Slovak had been outwitted, he must see that. At the very most he could attack the train and stop it, as he had done once before. Groczek hoped that he would. It would take quite a while to cut through that container and meanwhile the nearest police would have been summoned on the radio to the scene. Whether Slovak himself would take part in the operation or

178

not, Groczek couldn't be sure. It would be unlike him but this was an unusual case and in so far as no attempt had been made to relieve Groczek of the drugs on his way to Mostyn's, it looked very much as if Slovak had fallen for the train routine. He couldn't see it otherwise. Fallon had been wrong there. He had over-estimated him. Having pointed out to Groczek, quite rightly, that Slovak was not a Superman, he had fallen into the same error as Groczek had done earlier and assumed that Slovak knew everything, every move they were making. Slovak, however, did not. He might attack the train and if he did, successfully, that is – and that was by no means sure – he would get cans of chalk for his effort. Mostyn's chopper was unassailable.

What fascinated Groczek now was what Slovak would do. Somehow, he found it hard to believe that Slovak would simply fade away, that having failed to secure what he came for, he would simply disappear again. He could not believe that. Yet what else could Slovak accomplish? Had the whole thing been a blind, nothing but a game, a bizarre kind of practical joke? Had it never been Slovak's intention to take the drugs, but merely to put the fear of God into Groczek and nothing else? Was Slovak sitting, at this very moment, in his house just out of town, smiling to himself and with no intention whatsoever of doing anything at all?

Groczek felt a cold and clammy hand pass over his brow as the thought touched him. Fallon, finding Groczek still pre-occupied and not disposed to talk, finished his drink and went back to his own office. Groczek continued to sit, pondering this new thought that had taken possession of him and wondering where it led him. It led him, of course, precisely no-where, except into a state of acute embarrassment at having been made such a fool of, if, in fact, that were the case. In one way that was of little importance, certainly put against the kind of fool he would have looked had he actually lost the drugs. He could not have lived with that. That would have

179

destroyed him. But was there not, too, a certain loss of face in the heroin arriving safely at its destination, threatened nowhere at all along its route, with no further word or whisper from Slovak and the whole elaborate process of transportation seen for what it was – a product of irrational fears and unnecessary panic?

He began to pace the office again, restlessly, feeling a growing concern as the image he might shortly be presenting to the public appeared less and less favourable to him. Had he been entirely wrong in his assessment of the situation? Had Fallon been right when he suggested that he needed a rest, with the concomitant hint that he was beginning to break down? Was his mind breaking down? Nothing was impossible. The hospitals were full of over-worked and over-strained minds that had, somehow, got everything out of proportion and ended by confusing fantasy with fact? Wasn't that, in a way, what he felt Slovak himself was doing? And now supposing he had got that wrong? Would it be so remarkable? The burden of office in these last few years had been enormous. He was in no doubt of that. He had felt, at times, unable to cope with it all, yet he had driven himself to cope with it and had succeeded. But at what price? What had he unknowingly paid?

He felt himself sweating again. He wiped his forehead with his handkerchief and poured himself another drink. He had intended to occupy himself with work he had neglected until he received news of the safe arrival of the drugs but he now found himself unable to think of anything else. He looked at his watch and found, to his surprise, that the time had slipped away rapidly and that he had been back in his office far longer than he would have dreamed. He sat down at his desk and picked up some papers but found he could not concentrate on them. His mind kept returning to Slovak and his own predicament. He could not leave it alone.

What if Slovak's presence, here in the city, had nothing

180

to do with the drugs? What if he had come here for something else, a payroll, a bank, anything? What if he had taken in the situation at a glance and with his usual ingenuity and knowing that Groczek would wonder what he had come for, deliberately planted in Groczek's mind the thought that he had come for the drugs? That would have blinded Groczek utterly. While every nerve in himself and his force had been switched to guarding the heroin from Slovak, would this not have provided Slovak with the ideal opportunity to operate elsewhere almost at will?

Groczek stared out the window of his office, his face ashen grey as the realisation poured into him that his collision with Slovak may have resulted in nothing more than sending him flying off the wrong way, while Slovak had pursued his course undeflected. Groczek had not so much collided with Slovak as bounced off him and been sent careering off along a line elaborately plotted by Slovak beforehand. So strong was this sudden conviction of the truth of this that he felt, for a moment, nothing at all except a dull astonishment that he hadn't considered it earlier. And so gripped was he by this conviction that it took some time for him to readjust his mind to the words Fallon was shouting at him from the open door. He had so utterly dismissed from his mind the thought that Slovak's interest was, or had ever been, in the drugs that he could not relate what Fallon was shouting at him to any problem that he felt he had at that moment. 'The train,' Fallon shouted, for the third time, pointing at the phone on Groczek's desk, 'the train! They've hit the train! Pick up the phone! The local sheriff's on!'

In exasperation, Fallon strode over to the desk and picked up the receiver and held it out to Groczek. Groczek's mind began spinning, trying to find the right holes for the words to slot into. All his agonising doubts disappeared. Certainty and conviction took their place. He seized the telephone receiver and spoke into it. 'Chief Groczek,' he said, 'give it to me.'

181

He listened. Fallon watched him. Now and then he nodded, grimly, and once said, 'Where? Groton? Where's that?' and then listened again. Then he said, 'Thanks. Keep me informed, I'll be here. Any sort of lead, let me know,' and hung up.

He looked at Fallon. There was a grudging sort of admiration on his face, permitted only by the huge sense of relief that he felt. He nodded. 'They hit the train, like I said they would.'

'Where?'

'Groton. It's a hundred odd miles down the line. A small, disused station. It was closed years ago. There's grass growing over the tracks. They overpowered the signalman and took over the box. They switched the train off the main line and into the disused station. It's two or three miles from the main line.'

'Did they cut through the container?'

'No. They had a mobile crane waiting. They lifted the container off the platform and put it on a waiting truck. It's just disappeared. The police are out looking for it now.'

Fallon pursed his lips and whistled. 'Not bad. They took the whole lot.'

Groczek rose from his seat and let out a long sigh. He walked back to the window and stared out over the city.

'You were right,' Fallon said.

Groczek nodded. 'Yes, I was right.'

'And I was wrong.' Fallon shook his head. 'He's cleverer than I thought.'

'Yes, he's clever. But he's got 200 pounds of chalk for his pains.'

He looked at Fallon, and Fallon saw the glint of satisfaction in his eyes. Well, he couldn't begrudge him that. Groczek had acted on his instincts and his instincts had proved him right. Groczek had a right to feel satisfied, even to feel a sense of triumph.

Fallon got up to go but Groczek waved him back to his seat. He wanted to talk. He wanted to bask for a while in all

182

the warm relief of it and even in his deputy's quiet admiration. He didn't want to savour it all alone. He had been too much alone lately, too much, at least, *on* his own.

The phone rang again twenty minutes later. Groczek nodded to Fallon and Fallon picked up the receiver. He listened for a while, making a few notes on a pad with his pencil and then hung up.

'A cop's just found the container. They'd cut through the door, mesh, the lot. They've cleaned everything out except two or three cans that fell out in their hurry to get away.'

'What about the guards?'

'They're O.K. – just knocked about a bit.'

'Couldn't they have radioed where they were being taken?'

'Apparently the windows were blocked off from the outside and anyway, the gang had some kind of interference machine going. After the first few minutes the radios failed to maintain contact. The local police have set up road blocks. Maybe they'll pick up some of the gang?' Groczek nodded and there was a short pause. Then Fallon said, 'Well, that's that, I guess.'

Groczek nodded again but didn't answer. He was suddenly tired. The first rush of relief had drained away. He had woken, it seemed to him, from a nightmare. The relief had been in knowing he had woken. Now he wanted to be on his own again. Fallon saw it and went out. Groczek walked over to his desk and sat down.

He felt an immense desire to go and see Slovak. Slovak's face kept coming back into his mind and he knew that, sooner or later, they would have to meet again. He was intensely curious to see what the man's response would be and how he would have taken it all. Groczek felt, somehow, that he would be there now, at the house, possibly following up in his mind every stage of the robbery, seeing every detail happening as he had planned it. Soon they would bring him the stuff, though not to the house, and Groczek would have given anything to be present at that meeting.

183

He toyed, for a moment, with the idea of phoning the house and telling Slovak himself but he resisted the idea. He would let him wait, wait for the call he would be expecting that would tell him everything had gone according to plan, wait for the arranged meeting, the cans to be opened. He contented himself with the image of Slovak staring down into the cans of powdered chalk.

Groczek laughed, laughed out loud as the vision of Slovak's face struck him, the expression on it like that of a man with toothache who had unaccountably pulled out the wrong tooth. All that he had prophesied for Slovak was coming true. What he must now bend his mind to was proving Slovak's involvement with the robbery.

The intention that formed itself inside him at that moment was of such iron resolve that he reached out at once to call Fallon to his office to discuss a detailed plan of action, but as he did so, the phone rang under his hand. He picked the receiver up. 'Yes?' he said, impatiently.

'Chief Groczek?'

'Yes. Who's that?'

'Dr. Erdman, chief chemist at the labs in Boston.'

'Has the stuff arrived?'

'Yes, that's why I'm phoning. It's all here on my desk. I've got it in front of me. Your heavy squad just brought it in from the chopper.'

'Good,' Groczek said, with grim humour, 'I'm glad it didn't end up in Cuba, anyway. Thanks for phoning.'

'Not at all. I take it the real stuff's on the train?'

Groczek, about to replace the receiver, paused – and his heart missed a beat. Slowly, he put the receiver back to his ear. 'I'm sorry,' he said, 'I didn't exactly hear what you said?'

'I said,' Erdman repeated, 'that I take it the real stuff's on the train? This stuff's chalk. It looks like heroin, as everyone knows, but it's chalk. We must have got hold of the wrong end of the stick down here.'

Everything about Groczek had gone very still except his heart which had begun to pump wildly, producing a throbbing like a drum in his head. 'It can't be,' he said, hoarsely, 'it *can't* be!'

'Well, it is,' Erdman repeated, irritably, 'do you think I don't know the difference? It's here on the desk. I'm tasting it, smelling it. I tell you it's chalk. Have we made a mistake or have you? Hello? Hello? Are you still there?'

'Yes,' whispered Groczek after a pause. His mouth had gone completely dry and he kept swallowing in an effort to raise more voice but none would come.

'Well, what do you want us to do, wait for the stuff on the train? Two of your men are here, Wexler and Spivack, do you want to speak to them?'

Groczek shook his head slowly as if Erdman were in the room with him and replaced the receiver, hearing Erdman's voice calling, 'Hello? Hello?' as he did so. No, he didn't need to speak to Wexler or Spivack. He didn't need to speak to anyone. He sat there, ashen grey, back once more in his old nightmare. He saw what had happened. In one blinding flash of insight, he saw how it had been done. It was like some monstrous conjuring trick, but he saw through it. His head nodded up and down like a puppet. 'Of course,' he whispered hoarsely, 'of course,' and he went on nodding to himself.

Chapter Eleven

The phone rang and rang on Groczek's desk but he didn't answer it. A paralysis of the will had overtaken him. It was as if his muscles refused to obey the commands of his brain or perhaps no commands were being sent out at all. He sat at his desk motionless, staring sightlessly down at the blank pad in front of him. One phrase of Rosetti's from the file went round and round in his head – 'This man is no ordinary criminal'. He had read it and dismissed it, dismissed it with contempt as the proffered excuse of a police team that had simply failed to do its job. What excuses could he now offer?

In a way, he had less excuse to offer than they. They, after all, had simply come up with a theory, a theory that there was a mind at work behind some of the most spectacular robberies of the last decade or more. They had investigated it. They had found strong evidence to substantiate the theory but admitted they lacked proof. On that basis they had simply sought to warn any of their colleagues who might cross Slovak's path to take extra care, to watch him most closely, and be surprised at nothing. They, themselves, had at one point been taken by surprise but that, at least, was understandable. At each stage of their investigation, until the last, they might have been investigating nothing more than a figment of their own imagination.

Groczek, on the other hand, had had the benefit of their advice. He had spurned it arrogantly. It was not even as if the man had slipped into the city, moving quietly about unknown and unnoticed. He had flung himself into Groczek's path – literally. Groczek had recognised him. His long police training had instantly spotted the face and his brain had instantly flicked through the cards indexed there and come out with one marked 'File'. He had procured the file, studied it, had Slovak constantly watched. He knew – every cop's instinct had shrieked at him – that Slovak was not here for a rest or on a social visit, that he had come to pull a job. He had even hit on the nature of that job in one blinding flash of inspiration, taken all precautions to defend the property in his possession and which, he had realised, was the sole and naked object of Slovak's visit – and still he had lost it. He had lost it – and he knew how.

More words in Rosetti's file flew back into his mind as he sat there. *'We watched him plan the train robbery outside of Detroit.'* and again, 'We had witnessed what seemed to us an extraordinary conjuring trick. Before our very eyes and under our very noses he had accomplished what he had wanted to accomplish while seeming to accomplish something else or, if you like, nothing at all.' There, they had told him! Nothing could have been made plainer. They had, in their way, rehearsed it all for him, yet he had learnt nothing. In his arrogance and his impatience he had simply repeated their mistakes.

His vanity had been huge, he recognised that now. It had swallowed up everything, caution and commonsense alike, until the very last, and then, as vanity will, bereft suddenly of its insubstantial support, collapsed into empty panic. He was left in the position of a man who had bullied and been whipped. He was like a cock who had crowed and strutted his little hour in the yard and then had its neck ignominiously wrung.

A shudder went through him, the maximum of his movement in that immeasurable time he sat in the quiet of his office after that call from Erdman. He groaned, not inwardly. The sound was expelled upwards and outwards from his body, offered to the world as one might send out a bird in hope of finding land. The truth was he was drowning and he knew it. Everywhere he looked was water. His feet would touch nothing solid, not again in this life.

The door opened and Fallon appeared. 'I thought you'd gone out,' he said, and his voice was shaking, 'you didn't answer the phone. Have you heard? Wexler's been trying to get hold of you from Boston. The stuff they took off the chopper was chalk. I don't understand it? What happened?'

It took all of Groczek's will to lift his head and look at him, and when he finally did, Fallon saw a face that had aged beyond imagining. 'Did you hear me?' he asked, and Groczek nodded. 'Well, what happened? The stuff never arrived. What the hell's going on? Where is it? Who's got it?'

'Slovak's got it.'

'Slovak?' Fallon stared at him. 'What do you mean "Slovak"?'

'*Slovak's got it*,' Groczek said, whirling round on him again in a fury, but the voice was no more than a violent whisper, 'he's got it, don't you understand?'

Fallon stared at him. Nothing made sense. The junk had been put on the chopper. Who had interfered with it? 'Was there a mix up – in the security van, I mean? Did you put the real stuff on the train after all?' Groczek's look might have withered him then and there in other circumstances, but it meant nothing to him now. 'Well, did you?' he shouted at him. 'Tell me, for Christ's sake!'

'No, I did not,' Groczek said, icily, 'the chalk went on that train, you can rely on that.'

He got up from his desk and moved away from him. He stood with his back towards him and stared out of the window. How could he tell him? Every word he said, however carefully chosen, would be greeted with a look of utter incredulity. He couldn't face what he had suddenly become, a cop who had, in broad daylight and before the whole world been made a monkey of. He would have to admit it soon. He would have to make a full report. But he wasn't ready yet. He had to have time, time to compose himself, time to think what he would have to do.

Seeing that he would get nothing from Groczek by way of explanation, as yet, Fallon said grimly and trying to control the rising tide of fury that was sweeping over him, 'Well, let's go, then! If he's got the stuff, let's go and get him.'

Groczek shook his head. 'I can't prove he's got it. Not yet.'

'Is there anything you suggest that we *can* do?' Fallon asked, coldly. 'Shouldn't we at least tell the world that the

188

police force of this city has been robbed of ten million bucks' worth of heroin?'

'I need time to think,' Groczek answered.

'Well, wouldn't it be better if the news came from us than that it just leaked out, as it's going to, and looked as if we were just trying to cover up?'

'It'll take time to leak. That may be precious time.' For what he wasn't sure, but every voice inside him urged him to stall. Or was he simply refusing to face the facts?

'We'll have to notify narcotics,' Fallon said, 'we've got at least to do that.' Groczek nodded. 'Do you want me to do it? Shall I call them?'

'I'll do it,' Groczek said, 'that's my job. But don't talk to the press. Not yet.' Fallon shrugged and turned to go. 'Is anyone watching the house?'

'No. Mednik was, but I pulled him off it when we got back to the office. There seemed no point in leaving him there – knowing everything had gone so smoothly,' he added with a touch of sarcasm. 'But I'll send him back up.'

'I'll see to it,' Groczek replied. He turned to him. 'Perhaps you'd better go and look over the containers, talk to the local police, see what they've found out.' He looked at his watch. 'By the time you get there it'll be coming on dark. You may as well stay overnight.'

Fallon nodded. 'Well at least that's something,' he said, sourly, 'and I still think you ought to talk to the press. However, it's your baby,' and he turned and went out.

Yes, it was his baby, unwanted though it was, but he wouldn't announce its birth, not yet. He needed time. Fallon couldn't understand that and he couldn't tell him, but the idea of what he had to do was already forming itself in his mind. The time he needed was to bring himself to the point of being able to do it.

He called narcotics and spoke to Lamont, the head of the bureau. There was no way he could delay that. It would

189

have been a dereliction of duty to have put it off, but it took an enormous effort of will to pick up the phone.

Lamont listened. Groczek made it simple. When he ran over in his mind what precisely he would say to him, the story began to look so complicated and, finally, to take on so ludicrous an air, that he decided to report just the facts and leave it until later to go into detail.

'Are you saying,' Lamont asked, and he heard him laugh uncertainly at the other end of the phone, 'are you saying you've been robbed?'

Groczek licked his dry lips and swallowed hard. 'That's about the size of it,' he said.

'The junk you lifted from that mob – I mean, the stuff we knew about?'

'That's right.'

'What – the lot? I mean – all 200 pounds of it?'

'The lot.'

'They got it back? From the police?'

'No, it wasn't them. Not the same people. It was someone else.'

'Someone *else*?'

Groczek didn't reply. He didn't want to go into detail. He heard Lamont saying something to someone else in the room and heard, faintly, someone say, 'Jesus! He must be kidding!' Then Lamont returned to the phone. 'Listen – you wouldn't be putting us on, would you? I mean, a joke's a joke, but . . .'

'It's *gone*,' Groczek snarled, 'I'm just reporting it.'

There was a short pause, then Lamont said, 'I see. I'll get someone down there tomorrow. Just let me get this straight, though. You were shipping the stuff to Boston – yes, we knew about that, we okayed it. The train was hit and . . .'

'Look, I'll explain it all when your man gets here.'

'Do the press know?'

'Not yet.'

'Is there any chance of recovering the stuff before they do?'

190

Groczek took a deep breath. 'Maybe. I don't know.'

'Jesus Christ, the pushers'll be dancing in the streets when they hear. Any leads?'

'One or two.'

'All right. We'll dig out every agency likely to handle the stuff and put them under surveillance. I guess we can rule out the small fry. Jesus Christ,' he said again, '200 pounds of junk! I don't believe it. I mean, you'd already got it, that's right, isn't it? It *is* the same stuff, I didn't get that wrong, did I?'

'No,' Groczek said, grittily, 'it's the same consignment, the one you knew about.'

'It's the same stuff,' he heard Lamont repeating across his hand covering the mouthpiece, 'I told you, I didn't get it wrong,' and then, as the mouthpiece was uncovered, 'By the way, who had charge of the operation? Have you put him on suspension?'

'It was me,' Groczek said coldly and hung up.

Everything had gone as Slovak knew it would. The phone call he had just received confirmed it. No detail had been overlooked. He had brought off what he had come here to do, almost, anyway. He wasn't finished yet. The last stage had yet to be completed but he had no doubts that it would be. That stage was perhaps the most important of all, but it was all there, in his head, and it would be realised shortly with the ruthless thoroughness that he had realised everything else.

He felt immensely tired. The strain had been enormous, greater than he had ever known it before, physically and mentally. He felt that the achievement had, in fact, and certainly in part, destroyed him, that his mind, having encompassed the idea in the first place and then brought it all to fruition, would never again be the same. It seemed to him that in the process the strain had been so great that his brain had suffered a permanent damage.

191

Of course, he knew that was foolish. One might, with too great an exertion, damage muscles or destroy tendons, but the mind did not tear as a result of great effort. Only it *seemed* to and he recognised this as a warning, a warning that he was nearing the end of his career. He couldn't go on forever. He was not young anymore and working alone had become too much of a strain. Besides, there was nothing left for him to accomplish. He had done it all.

He wondered to himself what precisely Groczek would now do and found it difficult to predict his next step. It was not simply the loss of the drugs that would break him. It was the humiliation. When the news broke, as it soon must, Groczek would stand before the world like a man who had lost not only his wallet in a crowd but his trousers as well. The laughter that would sweep the country would simply blow him away.

Oddly, for he could see no connection between the thoughts, he found his mind turning to Maggie. He felt a great desire to talk to her and a sudden panic at the thought that she might not be there when he phoned. He wanted to hear her voice. He wanted her to hear his. He was frightened, suddenly, that she was not thinking of him, and his continued existence, he knew, depended on her thinking of him. If she ever gave up that thought, he had a feeling it would be the end of him.

He grabbed the phone and began dialling the number. He felt his heart beating wildly as he heard the phone ringing and ringing at the other end. Was she there? And if she was, was she alone? He felt something drop inside his stomach as the phone was picked up at the other end and heard her voice saying, 'Hello?'

He didn't answer at once. He had a wild urge to hang up, *not* to speak to her. Having heard her voice it seemed enough for him, that if he spoke to her now she would know the reason for his call. He heard her repeating, 'Hello? Hello?' and then, 'Who is it?' and there was a long pause. And then she said, 'Is that you, Frank?'

'Yes,' he said, 'it's me.'

'Do you know what time it is? It's after midnight.'

'Is that late for you now, Maggie?' he asked.

'I was in bed.'

'Alone?'

There was a long pause, and he wished he hadn't said it. Then he heard her say, 'What do you want, Frank?'

'I don't know,' he answered, 'I don't know why I called. Just to hear you maybe.' There was no answer. Then he said, 'How have you been? You never called me?'

'No.' A pause, and then she said, 'I'm all right, Frank. Are you all right? Is everything in the house all right?'

'Yes, everything's fine.' He waited for her to say something but there was another silence at the other end. Then he said, 'You wouldn't come over here, Maggie, would you?' and the effort it cost him to say it sent a pain shooting across the front of his brow.

'Now? Frank, I'm in bed. And even if I weren't – I told you, it's better if we don't meet.'

'It would be nice if you came over, Maggie. I'd like to see you.'

'Is anything wrong?' She sounded suddenly anxious.

'No, nothing's wrong. Everything's fine, as a matter of fact. It couldn't be better. It's just that – it's so lonely here.' He stopped. He was going to say, 'without you' but the words wouldn't came. Instead, he said with a little laugh, 'Have I rated a thought with you now and then?'

There was a slight pause, then she said, 'I'm going to hang up now, Frank.'

'No, don't hang up, Maggie,' he said, and then, with another small laugh, added, 'it took quite a lot to call you.' There was no reply and he added, 'Maybe I could come over there?'

'No.' Her voice was sharp and final. There was a short pause and she said, 'Look, why don't you call me in the morning?'

'The morning?' He heard his voice sound distant and vague. He repeated the word as if it had small meaning for him. 'I don't want to see you in the morning, Maggie, I want to see you now.' A note of urgency had crept into his voice which he had been trying to keep out.

'It's not possible,' she said. 'Look, I'm going to hang up. If you want to call me in the morning you can but please understand, Frank, the situation's not the same anymore. You *must* try to understand. I'm getting married. We can't go back to where we were. Nothing you can say will . . .'

He hung up, cutting her voice off dead. He didn't want to hear all that. He shouldn't have phoned. He'd done it in a moment of weakness and he wished now that he hadn't. And maybe, too, it was the wrong time. He hadn't realised quite how late it was. His mind had been so preoccupied all day with the progress of the operation that the time had simply slipped by. Well, there was another day tomorrow. He was tired, immensely tired, but he was at peace with himself. Everything was working out well, except for Maggie, but that would come.

He went out of the living room, switching off the one table lamp he had had on, crossed the hall and went upstairs to the bedroom. He undressed, got into bed and switched off the light.

He dozed fitfully for a while, half awake and half asleep, and found himself in a dream state, back inside his classroom. He was standing up in his desk. Everyone was looking at him. His teacher stood before him, a ruler touching him under the chin, and he was conscious that he had been asked the one question that he knew he did not know the answer to and that his life, his very existence, depended on his knowing it. He

194

could feel the deep despair inside him that came with that knowledge that there was no way he would ever find the answer to that in the time. And all the while, his teacher prodded him with the ruler under his chin and said, 'Well, Slovak, well?'

The lamp at the bedside table was suddenly switched on, bringing him awake, and he stared into the muzzle of a revolver and heard Groczek saying quietly, 'You didn't really think I'd let you get away with it, did you?' Slovak stared at him. Groczek was bending over him, smiling, the gun touching Slovak's chin. 'Get up,' he said.

'What's this?' Slovak asked.

'I want the junk,' Groczek said, quietly, 'where is it?'

Slovak stared at him for a long time, and then slowly he shook his head. 'No,' he said.

'Get up. Get dressed.'

Slovak didn't move. The black barrel of the revolver chucked him under the chin again, impatiently. Slovak pushed aside the cover of the bed and got out. Groczek moved away from him, his face cold and expressionless. Slovak put on his trousers and his shirt. 'Where are we going?' he asked.

'Just get dressed.'

Slovak laughed. 'Isn't this a little melodramatic?'

Groczek said nothing, but his eyes never left Slovak's face. When Slovak had finished dressing he said to him, 'Turn round.' Slovak turned round. He heard a slight clink of metal behind him and then felt his hands pulled behind him and handcuffs snapped onto his wrists and locked. He turned round as Groczek stepped back. 'Walk down the stairs,' Groczek said, waving the gun towards the door.

Slovak turned and walked slowly out of the room. Groczek switched off the bedside light and followed him out. He walked down the stairs after Slovak, and as Slovak came to the bottom, turned him roughly in the direction of the front door and

195

pushed him forward. Slovak halted in front of it and Groczek opened it.

Slovak looked at him. 'You don't need to go to all this trouble just for an arrest,' he said, amused.

'Walk outside,' Groczek replied.

Slovak shrugged. He stepped outside. A wind had sprung up and he could hear the barn door swinging on its hinge. Groczek snapped off the light in the hall and closed the front door. He pushed Slovak in the direction of the barn. Slovak walked towards it with Groczek just behind him. Slovak stopped in front of the barn door and Groczek opened it and pushed him inside. Slovak stared round but it was dark inside and he could see little. He turned to look for Groczek and as he did so he felt a rope slipped quickly over his neck and pulled tight. At the same time, the light in the barn, a single, naked bulb, hanging from the centre, was snapped suddenly on.

Slovak looked at the rope around his neck and followed it up to the beam over which it had been looped and then looked at Groczek who stood some feet in front of him, watching him. He saw Slovak's puzzled look and nodded. 'I'm going to hang you,' he said.

There was a deathly silence. Slovak was not sure whether to laugh or not. He stared at Groczek. There was something chilling about the man's total lack of agitation.

Groczek nodded again. 'I'm going to hang you – unless I get that junk back.'

For a moment, Slovak said nothing. Then he shook his head slowly and said, 'You wouldn't hang me.'

'Why not?'

'It's not your style – you know that. What's between you and me can't be settled by a murder.'

'And just what do you think is between you and me?' Groczek enquired, with a soft politeness.

196

'Why,' Slovak laughed, 'who's best, Groczek, who's best? If you murder me,' he said, 'you'll never know. And you *have* to know. So you and I have to battle this out – but according to the rules, you know that.'

Groczek didn't answer at once but merely stared at him. Then he said, quietly, 'Where's the junk?'

Slovak laughed again. 'You've got to find it, that's the point! And then you've got to get *me* – prove I took it, because that's the point, too, isn't it? But according to the rules, Groczek, the rules. The rules are everything.' He shook his head. 'And they don't include murdering your opponent.'

'I'm asking you for the last time – where is it?' Groczek said. Slovak stared at him, saying nothing and quite composed. Groczek said, 'Get up on that chair.'

Slovak looked at the chair standing next to him, then looked again at Groczek and shook his head. 'You're bluffing,' he said, 'you disappoint me. I don't kid that easily, you should know that.'

'I can drag you up.'

There was a short silence and then Slovak shook his head once again. 'You're not going to hang me. And I'm not going to tell you where the junk is. So why don't you just take this rope off and go home – and figure out the next move? It is your move, Groczek.'

For a brief moment Groczek stared at him, clearly weighing Slovak's resolve against his own. Then, with a sudden, vicious jerk, as if seized with an immense and maniacal access of strength, he pulled the rope down and down, lifting Slovak off his feet by the neck. Slovak made a harsh, gurgling sound, his feet kicking wildly in the air as he rose higher and higher.

Groczek held him there for a moment, watching his face turn purple, and then slowly let him down. 'Where is it?' he asked again, quietly.

As the rope slackened a little around his throat, Slovak

gasped for air, tried to suck it in and speak but he could find no voice. All he could do was to shake his head at Groczek. Again Groczek jerked the rope down viciously, pulling him up by the neck and left him dangling there for a moment. Then, once again, he let the rope slowly down until Slovak's feet touched the floor. 'Where is it?' Groczek repeated. 'I warn you, this is the last time.' Slovak stared at him, his head lolling to one side, his mouth open, his tongue protruding like a dog's in a drought, but still he shook his head and again Groczek jerked the rope up and this time wound it round the end of a peg on the wall to keep it taut. Slovak's feet kicked wildly against the air, and he heard Groczek's voice coming to him, breaking in over a noise like the rushing sea that filled his ears.

'You see, Slovak,' Groczek said, 'rules are for others. A really great man sometimes has to make his own. And I just made a new one, that no matter what—scum like you shouldn't profit from the fruits of their crime.'

Slovak felt a tremendous pressure building up inside his head as if shortly it would explode. He knew he was rapidly losing consciousness and he fought to hold it. He felt the handcuffs slipped off his wrists and his hands weakly clawed at the rope around his neck, but there was no strength left in his hands, try as he might, and they fell back again helplessly. Groczek's voice was coming to him in waves of alternate loudness and softness. Dimly, he heard him say with a laugh, 'It'll take about ten minutes. Sorry about that. I'd like to have broken your neck, but – one needs special machinery and they don't make it any more.'

He heard the chair kick over beneath his feet which were now still, though his body turned from side to side. He heard the door open and felt a gust of wind, but it was all happening a long way off and everything inside him seemed to be closing down. The singing in his ears lessened, as if that, too, was a noise going away from him and a feeling of peace began

slowly to seep into him. He was floating. He was bobbing
gently about. There was no pain and no agony anymore.
There was nothing at all.

Chapter Twelve

Groczek paced the main building of the airport waiting for the
plane to arrive. It was bringing Lamont's man. Lamont had
called him that morning and told him what time the plane
would be in. Would he meet his man at the airport? Groczek
had said he would. Were there any further developments? No,
Groczek had told him, none so far. He was waiting for Fallon
to return. Perhaps there would be some news then.

Groczek was in a state of considerable agitation. He had
returned home after his confrontation with Slovak, put the car
away and let himself quietly into the house. His wife was in
bed and asleep. He had let himself into the study, shut the
door and poured himself a stiff drink.

He was shaking. After Fallon had left the afternoon before,
he had left the office building and driven out of the city and
into the country beyond. He had stopped the car and simply
sat there, hour after hour, turning over and over in his mind
what he should do. And yet, he knew what he was going to
do, knew it before he left the office, knew it as he sat there
looking for other ways, looking for other solutions. The more
he searched in his mind for alternatives, the more he saw that
it was already made up. There was a time when the law was
irrelevant, when its net was simply not wide enough for the
catch to be made.

As he paced his study to which he returned later that night,
as he constantly passed and passed again the relics of his days
in Vietnam, he knew that his whole life had been, in a curious

199

way, a preparation for this moment and that though his anxious mind strove to find ways of evading that moment, of drawing back from it, he knew that he must go forward and meet it. Slovak would yield up to him the drugs or Slovak would die. Groczek's prevarication was no more than an idle way of passing the time until Slovak would, most likely, be asleep.

What he would have done had Slovak not been in the house he wasn't sure. Oddly, he had never doubted that he would find him there. He was certainly not a man to run. Slovak never ran. It was more than likely that Slovak would expect him to call, sometime, though not likely that he would expect him to call with such a grim purpose. Still, Slovak *was* there. He had found him asleep and left him dead in the barn.

Had he expected Slovak to yield up the drugs? Groczek didn't know. One could never be sure what a man might do faced with the alternative Groczek had offered, at least not a man like Slovak. The problem was not so much that Slovak might value the drugs too highly, as that he might put Groczek's determination too low. The man's mind was subtle, infinitely subtle, and the refinements of his thought might serve, in the end, to hang him, did, in fact, serve to hang him. He had imported into Groczek's mind a subtlety to match his own, but there Slovak had made a mistake. He had been too clever by half. He had refined Groczek's possible reactions out of existence. He had expected applause where Groczek had simply smashed up the scenery.

When he got home he had found himself shaking. The ice-cold calm that had taken possession of him when he had set out was gone by the time he returned. Inevitably he had begun to ask himself if he had done the right thing, if he hadn't, in disposing of Slovak, said goodbye to the drugs once and for all. He had to face that possibility. He *had* faced it earlier before he set out, but not seriously since the thought had been mixed with the possibility that Slovak might, after all, give up the drugs, but now that route was finally closed. Still, he did not regret it. In a way he knew it had become more important to him to dispose of Slovak than to recover the heroin. There had been from the first, in their confrontation, an absence of half measures that both had recognised.

Now, as he paced the airport building, waiting for Lamont's man to arrive, all that had been settled in his mind and gave him no cause for anxiety and yet he was in the grip of an agitation that stemmed from a source altogether different and unexpected, so unexpected that its effect on him had been shattering.

All that morning, while he sat in his office, toying idly with work he couldn't concentrate on, his mind had returned again and again to Slovak and to the barn. Partly it stemmed, he knew, from his sense of guilt. Had he left any evidence to implicate him in Slovak's murder? Would the hanging stand up to medical examination as a suicide? Was it important that it should? If it were, despite his setting of the scene, viewed as murder, would it not automatically be assumed that it had been committed by some of Slovak's criminal associates?

He was partly comforted by the thought that he would, himself, take charge of the investigation once the body had been discovered, as discovered it surely must be. Surely? By whom? And when? Who would go to the house? Tradesmen? It seemed unlikely. The girl – what was her name – Margaret Phillips? Possibly, but then again, she hadn't been seen to visit the house. Wasn't it likely that it might take weeks for the body to be found?

He found himself unable to face this prospect. He wanted to confront the discovery of Slovak dead *now*. He was impatient for it to be brought into the open. It unnerved him – to have it hanging over him all the while, unresolved, to contemplate it constantly as something that would turn up in the future to be dealt with. He felt unable to live with that knowledge alone. He wanted it shared by others so that he might

201

investigate it properly, go through the charade and act out his role. He wanted it there, in front of him, in front of Lamont's man when he arrived. And besides, wasn't the evidence against Slovak dead far more overwhelming than against Slovak alive? As a policeman of long experience, he knew that to be true, that while a man was seen to be to some extent involved in a crime, the presumption of his guilt was far stronger when he was no longer there to argue his case. It offered the police an easy opportunity to close the case, an opportunity an over-worked force was always looking for.

He had, therefore, sent Mednik up to the house, telling him to bring Slovak in for questioning. It was a perfect excuse, and in the circumstances would be expected of him, and he had felt an enormous sense of relief once he had done it, to have got that out of the way. If his relief at having made that decision was enormous, however, the shock of Mednik's return had been even greater. Slovak was not there.

Groczek had stared at him in utter disbelief. What did he mean, not there? Had he looked around the grounds? There was an old barn there – perhaps he was working in there? Mednik, however, assured him that Slovak was nowhere to be seen. He had looked in the barn. It was empty, just bits of old machinery. He had rung the bell at the house and when he received no reply had forced a window catch in the kitchen – not much, doing no damage – and entered the house. There was no one in it.

Once again, the thought crossed Groczek's mind that he may be going mad, that perhaps he was, after all, on the verge of a breakdown. He well knew the force with which illusory events could take hold of the mind and convince it that they were real. A teenage boy had recently killed a stranger in the clear conviction that the stranger was his father. The threshold was narrow. Was he walking along it and stepping, from time to time, first on one side and then on the other?

He must have looked odd to Mednik at that moment, for

Mednik had said to him, 'Perhaps he's just gone out, sir, or maybe away for a few days?' Groczek had waved him away, out of the office. He knew that he must have looked shaken, shaken out of all proportion to the news Mednik had brought him.

What could have happened? Could Slovak have released himself from the stranglehold of that rope? It seemed incredible and the moment that he asked the question he dismissed it as absurd. No one could have done that. There were only two possibilities. Either some of Slovak's friends had arrived on the scene, found him, and taken the body away, or Mednik had called at the house but had *not* looked in the barn, had merely told Groczek that he had because he had become convinced, from the outside, that there was no one in there and wouldn't admit that he hadn't searched the grounds thoroughly.

The more he thought of this possibility, the more he became convinced of it. But he had to see for himself. He knew that he would have no peace of mind until he did. He had, therefore, taken his car and driven out to the house. It looked, as Mednik had reported, deserted and unoccupied. He had walked straight round to the barn and, hesitating a moment outside the door, suddenly jerked it open.

It was empty. The chair he had overturned was back against the wall where he had left it. The rope was no longer over the beam but had been coiled up and thrown in a corner.

Again, he wondered if he had dreamed the whole event, but he knew, *knew* that he had not. He had turned, then, and looked at the house. It had a silent air, an air that criminals sensed when studying a house for a break-in. He had walked up to it and tried the handle of the front door. It was locked. He had gone round to the kitchen window that Mednik had forced, opened it and stepped inside.

The house, as Mednik reported, was empty. He had gone from room to room but found no one. He had left by the front door and it was only when he was on his way back to the car, when he had paused and looked back at the house, that he thought he had glimpsed someone drawing back from an upstairs window, someone who had been observing him. The impression, however, had been so fleeting that it failed to convince him and he got into his car and drove back to the office.

By the time he had returned to the office his mind was in a turmoil of doubt and uncertainty and remained so as he drove out to the airport and waited impatiently for the plane to arrive. The arrival of Lamont's man seemed now of small importance to him, compared with the mystery of the disappearance of Slovak's body. He could not make it out. Neither could he work out how it might affect him. He had, however, no more time to dwell on this aspect of the matter, for the plane had arrived and its passengers were disembarking.

He stopped pacing and turned to face the direction from which the disembarking passengers would come. He did not know the man Lamont was sending out, though he had no doubt they would single each other out. His name, apparently, was Webster and he was, according to Lamont, an experienced man. He stood watching the passengers as they approached him, bunched together in groups, searching their faces for a man he was likely to recognise as one of his own, but he saw no one. One group after another passed him and went on out to the car parks and he was beginning to wonder if Webster had not, perhaps, missed the plane when he saw, some way beyond the last group, a man limping towards him. He walked steadily, but slowly, as if each step cost him an effort to shift his weight from one foot to another. He wore a faded, brown raincoat and a green fedora hat. In his hand he carried an overnight bag. And as Groczek watched him, limping steadily but inexorably towards him down the long hall, he was reminded, oddly, of how a man's doom might approach him in the daytime.

204

The man reached him, finally, and held out his hand with a wan, deprecating smile, as if to apologise for the time he had taken in covering the distance. 'Webster,' he said, 'FBI Narcotics.' He turned to a much younger man who had come hurrying up behind, a bright, cherubic looking man, and said, 'Bradley – he works with me.'

Groczek shook hands with each in turn. He was slightly disappointed at the general appearance of them. They were not like anything he had had in mind. He had expected something brisker, more efficient-looking, but it was unimportant. Webster was scarcely likely to succeed where he, Groczek, had failed. He would spend a couple of days here, make his report and leave.

Groczek led the way out to the car but found, to his irritation, that he had to stop and allow Webster to catch up with him and that, having caught up, Groczek had no alternative but to proceed at Webster's pace. The man's rhythm irritated him from the start and he found this was not solely due to the pace he was compelled to walk at, but had something to do with the way he thought. They were not compatible, but there was little Groczek could do about that.

They sat in the car, Bradley in front, Groczek and Webster behind in the back seat. They drove in silence for a while, Groczek turning over in his mind exactly how to tell the story to Webster while Webster looked, with his bright little eyes, at the clean, white city they were passing through.

'Never been to this city before,' Webster said, 'have you, Brad?'

'No, sir,' said Bradley, nodding with approval at the passing scene, 'but I've heard a lot about it. Sort of lives up to your expectations, too, doesn't it?'

'It does, Brad, it certainly does.' Webster looked at Groczek. 'It looks a very fine city, sir.' Groczek nodded, but didn't reply. There was another pause. Webster settled back in his seat and said, 'Well, I guess we may as well begin. All I know so far is

205

that the drugs were put on a train to Boston, the train was hit . . .'

'The drugs were stolen in court during the trial,' Groczek said, interrupting him, 'the train was irrelevant.'

'Pardon me?' Webster said, sitting up and looking puzzled.

'The drugs were stolen in court,' Groczek repeated. 'They were never put on the train.'

Bradley turned and looked at Groczek and then at Webster, who tilted his head to one side, as if to face square on a piece of information that was coming to him at an unexpectedly acute angle. 'The drugs were lifted in court,' he repeated, 'and not on the train?' Groczek nodded. 'Now, that's not what Lamont said. Lamont said . . .'

'Lamont didn't have the whole story. It was too complicated to explain on the phone.'

'I see,' Webster said with a touch of disapproval. 'I wish, sir, you had told Lamont the proper story, then I could have been thinking properly on the way down here. Now I have to get this notion of the train out of my head. That's awkward – the mind being what it is. However, that can't be helped. Let me get this clear, then. The junk was lifted in court during the trial?'

'Yes,' Groczek said.

'You've got that, Bradley?' Webster asked.

'I've got it, sir,' Bradley said, though he sounded as if he didn't much approve of it, 'it's a remarkable statement. I've never heard of that happening before.'

'Nor have I,' Webster said. He looked at Groczek. 'Well, sir, perhaps you'd better fill us in from the beginning. You go ahead. We'll just listen.'

Groczek took a deep breath. It was hard to know exactly where to start. However, start he must. 'Well,' he said, 'it begins with a man called Slovak, Frank Slovak, have you ever heard of him?'

'Slovak,' Webster mused, and shook his head. 'No, I've never heard of a man called Slovak.'

'He's a criminal, very big time.'

'He's got a record?'

'No, he's never been caught.'

'How do you know then? That he's a criminal, I mean?'

'Rosetti has a file on him in New York.'

'Rosetti.' Webster looked inquisitively at Bradley for a moment, and then nodded. 'Doesn't he run some sort of academic outfit?'

Groczek nodded. 'He's been putting together dossiers on several people. Slovak was one of them. He's what they call "an engineer". He masterminds very large-scale crimes.'

'I see,' Webster said, 'but, presumably, they have no evidence, otherwise he wouldn't still be floating around?'

'That's true,' Groczek replied. 'Anyway, he obviously heard about the haul of heroin we made and came here to get it.'

'Obviously?' Webster asked.

'Why else would he suddenly appear here?'

'I don't know,' Webster answered, 'but I guess he could have come for a dozen different reasons. I mean, do you have any evidence he came here especially for the drugs?'

'Not exactly evidence,' Groczek said, irritably, 'maybe not evidence that would stand up in court, but – there's no doubt in my mind, and there wouldn't have been any in yours either, if you'd been here.'

Webster laughed. 'Well, that's often the advantage of coming fresh to a scene, you know. Still, go on, sir.'

Another wave of irritation passed through Groczek. He was beginning positively to dislike the man. There was, in his tone, a patronising air and his questions were obviously born of a desire to impress. Why didn't he just shut up and listen? Did he imagine Groczek was some junior officer to be questioned and cross-questioned in this manner? However, Groczek had to

207

get through this part of the story, if Webster were going to begin his investigation. So he took another deep breath and ploughed on.

He went over the sequence of events from the beginning, leaving out only the strange meeting in the study and, of course, his visit to Slovak the previous evening. That he could not tell and the meeting would have made no sense to Webster, anyway. The events, when he reported them, seemed somewhat lame and lacking in substance but Webster only nodded thoughtfully as he listened and seemed rather impressed by the incidents in the repair sheds. 'That's an alert cop,' he said of Levin. 'Let me get this clear though,' he went on, 'what you're saying is that when Slovak appeared in court, you suddenly realised what it was he had come for?' Groczek nodded. 'And when you saw the heroin being wheeled out of the court, you realised that he was there to lift it?'

Groczek nodded again. 'I knew it as surely as I'd ever known anything in my life and as it turned out, I wasn't wrong.'

'And so convinced were you,' Webster went on, 'when you were battering on that door in the court building, that those drugs *wouldn't* be there, that when you finally got into that room and saw them on the trolley, you were so relieved that it never occurred to you that they'd already been switched?'

'It was the relief, I guess,' Groczek nodded, 'at seeing them there.'

'Your mind, in fact, had been tuned to the wrong station?'

Groczek nodded. It wasn't a bad description of it. A better description would have been that Slovak had deliberately tuned Groczek's mind to the wrong station.

'Clever,' Webster said, his eyes bright with admiration as he looked at Bradley. 'I must say, I might have behaved in the same way – given the circumstances.'

Groczek glanced at him gratefully. Well, the man was trying to make amends for his former manner. There was a touch

208

of sympathy in Websters' tone for the first time. 'He's made me look a fool,' Groczek said.

'Who, Slovak?' Groczek nodded. 'We can't be certain it's him,' Webster said.

Groczek turned and looked at him. Was the man a complete fool? Had he told him all this just so that Webster could waste time looking in other directions for the guilty party? '*I'm* sure,' he said, coldly.

'Because the drugs disappeared while he was here?' Webster asked. Groczek stared at him with undisguised hostility which Webster did not fail to note, for he smiled brightly and said, 'We must keep an open mind, mustn't we? We must avoid staying tuned to only one station.' The car was drawing up to the headquarters building now. Webster said, 'By the way, can you fix me up with an office while I'm here? I don't like crowding other people.'

'There's an empty one down the corridor from me,' Groczek replied, shortly, and got out of the car.

They followed him into the building and up to his office. Groczek walked past it to the end of the corridor, opened a door and went inside. The office had a desk, filing cabinets, shelves and the usual paraphernalia of a city detective's office. Webster nodded, satisfied. He went to the desk and sat down in the chair. He felt at home at once. He turned to Groczek and smiled. 'This is fine,' he said. 'Well, let's pick up where we left off. What you had in the safe were cans of powdered chalk, but you didn't know that?'

Groczek stared at him. He felt a wave of irritation pass over him, as if their rightful positions had, by some subtle process, been reversed and that he was now being questioned by an officer of superior rank, which Webster was not. However, he swallowed his irritation and nodded. 'We had to ship the stuff to Boston. Whichever way we chose, I knew, in my bones, it would leak out.'

Webster clucked sympathetically and shook his head. 'Those

leaks,' he said, 'no matter what you do, you can never plug all the goddam holes. We have the same problem. Go on, sir.'

'Well, I had a problem, and I knew there was only one way of solving it.'

'To act on your own?'

'Yes. To achieve top security, I had to do it all myself.'

'I can understand that,' Webster said, looking across at Bradley to see if he, too, could understand that. Bradley nodded and Webster looked once more at Groczek.

'I decided I wouldn't send the real stuff by train,' Groczek continued, 'but let everyone think I was. I made up my mind to send it by helicopter.'

'Of course,' Webster said, 'you didn't have the real stuff, anyway.'

'Of course,' Groczek said coldly, 'but I didn't know that, did I?' Webster nodded to confirm that that was in fact so. Groczek went on, 'So I made arrangements with Mostyn's to use their helicopter.'

'That was cute,' Webster said, 'not using a police helicopter. Go on, sir. It really is a fascinating story and I'm beginning to see why you were so jumpy.'

Groczek opened his mouth to continue when there was a knock on the door and Fallon came in. He was carrying four cans of water chestnuts. He nodded to Webster and looked at Groczek. 'I just got back,' he said. 'I brought these with me. They were dropped during the getaway and left in the train.' He put them on the desk.

'This is Fallon, my deputy,' Groczek said. 'This is Webster, FBI Narcotics.'

Webster offered his hand and Fallon shook it. Webster indicated Bradley. 'My assistant, Bradley.' The two men nodded at each other. 'Please go on, sir,' Webster said, 'you made arrangements with Mostyn's to use their helicopter?'

'I went back to the Oriental Spice Company. I borrowed

the same number of cases of those,' Groczek continued nodding at the cans in front of Webster, 'opened them exactly as the others had been opened, and filled them with chalk. I put the chalk on the train and . . .' He broke off as he saw where he was going.

'. . . and the chalk on the helicopter.' Webster finished it for him. He picked up two cans, one in each hand, and looked from one to the other. 'All you'd done was switched chalk for chalk.' He raised first one can and then the other. 'The heroin had already been taken.'

Groczek nodded heavily. It hurt like hell to have to tell it, but at least Webster was beginning to see now, how it had all come about. Webster was looking at the cans in his hand and shaking his head with admiration. 'It was clever,' he said, 'that took some brains.'

'They've been checked for finger prints,' Fallon said. 'There's one set on them but we can't match them.'

'Oh, well,' Webster replied, smiling, 'that's easy, Watson.' He looked at Groczek. 'I guess they must be yours.'

Groczek stared at him. Bradley smiled. How quick and simple Webster's mind was. Groczek nodded. 'Yes,' he said, 'they'd be mine.' He turned to Fallon. 'Did the local police come up with anything?' he asked.

Fallon shook his head. 'Nothing so far,' he said. He looked generally round at everyone. 'Do you need me any more?' he asked. Webster shook his head. Fallon nodded and went out.

'How far do you trust him?' Webster asked, as the door closed.

'Fallon?' Groczek asked. 'All the way.'

Webster nodded. He got up, put the cans in the filing cabinet, locked it and turned back to Groczek. 'I've got to admit, sir,' he said, 'you may well be right about this guy, Slovak. But, of course, you've been involved all along and it takes a little while for an outsider to adjust to the idea. It

211

seemed a little weak, at first, but it gets stronger. Maybe we ought to go up and see him? I'd like to look at him, size him up a little.'

'He's not there,' Groczek said.

'Oh?' Webster replied, enquiringly, 'Are you sure of that?'

Groczek nodded. 'I sent one of my men up there this morning?'

'What for?'

'I wanted Slovak brought in for questioning. But the house was empty. There was no one there.'

'Do you think it might be a good idea if we just went up there and – looked around? Of course, we don't have a warrant to enter the house but – if there's no one there . . .?' He smiled. 'Bradley can fix that, I'm sure.'

There was a pause. Groczek felt reluctant to go with Webster to the house. It was entirely irrational. There was no need to fear anything and yet, the disappearance of Slovak's body made him uneasy at the thought of going up there with anyone at all. Was he afraid that he might, by some unconscious action, give himself away? But the pause was going on too long, and he said, 'I think we should go and see that clerk at the court, the one who had charge of the room. He's involved in this, somewhere, he's got to be.'

Webster looked at his watch. 'The courts close at 4.30,' he said, 'it's gone that now. We can leave that till tomorrow. Let's go and look over the house.'

Groczek nodded. They left the office and went down to the street. They got back into the car and drove out of the city in the direction of Slovak's house. Webster said, 'You say you've never really met him?'

'Not really met him,' Groczek replied. 'Like I said, our cars collided when he first came here, but that's all.'

'Yes, you mentioned that. That really is a weird coincidence,' Webster said. 'I mean, it has a strangeness to it, don't you think, almost like the hand of fate? What do you

212

think about fate, Bradley?' he asked, almost playfully.

'I can take it or leave it, sir,' Bradley replied.

There was a silence in the car after that. They drove out of the city and onto the highway. Shortly, the house loomed up in front of them, the car veered off the road and came to a halt in the drive. Groczek, Webster and Bradley got out. They walked up to the front door and Groczek rang the bell. Webster nodded approvingly. It was right to make sure the house was still empty. No one answered, however, and Groczek rang again. They waited for a few moments more, then Webster nodded to Bradley. Bradley took out a ring with a great number of keys on it and fiddled about with the lock for a moment. They heard a click, Bradley pushed open the door and stepped back. Webster looked at Groczek and Groczek stepped inside the hall, followed by Webster and Bradley.

The daylight, though not gone, was fading and the hall was plunged in gloom. 'Let's have some light,' Webster said. Groczek looked round, found the light switch and snapped it on. He opened the door into the living room and went inside, followed by Webster and Bradley. Bradley snapped on a table lamp near the door and they all walked to the centre of the room and stood looking round for a moment. 'Nice room,' Webster said, appreciatively. Then he looked at Bradley. 'You start on the cupboard, Brad. I'll look through the desk.'

Webster took a step towards the desk, and paused, staring at Groczek whose eyes were fixed on the door behind Webster. Webster turned. A man was standing there, staring at Groczek. Webster looked at Groczek, as if expecting some sort of introduction, but when none came, he turned back to the man and said, 'Mr. Slovak?'

Slovak turned his gaze slowly to Webster and Webster felt the force of the man's personality as that gaze swept over him. Then Slovak nodded slowly. Webster said, 'This is Chief Groczek. I'm Webster, FBI Narcotics.'

'What do you want here?'

'We did ring the bell,' Webster smiled, 'you didn't answer.'

'I was resting,' Slovak said. 'What do you want?'

Webster studied him for a moment. Then he said, quietly. 'It won't work, you know? Robbing the public, that's one thing. Robbing the police . . .' He laughed. 'That's something else. That's – naughty.'

He laughed again, and waited for Slovak to reply, but Slovak had turned away as if Webster didn't interest him and his eyes were fixed on Groczek. He turned and looked at Groczek. Groczek seemed unable to take his gaze from Slovak's face. Webster turned back to Slovak. 'Do you know what I mean?' he asked.

Slovak turned and looked at him. 'What have you lost?'

'A whole lot of heroin.'

'Very careless.'

'Yes, wasn't it,' Webster replied, glancing at Groczek and smiling wanly. He turned back to Slovak. 'They've known about you for some time,' he said, 'the police, I mean. They can't prove anything yet, but they will, one day – you know that, don't you?'

'Is that what you came here to tell me?' Slovak asked, after a pause.

'I didn't come here to tell you anything,' Webster answered. 'To be frank, I came to have a look around, but . . .'

'You found me here and you didn't have a warrant,' Slovak answered slowly.

Webster shook his head ruefully. 'Life's just full of one damn thing after the other,' he said. 'We thought you were out.' He looked at Groczek accusingly and then returned to Slovak. 'Still, since you're here, and you've caught us unprepared, so to speak, let me say this before we go. Frankly, I don't know if you're behind this robbery or not . . .'

Groczek snorted contemptuously. Webster turned and gave him a hard look. He wasn't used to having his statements questioned in front of others. He turned back to Slovak.

214

'But,' he said, 'I'm pretty sure you could get a message to those who are.

Slovak looked at him coldly. 'Try Western Union,' he said.

Webster laughed. He turned and walked around the room, picking up ornaments, examining them and returning them to their place once again, as if to give the interview time to breathe, to take some of the tension out of it. He picked up a small, white marble bust and stared down at it. A quietness had descended on the room. He let it settle. He wanted Slovak to understand the importance of what he was about to say. 'We can't allow it, you know,' he said, finally, 'we won't allow it. There are some crimes we'll solve if we have to put every man in the force onto it, you know that. What has been done is – impertinent, to say the very least. We won't accept it, and we'll go to whatever lengths we need to get the stuff back.'

He paused for a moment to let the words sink in. He continued to stare down at the bust, letting no movement of his detract from the solemnity of what he was saying. Then, he went on quietly, 'Now, if we got back say, threequarters of the junk, and a tip off on, say a few of the guys who did the job on the train, we'd settle for that, eh, Chief?'

He looked up into the mirror above him. Groczek and Slovak stood frozen in the glass, like two statues set down opposite each other. Groczek's face was expressionless but there was a slight smile on Slovak's and Webster had the distinct impression that something was passing between them but he couldn't read what it was. He turned from the mirror and looked at Groczek. 'Well, Chief?' he said again.

The question seemed finally to have penetrated into Groczek's consciousness for he turned to Webster and said, 'I don't make deals with hoods,' and turned and went out of the room and out of the house. There was a pause. Webster bit his lip in annoyance. He looked at Slovak and said, 'Well, I do.' He waited a moment for Slovak to reply but when none came he turned and went out, followed by Bradley.

215

Slovak remained quite still after they'd gone, listening to the car doors slam, the engine start and the crunch of wheels on the drive as the car drove away. He had been expecting them. It was inevitable they would come to look over the house. Groczek would have explained in detail to Webster Slovak's involvement in the theft of the heroin and Webster would have wanted to come and see for himself. Of course, he hadn't expected to find Slovak there. Neither had Groczek – especially Groczek. Groczek would have reported that Slovak had left the house, disappeared, though he would not have reported that he had verified this himself. He would not have reported that he had come to the house because he could not believe, *would* not believe that Slovak's body was not in the barn. He could tell no one that. Slovak had watched his frantic arrival and even more frantic search and seen the man's face as he had paused at the door of his car in the act of getting back in, and looked back at the house. It was the face of a man who had spent a lifetime returning to a buried treasure and when he got there – had found it gone.

Slovak sat down, smiling to himself. That must have been the greatest shock of Groczek's life, greater even than the loss of the drugs. He must be feeling now as helpless as a cat in a well. Wherever he scratched and clawed he could find no foothold, and beneath him there was no rest. It must have seemed to him that he was trapped in a maze, that each new turning he took led him back to the point he started at. Above all, he must now be on the verge of a conviction that he was dealing not with a man, but with a wizard. Slovak had escaped, it must seem to him, like Houdini from nothing less than an iron safe thrown into a river. It must seem incomprehensible to him, the exercise of a power beyond Groczek's wildest imaginings. Slovak had seen that on Groczek's face when Groczek had first seen him standing in the door, had seen it in the way Groczek's eyes had desperately searched

Slovak's neck for signs of the rope, marks that would, at least, have convinced him that he had not dreamed the whole episode, but he could see nothing beneath the roll-neck sweater Slovak had worn. The shock to Groczek's system must have been, in those few minutes, like that of a rabbit emerging from his burrow and coming face to face with a cobra.

And yet the explanation was simple and had nothing to do with magic and, indeed, had nothing to do with Slovak himself. Slovak, as he now admitted to himself, had blundered, and blundered badly. It was the only time since he had come here that he had totally misread Groczek, had failed to predict how he would react. The shock of losing the heroin, after all his precautions and the subsequent despair, had jolted him totally out of joint, and out of joint he had reacted with the clumsy crudity of a man who had been lamed in a fight and compelled to resort to the jagged end of a broken bottle.

It had been effective. It had taken Slovak by surprise and if it had in the end failed, Slovak could claim no credit for it. He had swung helplessly from the rope, convinced until the last moment that Groczek would not go through with it and then, when the realisation began to filter through into his brain that he had misjudged the situation, he realised also that this was too late, that this was, in truth, the end, that he was floating, bobbing about, drifting out to sea. There was no pain anymore and no agony. And then there had been nothing at all.

He had come floating back from a vast distance. He felt he would never make it, had no desire to make it, fought against making it. But he was helpless. He was borne back. The tide was irresistible and he gave up the struggle as he had finally given it up when it had borne him away. He was too tired to fight it all over again. He let it bear him back.

He had heard voices, soft and whispering like a wind over water, and then the wreckage of a scene passed before his

217

eyes like bits of driftwood and he had begun to remember what had happened. Something had snapped inside Groczek and Groczek had made an attempt on his life.

That was odd and unexpected. What was odder still was that he should have had an accomplice. Slovak had seen no one else, yet he could hear a man's voice and it was not Groczek's. Had he been waiting in the car? Had Groczek changed his mind, relented, and cut him down before the light had finally died in him? It was mysterious.

The man's voice was saying, 'He'll be all right but we'll have to get him to a hospital.'

Hospital? He didn't understand. Why would they be taking him to a hospital? Did they mean a prison hospital? He had thought, 'I must get out of here. Groczek has something else in mind.'

He had found, however, that he couldn't move. His limbs were numb and all the movement he had been able to accomplish was to flick open his eyes. He had found himself staring up at the ceiling of a room. It was not the barn. Where had they taken him? And then he had heard the man's voice, once again, asking quietly, 'Tell me, how did you come to find him?'

'He phoned me about an hour ago. He wanted me to come over but I said, "no". It was too late. He hung up on me. And then, afterwards – I don't know, he sounded so . . .'

'Sounded what?'

'I don't know. Anyway, I did come over. The house was in darkness but there was a light on in the barn. I thought, perhaps he was in there though it seemed odd. I went in and found him. I thought he was dead at first. I couldn't think of anyone else to call except you.'

There had been a pause then. He'd had the feeling they were looking at him and he'd lain still. So it was Maggie. She had come after all. Well, that was lucky. It was his good fortune and Groczek's bad luck. Groczek would live to regret his

218

ill-timed visit. And that must be her doctor friend she was talking to.

Slovak had then heard the man's voice speaking quietly again. 'What exactly is he? I mean – what does he do?'

'Oh – he's in property and things,' he'd heard her reply vaguely.

'I see.' There had been a reflective note in the voice then, and it continued, 'And where, exactly, do you come in, Maggie?'

'I told you,' she had said, with a note of hesitancy, 'I was in love with him once.'

'I see,' the voice had said again, this time more doubtful. There had been another pause, and he had felt their gaze upon him again. Then the voice said, 'He's coming round. He may try it again. I'd better call the hospital.'

Try it again? What were they talking about? Did they mean Groczek? Did they mean Groczek may try it again? But they couldn't have seen Groczek and if, by chance, they had, surely they could not think Groczek would try again, in their presence, what he had failed to do alone? And then he had remembered the slipping off of the handcuffs, the overturning of the chair. Groczek had, of course, made it look like suicide and, quite naturally, that is what they had assumed had happened.

He felt strength flooding into his limbs for the first time since he had drifted back. He was weak, incredibly weak, but with a supreme effort of will he had put one hand on the back of the couch and another beneath him and had levered himself up into a sitting position. A man, a younger man than he, was standing by the phone, dialling. Maggie was watching him. Slovak had opened his mouth to speak but nothing had come out of it. He felt a terrible throbbing at the base of his throat and a terrible pain there. He hadn't been conscious of it before. Now, as he sat up, the pain was almost unbearable.

219

He had put his hands to his throat and felt the lacerated skin hot beneath his fingers.

He had opened his mouth once more and this time a rasping, strangulated sound emerged from him that he had not recognised as his own. 'Stop him,' he had said, 'stop him!'

They had both turned and looked at him. 'Frank,' Maggie had cried, and rushed towards him. He had levered himself onto his feet, his eyes fixed on the man holding the phone. He had pushed Maggie roughly away and propelled himself across the room, snatching the phone out of the man's hand. 'Get out of here,' he had said to him.

'Frank,' Maggie had screamed at him.

'Get out of here,' Slovak had repeated, his voice scarcely rising above a whisper, but such was the force with which he had said it that the man, who had taken a step towards him, paused.

He had stared at Slovak steadily for a moment, and then said, 'Listen to me. I'm a doctor. You just tried to hang yourself. You may try it again. For your own good . . .'

'Get him out of here,' Slovak had snarled, turning to Maggie.

Maggie had looked at the man, helplessly, as if wondering if it wouldn't be better, after all, if he went. The man had looked from her to Slovak. Then he said, 'If you'll take my advice . . .'

Slovak had taken a step towards him and Maggie had screamed, 'Frank, stop it!'

He had stopped. She had turned and looked appealingly at the man. 'Phillip, perhaps . . .'

He had shrugged and shaken his head disapprovingly. He had studied Slovak for a while and then turned to Maggie. 'You'd better not leave him alone – and call me if you need me.' He had gathered up his bag, put a hand reassuringly on her arm and squeezed it. He had given Slovak one last look and then gone out.

220

'How could you do that?' Maggie had asked, turning to him, 'he came here to help you.'

'Is that him?'

'Who?'

'Your – doctor friend?'

There had been a slight pause, and then she'd nodded. 'I called him when I found you. I got you down but I couldn't move you. Frank, you're ill. You must get to a hospital. If I hadn't arrived when I did . . .'

'Oh, stop it,' he had said, impatiently, and the pain in his throat throbbed again, making him pause for a moment. Then he'd continued, 'You must have just missed Groczek.'

She had stared at him. 'I what?' she had asked. 'What do you mean?'

'Groczek was here. He tried to hang me.'

She had looked utterly bewildered, her eyes wide and disbelieving. 'Groczek? Oh, Frank!'

'He was here, I tell you, he was here! My God, you think I'd try to kill myself?'

'But why? Why should he do such a thing?'

'He wanted the junk back. I've got it and he knows I've got it. He came to get it but I wouldn't tell him where it was. That punk policeman! I hadn't figured on that. He surprised me. I'm going to take him apart, Maggie. I'm going to shred him. When I'm finished with him, he'll wish he'd hanged himself!'

The effort of speech had made him feel giddy. His throat was raw and throbbing. He had put his hand to it and felt it tenderly, then walked unsteadily towards the couch where he had been lying and sat down on the edge of it. All this time she had watched him incredulously. Finally she had said, 'You've got the drugs? From the police? There's nothing in the papers?'

'It's too soon.'

'And Groczek came here? He tried to murder you?'

221

He had paused and sat there thinking for a moment. 'Groczek surprised me though; he acted out of line. It was crude. I expected something different.'

She had asked quietly, 'Does it ever occur to you, Frank, how much human misery there is tied up in that heroin?'

'There's human misery everywhere,' he had said, 'there'll always be human misery.'

She had stared at him for a while. Then she had come over and knelt in front of him, putting her hand up to his throat and touching the skin with her fingers. 'Your throat looks terrible. It ought to be dressed.'

He'd taken her hand and kissed it. 'I don't need it dressed.'

She had looked up into his eyes. She was still in love with him, he could see that, but he could see, too, that it was like a great stone on her chest when she thought of it. 'I don't think you should stay here. Come back to the apartment with me, for a couple of days anyway.'

'What would your doctor say?' he'd smiled at her.

She had shrugged. 'My conscience would be clear. I'd just be looking after you for a while.'

'Are you sure?'

'I'm sure. I love you, Frank, but I'm not going to marry you. I'm going to marry Phillip. But I'll look after you for a while, if you need me.'

He had stared at her a long time. He believed her. For the first time, he saw that he had really lost her. He pulled her towards him and held her close and she didn't resist. It was, he knew, their parting embrace. Then he had shaken his head. 'I've got things to do. I shan't be here, anyway, for a couple of days.'

'Why don't you leave for good? If you've got what you came for, why don't you leave for good?'

'I'm not finished yet.'

'With what?'

'With Groczek.'

222

'What more can you do to him?'

'Oh, I can do more, much more. You'll see.'

'But is it worth it?'

He had paused a moment to consider. Then, he had nodded. 'It's him or me, Maggie. He knows that, so do I. But I don't expect you to understand it.'

She had risen to her feet and stood looking at him. Then she had said, 'Goodbye, Frank,' and turned and walked to the door.

'Maggie,' he'd said, 'can I still call you – sometime?'

She had stood looking for a moment at him, and then, she'd nodded, turned and gone out. He had sat there quite still, listening to her car door slam, the engine start, and the car pull away. He had put his fingers to his neck and touched it. His throat hurt, he felt a sensation of burning there. It had been a close thing, the closest thing of his life. It had happened because it was totally unexpected. It was the one aspect of Groczek's behaviour he had been unable to predict. Never mind – what was about to happen, shortly, he could predict with fair certainty. He had arranged it all.

Chapter Thirteen

Webster and Bradley ate their breakfast in silence. The food at Madigan's was unappealing and the rooms uncomfortable, but the hotel was not far from the centre of the city and its prices accommodated their meagre allowance. Both were pre-occupied with the facts of the case, as they understood them. As far as they could pin them down they were very curious and amounted to little more than Lamont had told them in the first place – that a large quantity of heroin had disappeared after a train robbery.

223

Groczek's story – that the drugs had been stolen in court had thrown them somewhat off balance, and his description of the involvements of Slovak had an element of the bizarre about it. Webster was not disposed to believe in masterminds. In his experience, a crook was a crook, though he had known some clever ones in his time. The trouble was that at the moment all Groczek's explanation was entirely supposition when one really examined it, though he put it forward with such conviction, vehemence almost, that Webster found himself tilting, against his inclinations, to the side of believing it. Groczek, after all, was a very experienced cop, a cop with a very big reputation. He was, moreover, Chief of Police in this city and hardly likely to give vent to wild and unsubstantiated accusations.

The meeting, too, with this man Slovak, unexpected as it was, had not exactly borne Groczek out. Webster had played along with it, he had no option in the circumstances, and had let Slovak know in no uncertain terms that he was under suspicion. But the man's reaction, the way he had carried himself, had impressed Webster. If he were a criminal, he was like no criminal Webster had ever met, by which Webster meant that, on first meeting, Webster would not have taken him for one, and Webster had met an immense variety of them.

Of course, he had to accept that Slovak was, in some way, connected with crime. Rosetti had a file on him, which Groczek had seen, and whatever Webster thought of Rosetti and his little outfit, there must be some justification for Slovak becoming, for them, an object of suspicion. But there was nothing, so far as Webster could see, that connected Slovak with the theft of the drugs except Groczek's conviction, and that, after all, might exist solely in Groczek's imagination, *did* in a way, for there was no proof of any kind. One had to bear that in mind. Skilful as Groczek was, he could make mistakes, like everyone else. He could panic like everyone else, and who was to say at this stage that he had not simply panicked when Slovak arrived and had assumed what was yet to be proved?

Well, this morning, he hoped, would partly take care of that. Webster would go with Groczek and see the clerk at the court who had charge of that room, but there was something else that was bothering Webster.

'There's something going on between Groczek and Slovak,' he said. 'Do you feel that?'

'No,' Bradley answered, 'not exactly – unless you mean a lot of hate, which wouldn't be odd in the circumstances.'

'No,' Webster replied slowly, 'I didn't mean that.'

'What sort of feeling then?'

'Well, that's just it. I don't know. But there was something between them – something. In the way they looked at each other. It was – I don't know.' He stopped for a moment and searched for the right word. 'There was a familiarity between them.'

Bradley laughed. 'They didn't behave in a familiar way exactly.'

'Well, familiar doesn't always mean friendly, if you see what I mean. I only meant it was not a meeting of two men who were entirely strangers.'

'They had met before,' Bradley reminded him.

'The collision?' Webster shrugged. 'That wasn't exactly a meeting. They eyed each other across a few feet of road but, if that was all, if that was the only time they'd met, and not met since, I would have expected something else in that house.'

'Like what?'

'Well, curiosity?' He paused for a moment to get a reaction from Bradley, but Bradley merely waited for him to go on. 'Well,' Webster continued, 'here's a guy you've met once, briefly, and with no cause, at that moment, to take too much notice of him. Since then you've been reading about him in a file, you come to the conclusion he's your enemy number one as far as the drugs are concerned, and it turns out you're right

225

because he lifts them right under your nose. You meet him for the first time after that and what's your first reaction? You'd be curious, wouldn't you? You'd study the man properly. A cop surely would. Yet Groczek's first reaction seemed more like shock to me than anything else.'

'Well, he didn't expect to find him there. He thought the house was empty.'

'Because one of his men had been up there and seen no one? Slovak might just have slipped out for a while. Why should Groczek assume he'd gone altogether?'

'You forget,' Bradley said, 'Groczek thinks Slovak pulled the job. Naturally, he wouldn't expect him to hang around after that.' Webster nodded and bit his lip. That was a good point but then Bradley spoiled it for he went on, 'And anyway, he did ring the bell before he went in.'

'Well, then,' Webster asked, 'which is it? Did he expect to find him there or didn't he?'

'Couldn't it be a bit of both,' Bradley countered, 'couldn't he have thought he'd gone but just to make sure pressed the bell?'

'Well, maybe,' Webster conceded, 'but he was damned positive Slovak wouldn't be there when I asked if we could see him. But now, let me put another question to you. Which side of the door, facing it, is the bell on?'

'The bell?' Bradley stared at him for a moment and then thought about it. Then he said, 'The right.'

'No, it's on the left. It should be on the right. You'd expect it on the right but for some reason it's on the left. I looked for it on the right, naturally. Groczek didn't look at all. He put his left hand out straight away and pressed it.'

Bradley shrugged. 'Maybe he's more observant than you?'

'Then why didn't he notice the light switch in the hall straight away? I'd noticed it. He had to look for it.'

'Jesus,' Bradley said, 'you're groping a bit, aren't you?'

226

'I'm groping,' Webster nodded, 'what else can you do in the dark. And it is dark.'

'But you're trying to point me some place. Where?'

Webster shook his head. 'I'm not trying to point you anywhere at all. If I knew where to point you, I'd be facing in that direction myself instead of slowly turning circles.'

Bradley looked at his watch. 'We'd better pick up Groczek and get down to that courthouse,' he said. He threw down his napkin and stood up.

Webster did the same. 'And that's another thing,' he said, as Bradley started to move off. Bradley paused and looked at him. 'I get the feeling I'm being hustled.'

'Hustled?'

'Don't you? I get the feeling I'm being pushed into thinking one thing when maybe I'd like to think something else.'

Bradley stared at him for a while and then nodded and sighed. 'I know what you mean. Hurried along. Still, Groczek's the guy on the spot. Up to a point, you have to go along with him.'

Webster shook his head unhappily and started limping to the door. 'I just wish,' he said, 'he wouldn't push so goddam hard.'

They got into the police car that was waiting for them outside and drove to the headquarters building. They sat in silence in the car while the driver went in to tell Groczek they were here. After a few moments, Groczek came down and got into the car. He exchanged a 'Good morning' with each and settled down in the rear beside Webster. Webster smiled at him brightly. 'Any news, sir?'

'No,' Groczek said, 'there are dragnets out all over the area but nobody's been picked up.'

'Just vanished?' Webster shook his head in admiration. 'They rob a train in broad daylight and then vanish into thin air.'

227

'It's not important,' Groczek replied, dismissing it. 'The stuff was taken in court. Slovak had help from inside and I'm pretty sure I know who it was.'

They pulled up outside the courthouse and got out. They walked up the steps and into the building and took the elevator to the second floor. They stepped out of the elevator and Groczek strode impatiently along the corridor towards room 4B but paused half-way down as he realised, once again, that Webster was way behind him, limping slowly along. Webster smiled wanly as he came up to him. 'Sorry, sir,' he said, 'you're just going too fast for me. Is this the room?'

Groczek nodded. They had paused outside the door. Webster put his hand on the handle and turned it. The door opened. They stepped inside. The room was empty. Webster limped over to the window and looked out onto the alleyway below. He saw nothing that interested him. Groczek said, 'We left the drugs in here.'

'Is this where evidence is always kept?'

'Always. Ever since I can remember.'

'It's not exactly Fort Knox, is it?' Webster smiled.

'We've never had trouble before. I suppose people didn't think of things being stolen during a trial. Still, I agree, the security should be looked into. It's being looked into now in fact. Anyway the drugs were taken into court and then brought back. They must have been switched while they were in this room.'

Webster opened a cupboard door and looked inside. There were only boxes and files, nothing of interest. There was a sound in the doorway and they turned. The old clerk was standing there looking at them.

Webster said to him. 'You handle the evidence brought into court?' The old man nodded. 'You have charge of this room?' The old man nodded again. 'The drugs you had in here have disappeared.'

The old man shook his head. 'That's got nothing to do with

me,' he said. He looked at Groczek. 'They were taken out of here by the police. I've got a receipt.'

'It was chalk that was taken out of here,' Groczek snarled, '*chalk*!'

'Then it was chalk that was brought in,' the old man replied.

Groczek took a step towards him, his hands clenching in a surge of rage, but Webster put a restraining hand on his arm and he paused, glowering at the clerk. 'Do you think I'm a fool?' he asked, tight lipped. 'The drugs are gone – and they could only have gone while they were here! Now, you listen to me,' he went on, his tone changing a little, 'maybe you were tricked into it or maybe you were just bribed. Either way the courts will take a lenient view of a man your age if he turns out to regret having made such a mistake and does what he can to retrieve it. You help us and we'll help you. I promise you that. You've got witnesses here.' He looked at Webster and Bradley. 'They'll hold me to my word, though I don't need holding. I want those drugs back, and I'll go a long way to help anyone who helps me, no matter what he's done, you understand?'

There was a long silence. Webster, Bradley and Groczek stared at the old man, waiting. He looked from one to the other of them and his lips started to quiver, but it was with indignation, not remorse. 'We'd better have the chief clerk of the court in,' he said, 'and I'd better ring for my lawyer.' He turned to go out.

'Just a minute,' Webster said, 'just a minute.' He stopped the old man and smiled winningly at him. 'There's no need for lawyers and all that. No one's accusing you, not now. We just want your co-operation, that's all. Now, you want to help us, don't you?'

'I've been a decent man all my life,' the old man said, his voice trembling with emotion, 'a respectable, law-abiding man. I won't stand here and be accused by anyone.'

'No one's accusing you,' Webster replied, smiling.

'He is,' the old man answered, looking at Groczek.

'But I'm not,' Webster replied, 'and anyway, Chief Groczek didn't actually accuse you. He merely suggested that you might be in a position to help us. That's normal police procedure in a case like this.' Webster smiled at Groczek, looking for a nod of encouragement, but Groczek was staring hard at the old man and conceding nothing. Webster looked back at the clerk. 'How long have you worked for the court?'

'Thirty-five years,' the old man said, 'and nothing like this has ever happened before.'

'Thirty-five years?' Webster was impressed and looked at Groczek to see if he, too, was impressed but Groczek, clearly, was in no mood to be impressed by anything. This was, Webster sighed to himself, a closed mind. It wouldn't help. He turned once more to the old man. 'How long have you had charge of this room?'

'Close on twenty,' the old man said. 'We've had everything in here – valuables, everything. The procedure's all laid down. It was laid down before I got here. Nothing's ever happened.'

'Well,' Webster said, in a conciliatory tone, 'something *has* happened and naturally we have to investigate it. Now, you're an official of the court, you understand that?'

'I understand that,' the old man answered, as if he resented being spoken to like an idiot, 'and if that's all you're doing, that's different, but that's not all *he* was doing,' and he glared once again at Groczek.

'All right,' Webster said with a sigh, 'just let me ask one or two questions. The drugs came up on the trolley and were put in here?'

'That's normal,' the old man said.

'Then you left the room for several minutes. Is that normal?'

'Of course, it is! What do you expect me to do, piss up against the wall? That's a heavy oak door with a double lock on it. Who's going to get in there?'

'How long were you gone'

230

'Four minutes, at most. Even he couldn't get in there,' he added, looking again at Groczek. He sat unsteadily down on a chair, quivering with emotion. He took out a handkerchief and blew his nose loudly, and then wiped his eyes. He was clearly distressed by the situation he had been placed in.

Webster went over to the window and looked out again. 'Were there any window cleaners about on that day?' he asked.

'Windows are cleaned first Monday of the month,' the old man said, putting away his handkerchief, 'it wasn't window cleaning day.'

'Were there any repairs being done? Did you see any ladders anywhere?'

'I don't remember,' the old man said.

'He's lying,' Groczek broke in, 'can't you see he's lying?'

'You ought to be ashamed of yourself,' the old man shouted at him, 'trying to pin a thing like this on an old man! If the drugs are lost, you lost them, and you're just looking for an out! An out, that's what you're looking for, someone to pin it on!'

Webster looked at Groczek with some exasperation. It was certainly no help to have him there. His bullying tone was contrary to the methods Webster was in favour of using and was contrary to what he imagined a Chief of Police would adopt. Making allowances, Webster put it down to desperation, but desperation was at the very root of Webster's unease. There was altogether too much desperation from Groczek. Webster could understand it. To have had so large a quantity of drugs stolen from under one's nose was likely to make any man who had responsibility for them desperate. But desperation was helping nobody. Desperation blinkered a man, cutting out the signals coming in from other directions. It put his mind on one track and nothing would shift it, and what was worse, there was a real danger of others hooking up behind. 'Others' included Webster and he didn't like it. He didn't like being drawn along behind. Neither was he going to be. Without another word, he turned and limped out of the room and down the steps, not even waiting for the elevator and so out of the court building. Bradley followed him out.

Webster got back into the car and Bradley got into the front. They sat and waited in silence for Groczek to join them. A few moments later he did so, slamming the car door and sinking back into the seat beside Webster. 'We should have brought that man in for questioning,' Groczek said.

'I'm not ready for that yet,' Webster said, and there was another short silence. Then Webster said to the driver, 'Back to the office.' The driver started up the car and pulled away.

There was an uncomfortable silence in the car on the way back. Clearly each was at odds with the other, and that was unfortunate. It was not the best way to conduct an investigation though Webster had met the situation before. Outsiders were often resented and, if one were not careful, a spirit of non-co-operation developed which hindered the enquiry. Webster had to guard against that if he were to get anywhere, and one of the ways he could do it was to separate himself from Groczek and go off on his own. He would have to do it sooner or later and it might as well be done now.

When they arrived at police headquarters, Webster said, 'I'm just going back to the hotel, sir, I've got one or two things to do there. I'll call in later.'

Groczek stared at him, but he offered nothing further by way of explanation and after a moment Groczek nodded and turned and walked on into the building. Webster pulled the door closed and said to the driver, 'Back to the hotel.' He leaned back in his seat and let out a long sigh, shaking his head. 'I had to do that,' he said to Bradley, 'that man's kind of over-powering. He's in the grip of an obsession and he wants me to share it.'

'About Slovak?'

'About Slovak and about the stuff being taken in court.'

'Well, it seems a likely explanation,' Bradley said. 'The security in that court leaves a lot to be desired.'

'So does the security in most courts, when you come to think of it,' Webster replied, 'but that's not really the point. The point is,' and he brooded for a moment before coming out with it, 'if the stuff were taken in court, why was the train robbed?'

There was a moment's pause, then Bradley turned and stared at Webster for a moment. Then he nodded. 'Good question,' he said.

'Yes, it's a good question,' Webster replied, 'and it's been bothering me ever since Groczek gave me his version of the robbery. If Slovak already had the junk, why bother to rob the train?'

'Why didn't you ask Groczek?'

'Well, I was a little bit surprised that he didn't mention it himself, so I'm waiting for a while to see if he does.'

The car drew into the forecourt of the hotel and Webster and Bradley got out. They went into the hotel, ordered two bourbons in the bar and sat at a table sipping them. Then Bradley said, 'There is an explanation, you know?' Webster looked at him and waited. 'He robbed the train because he didn't want anyone to know he'd taken the stuff from the court.'

'Why not?'

'Because he didn't want to compromise the old man. Maybe that was part of the deal. If he'd bribed the old man to be absent from that room for a few minutes just at the right time, it was going to look pretty obvious that he had something to do with it.'

Webster shook his head. 'No Brad,' he said, 'if that were the case, Slovak must have known it wouldn't be heroin on that train, and that, once the theft was discovered, Groczek would be bound to conclude the stuff had been taken in court, anyway, and Slovak would be back where he started.'

'You're forgetting one thing,' Bradley said.

'What's that?'

'How could Groczek ever prove he'd put cans of chalk on that train?'

'But we *have* the cans of chalk in the . . .' Webster stopped as he saw the absurdity of it.

Bradley nodded solemnly. 'Exactly,' he said, softly, 'but Slovak couldn't have known that. That was a mistake. Slovak thought it would all be cleared out and *then* how would Groczek have proved it? That was just a piece of luck for Groczek when you come to think of it.'

There was a long silence, Bradley could see that Webster was impressed. It was a tortuous route to have gone but he had set out and arrived safely. Webster said finally. 'The only thing is, I don't believe the stuff was stolen in court.'

Bradley let go a long sigh. He'd had a feeling he'd been having it all too easy, but he wasn't beaten yet. 'Can you prove it?' he asked.

Webster shook his head. 'I can prove nothing in this goddam case,' he said, 'but I don't believe it could have happened.' He thought for a moment and then went on, 'Let's have some lunch, then take another look at that courthouse – without Groczek.'

Oddly Webster was feeling better, better than he'd felt since he arrived. His mind was working, he felt it to be working in top gear. It was not that the issues were becoming clearer to him. They weren't. It was simply that he felt a certain sense of release at being free of Groczek's brooding presence telling him what he was thinking before he'd thought it. If the issues were not yet clear, his mind, at least, was. The cloud that had seemed to envelop it since the moment he stepped off the plane had dispersed. He felt a lot better.

This was a curious case. It was pure thought that was going to see them through this one and it appealed to him. Fingerprints and footprints and patient, plodding police work were

234

not applicable. Neither, he added as an afterthought, were they available. But he felt that the problem was amenable to pure thought if he could concentrate his mind sufficiently upon it, keep to what he knew and refuse to be side-tracked.

A remark by the old clerk, blurted out in the moment of his extreme indignation, had lodged in Webster's mind and given him food for thought. It was that Groczek had lost the drugs and was simply looking for a scapegoat. Webster felt there was an element of truth in that. The same thought had crossed his own mind. He was well aware of the pressure on the police to get convictions in certain cases, no matter what, and in this case, when the police had been robbed rather than the public, the pressure would inevitably be all the greater. There would be, was bound to be, an enormous loss of face and a conviction, if not the recovery of the drugs, would go some way to restoring their public image. That that pressure was there, Webster did not doubt. He had revealed as much to Slovak when he had told him they would put every member of the force onto the case if need be to restore the situation. However, Webster was also aware that a false conviction would not satisfy him. He wanted the truth, in so far as he was able to arrive at it, irrespective of Groczek's feelings in the matter.

What Webster felt he needed, now, was another view, an altogether different view, a view of someone who had been close to the action all along but not leading it or pushing it. That person was clearly Fallon. He would like to talk to Fallon.

Before sitting down to lunch, therefore, he called Fallon at the office and asked him if he'd come over to the hotel after lunch. Fallon said that he would. Webster then sat down with Bradley to lunch and both ate in silence. Fallon arrived during coffee.

He ordered coffee for Fallon and when it arrived and Fallon was stirring his sugar into it, Webster leaned back and said to him, 'It's a weird business, isn't it?' Fallon nodded, but said

235

nothing. Webster said, 'What do you think – do you think Slovak's had a hand in this or not?'

Fallon shrugged. 'I don't know,' he answered, 'maybe he did, maybe he didn't.'

'Chief Groczek's pretty sure?' Fallon nodded. 'But you're not?'

'I don't know what I think any more. As you say, it's a weird business.'

'Why do you think he's so sure?'

Fallon was silent for a moment. He seemed reluctant to talk about it. Then he said, 'Perhaps because Slovak appeared in the court during the trial.'

'But it was a public trial. Perhaps he was just curious?'

'Well, it's all "perhaps",' Fallon replied with a touch of irritability. 'I've never seen so many ifs and buts in a crime before it was committed. I'm sick of those drugs. They've been nothing but trouble! Ever since the trial we've been hopping about, first this way, then that – we made too much of a production of it, as if there was nothing we could do to protect our own property. We should have just pushed the stuff on a plane or a train or into a car and sent it.'

'Too much of a production,' Webster repeated, thoughtfully, 'yet the junk was lifted.'

Fallon sighed. 'It makes us all look even sillier, doesn't it?'

Webster nodded and was silent for a while. Then he said, 'How did it all start? I mean, this thing with Slovak?'

'Chief Groczek recognised him.'

'When the cars ran into each other?'

'Yes. He's got a hell of a memory. He remembered he'd seen a file on him in New York.'

'Rosetti's?'

Fallon nodded and shrugged. 'From that time on he became convinced Slovak was here to pull a job.'

'Why?' Webster asked, leaning forward. 'Why was he so convinced?'

236

'I don't know.'

'Were you convinced?'

Fallon shrugged. 'I wouldn't say I was convinced, exactly. I didn't think much about it at all until later, till we got to the point of moving the stuff. But, Chief Groczek,' – he fiddled with the spoon in the cup while he thought about it – 'the Chief got over-obsessed by it, I think.'

'In what way?'

Fallon looked uncomfortable. 'Why don't you talk to Chief Groczek?' he asked.

'I've talked to Chief Groczek,' Webster replied, 'and now I'm talking to you.' Although he smiled as he said it, there was in his tone an unmistakable note of reprimand. Fallon flushed. He was unused to being spoken to in that way. He had expected Webster, as a colleague, to understand his reluctance to discuss his superior when his superior was not present, but Webster, apparently, had no sensitivity on such matters. He sat there, doggedly, unprepared to budge and quite prepared to sit there all day if necessary. Fallon finally said, 'He wanted him out of the territory. He wanted Slovak to know that we knew he was here and we weren't going to be taken by surprise.'

'Which, of course, is exactly what you were taken by?'

'As it turned out,' Fallon admitted, 'I guess you could say that.'

'How exactly did you let Slovak know this? Did you put a tail on him?'

'We had him watched. And – we harassed him a little.'

'Harassed?'

'Well, you know – pulled him in, turned the house over, that sort of thing. Nothing serious.'

'Those were Groczek's instructions?' Fallon nodded. 'In writing?'

'Well, of course not,' Fallon said, impatiently, 'a nod and a wink – you know as well as I do the procedure in these cases.'

237

'Perhaps not quite so well as you,' Webster replied, 'though I know what goes on. What did you think of all this?'

'I wasn't as worked up over Slovak as Chief Groczek was. It seemed a fairly routine affair. We knew he was here. He knew we knew. I thought we could take care of ourselves but, then, as time went on, I've got to admit I could see that maybe the Chief was right and that we had a problem.'

'You came to see it more his way?' Fallon nodded. There was a silence for a moment, and then Webster asked, 'By the way, what were Slovak's movements on the day you discovered the drugs were gone?'

'I can't tell you exactly.'

'You had the house under surveillance?'

'Well, we had – but when we put, as *I* thought, the drugs on the helicopter, I thought we were in the clear. There seemed no point in continuing to watch the house so I pulled the man off. We've got a manpower problem here, the same as everyone else.'

'Well, afterwards,' Webster continued patiently, 'after you discovered the drugs were gone, what then? You must have sent a man back up there?'

'Well,' Fallon said, awkwardly, 'I was going to send Mednik back up but the Chief sent me off down to the Groton area to talk to the local police and . . .'

'You forgot?'

Fallon bit his lip in vexation. 'No, dammit, I didn't forget. Chief Groczek said he'd do it – send Mednik up there, but I guess *he* forgot.'

'I see.' Webster paused and looked at Bradley enquiringly to see if he had anything to ask, but Bradley shook his head. Webster sighed. 'It certainly is the weirdest thing. There's this guy Slovak, a number one suspect before the crime and after – and not a shred of evidence against him. In its own, quiet way that really is amazing.' He shook his head and looked at Fallon. 'Do you have the car here?' Fallon nodded. 'You can

238

drop us at the court building. I want to look over that place again.'

They all rose. Bradley and Fallon walked out to the car and Webster limped slowly behind them. It had been useful talking to Fallon, though nothing substantial had emerged. Fallon had reluctantly confirmed his own impression that Groczek had, to some extent, panicked. Webster had wondered if this were not simply his own, jaundiced view, coming in from the outside, as it were, and seeing what appeared to be only a perfectly normal situation blown up out of all proportion, but talking to Fallon had convinced him otherwise. Fallon clearly, and understandably, had not wanted to undermine his chief's authority or to say anything that might call into question his chief's behaviour, but Webster could detect in Fallon a faint odour of contempt. His chief had fallen a little in Fallon's estimation.

Webster had noticed, too, that Fallon was still rather puzzled by it all, like a man who understands the facts but not the sense. Webster understood that puzzlement. Groczek's panic did not fit with the man, it was out of key, and clearly he was being asked by events to alter a long held assessment of Groczek's character. If all that had taken place could be traced back to this panic – the conviction that Slovak had come for the drugs, the elaborate precautions taken for their safety, the moment of mad hysteria in the court room – the panic, itself, seemed inexplicable. It was as if Slovak were exerting some mysterious influence over Groczek's behaviour, subjecting him to the baleful gaze of his evil eye.

Webster did not believe in evil eyes, but that there was a connection between these two, over and above that of simple antagonist in a drama that was commonplace in police experience, he was convinced of. He was certain that his own antennae had not misread the signals coming to him from that confrontation between the two in the house. He had seen something. Signals of some sort had been flashing be-

239

tween these two, but what? He had tried, earlier, to present this to Bradley but he had been unsuccessful. Yet the feeling had persisted. If he had had to put it into words, Webster would have said that what was coming from Groczek in that room, as he stood eye to eye with Slovak, was panic. There it was again. But panic about what? Whatever the cause, there was an odd relationship between them, of that there was no doubt. 'Strange' might be a better word – a 'strange relationship'.

Bradley and Fallon were already seated in the car when Webster got in. They all sat in silence while Fallon drove to the courthouse and pulled in at the kerb. Webster thanked him for coming over to talk to them and he and Bradley got out. The car drove off and Bradley looked at Webster. Webster nodded, turned and limped slowly up the stone steps that led to the imposing entrance to the building. 'Tell me, Brad,' Webster said, as he took the steps one at a time, 'what do we have?'

It was a familiar question, born of long intimacy, a request for a summing up of what one knew, as distinct from what one thought one knew. Bradley took a long breath and began, 'Well, sir, we have a very complicated set of facts.'

Webster shook his head. 'Wrong, Brad. We have a very complicated story. The facts are few and surprisingly simple. Ten million dollars' worth of drugs disappeared after a train robbery.'

Bradley glanced at him, expecting him to say more but Webster did not continue. His eyes were fixed on the neoclassical facade up ahead of him which it seemed might take him all afternoon to reach. Bradley kept pace with him. He was used to it. It caused him no irritation.

They entered the building. The court was not in session and there were few people about. They made their way to the courtroom in which the trial had been held and went inside. It was empty. They stood at the back of the court,

240

gazing round at it, recreating in their minds a trial and the trolley with the drugs on it. It wasn't difficult. It was a familiar scene to them. They stood there, silently gazing for a while, and then Bradley said, 'Well, here's a fact. The last time Groczek saw that heroin and *knew* it was heroin, was in this room.'

'How do you know that, Brad?' Webster asked, gazing at the exit door through which the trolley must have gone.

'Because what's the guy's name – the expert witness, Goldfine – testified that those cans contained heroin. That, sir, is a fact.'

'I didn't mean that,' Webster said, as he turned and limped out of the courtroom. 'What I meant was, how do you know that that was the last time Groczek saw that heroin?' Bradley stopped and stared at Webster, but Webster did not pause. He limped his way onward, out into the corridor and stopped at the elevator and pressed the button. Bradley came up behind him and waited. He said nothing. He had nothing to say. He wondered, though, if Webster were not being altogether too clever, too pedantic. It was not often that his chief irritated him but he had just done so. It seemed to him too smart a point to have made and not a particularly telling one.

The elevator arrived and they took it to the second floor. They walked along the corridor to room 4B. The door was not locked and Webster opened it and went inside. The room was empty. Webster limped slowly over to the window and stared out, looking round at the adjoining buildings. Then he looked at Bradley and shook his head. 'I can't see it, Brad, I just can't see it.'

'How it was done?'

'Not the way Groczek says it was done.' He opened the cupboard and looked inside but there was nothing of interest there. He turned back to Bradley. 'By Groczek's account, he could have stayed in that courtroom only a few minutes after that trolley went out and before it struck him what Slovak

241

was after. Say four minutes – even that's long, but say four. Say the elevator was waiting when the trolley came out so it went straight up. Groczek arrived here two or three minutes after the drugs had been brought in. Now, if Groczek's right, someone paid the old man to leave the room for those few minutes, while someone took the drugs out and put the cans of chalk in their place, someone for whom the old man had made a duplicate key.'

'You can't say it's not possible.'

'You can say it's verging on the impossible,' Webster argued. 'Frankly, for all practical purposes you can say it *is* impossible.'

'There could have been more than one person.'

'Brad,' Webster said, 'do you know how much is 220 pounds of heroin? Suppose each of those cans contained a pound. Suppose there is a dozen cans in a cardboard box. That's close to twenty boxes. Now with a court in session there are people walking about the corridors. They'd notice *something.* How would you get that many boxes in and out, in three minutes flat and in broad daylight? How? I don't see it. And one thing's sure, the old man couldn't carry them.' He shook his head and said again, 'I don't see it.'

Put like that, neither did Bradley. It didn't seem feasible. There simply wouldn't be enough time for the switch. But if it hadn't happened in court, as Groczek was convinced it had, how and where had it happened? As if reading his mind at that moment, Webster said, 'How much do we know about the helicopter and its pilot?'

'Not much,' Bradley said.

'Well,' Webster sighed, 'we may as well check it out. You never know.' He turned and limped out of the room again. Bradley followed him. They walked down the courthouse steps and waited for a taxi. Webster growled, 'Helicopters, trains, cans of fake heroin – such elaborate precautions.'

242

'Well,' Bradley offered, 'if he knew something was going to happen, you can hardly blame him.'

'No, you can't,' Webster conceded, 'only none of it worked, none of it. That's what bugs me.'

Bradley laughed. 'It must bug Groczek too. I'll bet he's sorry he ever suggested pumping that stuff back into addicts on maintenance.'

Webster turned slowly and stared at his colleague. 'It was his idea?' he asked.

'Sure it was.'

'How long have you known that, Brad?'

'Since lunch.' Bradley shrugged. 'Fallon mentioned it in the car while we were waiting for you. I guess I forgot to tell you. Why, does it make a difference?'

Webster stared at Bradley with eyes exaggeratedly wide, tilting his head to one side as if to examine him from a new angle, an angle he hadn't used before and that might reveal to him a clue to the explanation of Bradley's forgetfulness. Bradley looked a trifle sheepish and shuffled his feet on the sidewalk. Webster said, softly, 'I don't know, Brad. I don't know what difference it makes. I don't know what difference any damned thing makes in this whole cock-eyed business. That's the point. When I *know* that, when I know the difference things do make, I may just be on the way to finding out what they make a difference *to*! So let's not forget to tell each other what we know – I mean really know. There's precious little of it.'

And it was true. What they actually *knew* was very little. It was surprising how little it actually was. They were on their way now, a cab having been picked up, to Mostyn's, but Webster knew there would be nothing of interest there. As he understood it, the two detectives who had accompanied the drugs on the plane had not known until the last moment that they were going to do so. To suppose that the drugs had been switched, in some way, on the helicopter was prepos-

243

terous. It presupposed that the pilot, whoever he was, knew beforehand what he was transporting and during the flight had made a proposition to the two men travelling with him which had been accepted. Such a theory was absurd. It was even more stupid if one supposed, what was probably more true, that the pilot knew nothing beforehand of the value of the goods he was carrying. Of course, it was possible that Slovak had, himself, discovered by observation and deduction, Groczek's intention of transporting the drugs by Mostyn's helicopter and made approaches to the pilot, but even this depended on two highly improbable events, namely, that the pilot was corruptible *and* that Slovak knew which detectives were to accompany the heroin. It was absurd, all absurd, and Webster did not believe it for a moment.

These thoughts were confirmed rapidly at Mostyn's itself. Greenberg did not know beforehand what was being carried, though when he saw the boxes, which had received considerable publicity in the press, he guessed what they contained. As for the pilot, he was Greenberg's elder brother and the possibility of a rich, successful and, until now, perfectly respectable, elder son of a huge family business being either approached by Slovak or proving susceptible to his approaches, was manifestly out of the question.

When Webster and Bradley left Mostyn's, Webster felt that he had travelled full circle. He had staggered back to the point he had started from. There was chalk on the train and chalk on the helicopter and he could not believe the heroin had been taken in court as Groczek said it had been. Where, then, had it gone? Was it possible – and the thought had been throbbing in the back of his mind for some time, he recognised that now – was it possible that the only person who knew the answer to that was Groczek?

Webster felt his heart beat a little faster as he arrived at that thought, not from excitement, not from a sense of having, at last, found a trace of his quarry, but from the enormous and unpleasant implications of it. Was he on that dreary road of uncovering corruption on the very grandest scale, a scale that would shake the foundation of the force throughout the country and do them all immense harm by damaging, once again, the integrity of those charged with keeping law and order? Was there to be another scandal and was he, Webster, to be the instrument chosen to lance it like a boil and let the pus out? Webster couldn't believe it, didn't want to believe it. He thrust the thought aside.

The day was fine, warm but not too hot. Webster wanted to walk. He had felt shut in ever since he got here and he had no desire to return to the office or the hotel. He limped slowly along the street and Bradley fell into step beside him. Neither spoke. Webster was not in the mood for discussion. The thought he had cast aside a moment before had returned again, looming up, as it were, ahead of him. He had no choice but to confront it and confront it properly.

What did it entail – that Groczek had, on his own, decided to take the drugs for himself, to dispose of them and salt away the money? Had he decided that the time had come, having for so long, and for comparatively so little, looked after the public, to look after himself? It was not new. It had been done before, though perhaps not on quite so grand a scale. Every time it happened the force took a terrible beating. The public's faith was undermined and their cynicism grew. There was, as a result, a tendency always to cover up, but Webster had nothing but contempt for that. To cover up merely spread the corruption. It bred faster, like a mould in a warmer room. One had to be ruthless and cut it out. Was he now confronting such a case, despite his reluctance to do so?

Whichever way his mind turned it seemed the only logical explanation. Groczek had had control of the heroin from the start. He had had it under lock and key. Since the time the junk had been seized and until it was brought into court for

245

the trial, only Groczek had had direct access to it. He had told Webster, in fact, in his insistence that the drugs had been taken in court, that only he, Groczek, had had the combination to the safe in which they had been kept, telling him this as proof that no one could have got at the drugs in the vault and that they therefore *must* have been stolen during the trial. But, by the same token, if no one else but Groczek could have lifted them from that safe, he alone must become suspect if it were found that the drugs had disappeared, perhaps before they ever went into court? No, that was not possible. Goldfine had testified that the stuff in the cans was heroin. *After* then, after they had been brought back? Was that reasonable? Was it reasonable that a man like Groczek would act in such a way that the finger of suspicion must inevitably and immediately point at himself? Webster confronted that question and answered it, almost with a sense of relief, in the negative. It was not reasonable.

But was that, then, the reason for the invention of the court story and the use of Slovak as a scapegoat? That was certainly more reasonable, that knowing he, himself, must become suspect number one, the moment the drugs were found to be gone, Groczek seized on the presence of Slovak in the court to concoct the whole story with which he had confronted Webster on his arrival. It was ideal, since it was so highly plausible. All suspicion would then be turned on Slovak, a man suspected, anyway, of engineering very large robberies. Though it may not remove suspicion entirely from the minds of some that Groczek had, himself, lifted the drugs, the weight of suspicion must inevitably fall heaviest on Slovak. He would be a natural. If the drugs were never found, nothing would ever be proved and even if some of the labour involved in the train robbery were picked up, what would they have got but chalk, bearing out Groczek's claim that he had, in all good faith, taken every conceivable precaution?

Only, as he said, the drugs had been stolen in the court-room.

And there he was back at that damned train again. Who had organised that robbery? Groczek? That was feasible. He might have done that to cover himself, expecting – and this was the reverse of Bradley's reasoning which implicated Slovak – expecting the train to be cleared out. What he had not foreseen was the dropping of the cans. Had it been cleared out, then who was to know . . . ? But Webster stopped there. It was already absurd. Why should Groczek organise the robbery of a train? What advantage was there to him? If he had the drugs, and he had his story of how they were taken in the court, what more did it prove to have the train robbed? The drugs could not be stolen both in court and from the train. And if the chalk Groczek said he had substituted for the drugs had arrived at Boston, it would prove only that Groczek had taken precautions as he had seen fit. It would not in any way invalidate the theory that the heroin was taken by Slovak in the court.

Webster's head was spinning. He simply could not break out of the circle. Nevertheless, he thrust his hands deeper into his pockets and attacked the circle again. If Groczek had not organised the robbery of the train, it had to be Slovak. The possibility that there was yet a third party working on a similar scheme was too absurd even to contemplate. That it was Slovak who had robbed the train seemed, on the face of it, more reasonable, since it was in accord with Webster's conviction that the drugs could not have been switched during the trial in the time available, and therefore Slovak must have thought the drugs were on the train. In that respect Groczek's ruse would seem to have worked. But the drugs were not on the train and if Slovak had robbed it all he had got was cans of powdered chalk. Where, then, were the drugs? Who had got them? Groczek? Webster shook his

247

head as if to clear a swarm of bees around it. He had just been through that. It didn't make sense.

They were, by now, nearing the headquarters building. Bradley, who had walked alongside him in deepest silence all the way, now looked at him and said, 'Well, sir, are the facts still as simple?'

'I come back and back to the simple fact, Brad, that $10,000,000 worth of heroin disappeared after a train robbery. The heroin wasn't on the train and yet the train was robbed. Why?'

'Ask Groczek. If he's so sure the stuff was taken in court, maybe he's got an explanation?'

Webster nodded. Maybe it was time after all. Since he was, as Bradley said, the one who was pressing hardest for the acceptance of his theory that the heroin had been stolen in court, he should have his own ideas about the robbery of the train.

He met Groczek in the corridor as he limped along towards his own office. Groczek's face looked anxious and drawn and he may well have seen them coming from the window of his office, for his appearance in the corridor was an act of impatient interception. 'Well?' he asked.

Webster smiled wanly at Groczek and patted his lame leg. 'I've just got to rest this,' he said, turning and limping off along the corridor, 'but there's a question that's been bugging me ever since you told me that story of the drugs being lifted in court.'

'What's that?' Groczek asked, falling into step beside him.

'Well, sir, it's this,' Webster replied, putting his hand on the handle of the door into his office and pausing, 'if Slovak took the stuff in court, as you suggest, why did he bother to rob the train? You must have thought of that,' he added, and opened the door and went inside.

Groczek followed him slowly in. Bradley came in afterwards and closed the door. Webster went to his desk and sat down. 'Damn foot,' he said, rubbing his ankle, and then, '*Had* you thought about that, sir?'

'Of course, I had,' Groczek answered.

'What do you think, sir? What's the answer?'

Groczek stared at him impatiently. 'It's not important,' he said, 'Slovak could have done it for several reasons?'

'Such as what?'

'I think he robbed the train to cover up the fact that he'd stolen the stuff in court.'

'Why should he want to cover it up? Why was it so important to him once he had the drugs?'

'He's a – a private man. He likes to operate in the dark. He couldn't have done it on his own, he had to have co-operation from inside. Most robberies of this kind depend on that. In this case it was the old clerk, I'm certain of it. I think robbing the train was to cover the old man. Only he made a mistake. Some of the cans were dropped in the getaway.'

'Yes,' Webster nodded, 'that was Brad's idea, too. There are two things wrong with it. First, I just don't believe that Slovak would go to all that trouble just to cover the old man. It doesn't make sense to me. I don't say it's impossible, but I do say it's damned unlikely. Second, I don't believe those drugs could have been switched in the time available between their arrival back in that room and your arrival at that door.'

'I tell you that's how it was done,' Groczek said, grittily. Webster shook his head. 'Then there must have been two gangs.'

'Two?' Webster echoed.

'Two.'

'Slovak and one other?'

'Yes!'

'Working independently of one another?'

'Yes!'

'And with but a single thought?'

Groczek stared at him, swallowing hard. He could see, as

249

soon as he'd said it, how far fetched it was, but the faint tone of contempt in Webster's voice riled him. 'Then you tell me,' he snarled, 'since you're so clever, what the answer is.'

Webster shook his head, mildly. 'I don't know the answer. I'm just, in a way, thinking aloud. And obviously, I'm not that clever.' He shrugged. 'But there's been so much dust flying around here . . .'

He broke off. He was getting nowhere again and succeeding only in antagonising Groczek. That hadn't been his intention and it surprised him once again to see how easily Groczek lost his calm and seemed unable to pursue the matter in a spirit of objective enquiry. After all, weren't they both after the same thing? Despite his earlier doubts about Groczek, he had put them firmly aside. Reasoning it through had led him nowhere. He was not, therefore, accusing the man of anything, so why was he so touchy? Perhaps it was in his, Webster's, refusal to accept at its face value Groczek's theory that the drugs were taken in court? Was the man so pigheaded as to be unable to concede that he may have been wrong and that they must all now look elsewhere for an explanation?

'Let me,' Webster said, cooling it, touching the air with the fingertips of his outstretched hands as if trying to calm a fluttering agitation he saw there, 'let me state the only fact I know – that a lot of heroin disappeared after a train robbery.'

Groczek said, grimly, 'It disappeared during the trial.'

'I don't *know* that,' Webster replied.

'I'm telling you!'

'I know you're telling me,' Webster answered, getting more and more annoyed, despite himself, 'but that doesn't make it a fact, it . . .'

'For Christ's sake,' Groczek snarled, 'the heroin was stolen in court! It was chalk that was put on that train, chalk! What the hell do you think you've got in that cupboard? Have you forgotten? Whoever robbed that train got cans of

250

goddam chalk! The heroin had been taken earlier!'

Groczek's voice had risen to a note that stopped short only of a scream. The veins in his head were standing out, and his face was almost purple with frustration and rage. But it wasn't that that engaged Webster's attention. It was something else, a thought that had entered his mind, hopped into it like a bird.

He turned and looked at Bradley, then at Groczek. Both were staring at him, staring at him as one might stare at a man experiencing a divine revelation and who would, in a moment, transmit the message and so change the world for all time. They saw Webster rise, like a man in a trance, turn and stare at the filing cabinet behind him. He took from his pocket the key, inserted it into the lock and opened it. He stared down at the cans of chalk Fallon had brought back with him. He put his hand in the drawer and took one out. He turned and looked at Groczek.

Groczek was watching him. Beads of perspiration had broken out on his forehead, the product of some ghastly premonition that had suddenly gripped him, as if Webster's insight had been matched by one of his own. Or, perhaps, the flash of Webster's sudden intuition had seared Groczek's mind too. All the voices of reason struggled with that premonition, tried but failed to overthrow it. Yet it was the voices of reason that burst from him in one, last, desperate endeavour to reassert the primacy of the real world, the world of fact, the world of order and of things known. 'It's chalk,' he cried, 'we *know* it's chalk! It came off the train!'

Webster sniffed it, then shook a little onto the palm of his hand and put the tip of his tongue to it. He looked at Groczek. 'It's heroin,' he said, 'taste it.'

Groczek stared at him. It couldn't be. What was he saying? It was chalk. It came off the train. Groczek had put it there. 'Taste it,' Webster repeated tonelessly. It was like a dream. The premises were absurd but all that followed, followed with

251

relentless logic. He put out a finger and touched the powder in Webster's hand. He put it to his lips. Webster watched him, his eyes narrow and glinting. 'It's heroin,' he said, once more, 'I just assumed it was chalk.'

There was a long silence. Bradley, who had been leaning up against the door, had pulled himself upright and was staring at Groczek. Groczek kept swallowing, as if trying to say something but his lips worked soundlessly and nothing came out. And then he laughed – but Bradley heard the edge of hysteria in it. 'My God,' Groczek said, 'don't you see what he's doing? Don't you see it?'

Webster shook his head, slowly. 'No, sir.'

'He's trying to make it look . . .' He broke off again, swallowing hard, as if the lump that was in his throat was growing larger by the moment. 'You can't seriously think,' he began again, and stopped, and started once more. 'Christ, he *wants* you to think I'm involved! That's why the train was robbed, don't you see? He planted those cans! He wants you to think I'm working with him! It's a blind, don't you understand? To make it look as if I put the *drugs* on the train!'

He stared from one to the other, searching, pleading for a glimmer of understanding, but their faces were grey and unmoved. He couldn't believe it! It was impossible that they didn't understand. 'But you *can't* think . . . you're not going to be taken in by . . .?' It was insane! All around him the universe seemed to explode inwards with a series of lights and thunderclaps. 'You're being fooled, can't you see it?' he cried. 'He's got you on a string! He's out there, now, leading you like a bloody puppet every inch of the way! YOU'RE BEING BRAINWASHED!'

There was another long silence. Webster stared intently at him. Then he asked, 'Can you think of any reason why he should – frame you, I mean? Getting the drugs, that's one thing, that's his business, but . . .'

'He hates me! He wants to destroy me!'

252

'Hates you? Why should he? What is he to you or you to him?'

Again Groczek swallowed hard. This was hard to tell. How could he make him see it? How could he explain what there was between him and Slovak? It was all so insubstantial and yet so real. 'I – I tried to get him out of the city. I – I pushed him around a bit.'

Webster nodded. 'I heard about that. But why? Why was it so important?'

'I didn't want him here,' Groczek said, looking again at Bradley, but there was no more undertsanding there and he turned back to Webster. 'He's scum,' he said, violently, 'scum! I know that kind. I grew up with it. Bright boy from the slums, wins scholarships but no moral fibre, no backbone, a born criminal type. I told him so, that's why he hates me!'

'When?' asked Webster softly.

'When?' Groczek repeated like an idiot.

'When did you tell him?' Webster asked even more softly.

Groczek felt his breath coming in short, hard gasps. He saw at once that he'd slipped, that so keen had he been to convince Webster of one thing, that he'd merely succeeded in confirming a suspicion that had been present in his mind all along. But he ploughed on, desperately. 'He – he came to my house once. He came to threaten me.'

'So you have met – subsequent to the collision, I mean?' Groczek moistened his dry lips and sought for the right words that would retrieve the situation, but he couldn't find them and Webster was going on, 'More than once?'

Groczek shook his head. Again his lips moved soundlessly for a moment, and then the voice came, but it was no more than a hoarse whisper. 'No. Just the once.'

Webster nodded gravely but said nothing for a moment. He, too, seemed preoccupied in choosing his words carefully, words that would now put everything straight for him. He had made too many mistakes, he didn't want to make another. He felt, now, that he would not. 'From the start,' he said, finally, 'I was thrown by the story you told. It didn't make sense and yet, in a way, it did. I came here to investigate a simple train robbery and the disappearance of a large haul of drugs. And then you explained to me what had happened. It took me in. It was a complicated story, but it took me in. Then, when I began to think about it, it didn't add up. It didn't add up because it seemed to me impossible that those drugs could ever have been switched in court as you said they were.'

'They were, they were,' Groczek whispered.

Webster shook his head. 'No, they weren't. And it was only when I put that firmly out of my mind, that I began to look in other directions. I even considered you having engineered the whole thing and using Slovak's presence here as a sort of fall guy, but that didn't add up when you reasoned it through. What I hadn't considered, what never crossed my mind, was that you were both working hand in glove. It was beautiful, wasn't it? All the suspicion would point at him, and he didn't mind that, he'd had all that before. He didn't mind it, because although he'd be suspect, there wouldn't be a shred of evidence that could stand up in a court and convict him.'

'That's not true,' Groczek whispered, 'I tried to get him out of the territory. I harassed him, Fallon knows that!'

'No. What you did was to cover your association with a known criminal by appearing to harass him, that's what you did. And that was clever.'

'You can't believe that,' Groczek said, 'you can't! He's framing me, I tell you! You're thinking just the way he wants you to think!'

'Do you expect me to believe,' Webster asked, with a cold contempt, 'that he went to the trouble of robbing that train just to put heroin *on* it?'

But it was true! How could he make him see? If it was so clear to Groczek why wasn't it clear to *him*? Why? Because

Webster didn't know Slovak, didn't know him the way Groczek knew him, the subtlety of the man, the depths of his resources or the lengths he would go to accomplish what he had set his mind on. He had to make Webster see this, had to! But the words had all dried up, the thoughts in his head were no longer clear. Everything was becoming a terrible muddle as between chalk and drugs and train and court. Everything was being stood on its head. What had he done? What *had* he done? He was, for a moment, suddenly unsure. Had he, by mistake, or by some strange, subconscious design, put the drugs on the train? Was that possible? Was Webster right?

However muddled Groczek's mind was at that moment, Webster's mind was utterly clear. He was shaking his head slowly, and going on, 'No, I don't believe that. I'll tell you what I believe. I believe you conceived this idea from the beginning but to do it on your own was to point the finger of suspicion straight at you. To do it with someone else, however, would put you in the clear. You found Slovak. Slovak was ideal. You talked to him. You put to him what you had in mind and he accepted. You put the drugs on the train and he was party to that information. All the rest was nothing more than an elaborate device to protect yourself by appearing to be a man who had taken every precaution, every conceivable precaution – but had been outwitted. I believe there is, here, a conspiracy to rob. That's what I believe.'

The room had gone incredibly quiet. Even the noise of traffic from the street outside seemed muted and far away. There was a singing in Groczek's head that made everything seem to come from a vast distance, even Webster's voice. It was as though he had crashed at high speed into a wall and lay shattered on the side of the road in that half-world between the living and the dead. In that limbo state he saw Webster rise from his desk like a shade in hell to announce his punishment and the term of his sentence. 'Chief Groczek,' he said,

255

'I regard you as under the very gravest suspicion. I shall ask to have you suspended while I complete my investigations.' Groczek said nothing. His brain seemed to have frozen in his skull, his eyes to have rusted in their sockets so fixedly did he stare at Webster. Then, without a word, he turned and walked out of the room.

Chapter Fourteen

Webster's arrival at a point in his investigation that gravely implicated Groczek in the robbery had stunned Groczek. His brain, he felt, had seized as a consequence, impacted. Nothing came from it. It ceased to be a living thing directing his energies and his actions. He had the impression that it had congealed, and when he had walked out of the stony silence of Webster's office it was not, in any sense, an acknowledgement of Webster's right to suspend him or a total acceptance of Webster's view of his position, but rather a response on a much lower level to an instruction to remove himself from their presence. On that level, he was obeying no more than the whispered voices of an instinct for life that still murmured inside him. If he were to save himself, his brain must thaw and begin pulsing again, and this would not happen until he had left Webster's icy presence.

It was only when he was at the wheel of his car and driving himself home that his brain began to function sufficiently for him to realise that he could not at all remember the intervening gap of time between leaving Webster's office and sitting at the wheel of the car. Yet he must have returned to his own office, taken his hat and his coat, walked out of the building, into the car park, got his car and driven off. He remembered nothing of it.

But now a little warmth was flowing back into his brain and the full horror of his situation was flooding back with it. He was like a man awakening from an anaesthetic to find a leg gone and remembering no reason why an amputation should have been carried out at all. He wanted to scream for someone to rush in and reassure him he was mistaken, that all was well and that both his legs were there, but he knew that he could not scream, that if he did, no one would hear him and that what he saw, or rather saw the absence of, was nothing less than the stark reality of his situation and that no amount of screaming would change it. And yet with the horror there came, too, the realisation that he had not been taken entirely by surprise, that, in some way, Webster's actions were a fulfilment of a premonition he had had ever since Webster's arrival, a premonition that this man had arrived to complete the final act of a drama that was being played out between himself and Slovak. He had pushed it aside for it made no sense, and yet the feeling had persisted that Webster had come, not for Slovak, but for *him*.

At first, he had put this down to his own impatience with an outsider to whom everything, every detail, had to be explained and gone over, and having been explained and gone over, and then questioned, either outright or with bright little eyes and deprecating smile. Everything had seemed so clear to Groczek, yet the more he explained, the more insubstantial the explanation had become. He had seen it wilting under Webster's gaze as he held it out to him, seen it shrivelling in his outstretched hand. Webster had brought his own views with him, Groczek had seen that from the first, and although he listened, or appeared to listen intently, he did not hear. Groczek had hoped that this would change, as Webster prodded and poked about, but nothing changed. From the first, he had seemed relatively disinterested in Slovak, as though Slovak could not possibly be the key and had, instead, twisted and turned in a mass of irrelevant material. That seemingly irrelevant material had twisted and turned into an unexpected shape – an iron finger that pointed straight at Groczek.

Groczek felt a cold shiver run through him. Such was the power Slovak had revealed himself possessed of that Groczek knew that whatever else there was to be accomplished, Slovak could do it. What that was, or how it would be done, he could not imagine, but he well knew, now, that if all Slovak had done so far was to push him off the edge, Slovak was, at this very moment, arranging the time and place in which he would hit the ground. And Groczek felt powerless to prevent it happening. He was in free fall. There was nothing between him and the earth. Tomorrow the news would break in the press and his suspension would be banner-headlined all over the newspapers. The day after – who knows? Groczek shivered again at the thought of spending time in his own jail. Men had imagined worse hells, but none, in reality, could measure up to that. Groczek knew that he would rather be dead. Did Slovak know that too?

By the time he arrived back at the house he had struggled through so many ways and byways of thought on this whole episode of his life and its possible ending that he was in a state of utter exhaustion. His hands were shaking on the wheel, and so preoccupied was he that twice he narrowly avoided a collision. He parked the car and as he put his key in the lock he wondered what he would say to his wife, how he would break to her the news that was bound to break the following day, but remembered that she had gone to her sister's for a few days and would not be home. He felt momentarily relieved at not having to face her, but as he closed the door and was about to walk on into the study he paused. He had the distinct feeling that someone was in the house, that he was not alone. It was, when he thought of it, more than a feeling for he realised that he had heard, or thought he'd heard a noise coming from upstairs, a noise that had

258

coincided with the closing of the door, so that he could not be certain if he had heard it or not.

It then occurred to him that perhaps his wife had not gone to her sister after all and he called out to her, 'Mary, is that you?' There was no answer. He called again but there was only a deep stillness and yet the impression persisted that someone was in the house with him. He listened again, perfectly still. He heard a creak from upstairs and then silence again. He took out his side-arm, put a hand on the banister rail and moved silently up the stairs. He reached the upper landing and paused, listening. He could hear nothing. He was quite close to his bedroom. He put a hand on the handle, flung the door open and leapt inside. The bedroom was empty. Nothing had been disturbed. He stood there, staring round the room. He noticed that the hand holding the gun was shaking and he felt a dribble of sweat roll down the back of his neck. He moved swiftly out of the room and rapidly inspected the other rooms, throwing open the doors and looking inside, but he found no one. He paused, once more, on the landing and listened. Outside, and some way off, he heard a car start up and drive off, but he realised that it was only his state of tension that made him notice the sound at all, a sound that in other circumstances wouldn't have registered.

He walked back into his bedroom and looked round it again. It was in perfect order, as his wife would have left it. He kept no valuables in the house and so did not feel the need to check drawers and closets, and it was most unlikely that any thief breaking in would have put everything back so neatly. Nevertheless, he could not rid himself of the feeling that for a moment he had not been alone, and yet that feeling could have so easily been the product of his state of mind.

He went down to the study and closed the door. He sat down at his desk and dropped his head wearily into his hands. The full extent of the horror that had engulfed him in Webster's office now struck him like a tidal wave, and the

259

extent of the horror that was yet to come followed in its wake. He knew there was no escaping the end Slovak had planned for him except, perhaps, by fashioning his own.

He stared at the revolver he had laid down on the desk. It offered him a solution. There would be no explanations needed to his wife, no trial, no sentence. His wife's absence from the house seemed especially arranged for the occasion. He would not have wanted to have done it elsewhere. His study was the right place to take his leave in. He picked up the gun and pointed the barrel at the centre of his forehead, staring into the black hole that faced him. It was all so simple. The eye of the gun held him fast for a moment. Then he laid the gun down.

He rose from the desk and paced the room rapidly and restlessly. He wasn't ready yet. It simply could not be the end, not yet. There must be another way. He stopped. Yes there was a way. What Slovak had done, Slovak could undo. How, Groczek could not see, but he saw that Slovak could accomplish anything. He saw, too, what it was that Slovak wanted – Groczek's unconditional surrender, his acknowledgement of total defeat. He had challenged and he had lost. He had dared to set himself up as Slovak's equal and now, if he were to concede that he had been wrong, if he were to bare his head and extend his neck in the presence of the master, would not Slovak relent? Groczek didn't know but he felt that it was possible. Slovak had the drugs. He had won every point in the game. What more could it profit him to achieve? Groczek could offer him the one and only satisfaction that was missing, the sight of Groczek, abject in defeat, taking Slovak's foot and placing it on his own neck. Groczek was prepared to do that. It was, after all, no more than the truth, and if the humiliation would scar him for life, at least his life would be returned to him. But would it be enough? Groczek wasn't sure, but he felt he knew Slovak well enough to make him think the attempt was worth making.

He couldn't go to the house, that was too dangerous. He couldn't afford to be seen meeting with Slovak. He was sure Webster would be watching both him and the house by now. But he must talk to Slovak and arrange to meet with him, somehow. He picked up the phone and called the house.

The phone rang and rang at the other end. Groczek sat there listening to it, a deeper and deeper despair gripping him as the bell rang and rang but no one answered. Then as he was about to hang up, the receiver was lifted at the other end.

There was silence. No voice came down the wire. Groczek said, desperately, 'Hello? Hello? Slovak, is that you?' Again there was nothing. It was as if he had been misrouted to a grave and a passing ghost had removed the receiver to avoid disturbing the occupant. But Groczek knew, *knew* there was a living presence at the other end, listening, and that the presence was Slovak. 'Slovak, is that you?' he repeated. 'I know you're there. Please answer!' And when there was again no response, he went on, 'I must see you! Please! Can we meet somewhere?'

There was another long silence. The sweat was rolling down Groczek's face and dropping onto the pad in front of him. He waited and waited, but still no sound came from the other end. For what seemed an age he just sat there with the phone at his ear, listening to what seemed to him a cosmic silence in which nothing lived. Then, a voice came out of that eternal silence and it was Slovak's. 'We shouldn't be seen together, Groczek, you know that,' and Groczek heard the note of amusement in the voice.

'We can meet in a crowded place – anywhere – you name it.'

There was a short pause, then Slovak said, 'I'll be at the stadium at nine o'clock. I'll leave a ticket in your name.'

'All right. Only be careful. They'll be watching the house. Webster, I mean. He's the man from narcotics. He's investigating the . . .' His voice choked on the word.

261

'Robbery?' Slovak supplied, with the same hint of amusement in his voice, the word. 'Don't you worry about me, Groczek. Don't you worry about me.' There was a click at the other end as the receiver was put down. Slowly Groczek replaced his own. He felt drained. In those few words he had poured out the last few, precious drops of his spirit. So complete was the exhaustion that overcame him that he put his arms on the desk and his head sank wearily onto them.

He awoke with a start and looked at his watch. He saw that it was already nine o'clock. He leapt to his feet, slipped the gun into his pocket and hurried out of the house. He paused outside, looking round. It was dark, but he could see nothing that gave him cause to believe he was being watched. He got into his car and drove out to the stadium, taking a meandering route through the city to spot any following cars, but there seemed to be none. He arrived at the stadium and put his car in the car park.

The city had built the stadium at great expense in concrete and glass. The great expense was an affirmation of the principle that money was not everything. It was beautifully equipped. Baseball and football were played there, high schools held their athletic meetings there and, in season, dogs were raced there at night and betting allowed.

The stadium was packed, the track held in the glare of floodlights. As Groczek entered, holding the ticket he had found waiting for him, the crowd was on its feet cheering home the winning dog. Groczek found the entrance to the tier of seats in which his own was located and mounted the stone steps to the top. The crowd was vast, stretching on either side of him. He looked down at the row and number marked on the ticket and saw that it was down the steps and towards the front. He made his way down until he stood opposite the row. He looked along it. He saw that there was one seat empty and that it was his own, but on either side of it sat a man he did not know.

262

He turned, puzzled, and looked about him. The loud-speakers were announcing the next race and there was a general movement among the crowd as they drifted out to place their bets. Men in white hats and coats and carrying trays loaded with beer and snacks were moving up and down the gangways. Groczek's eyes lifted to the long glass wall of the restaurant and bars that overlooked the rear of the stadium and was brilliantly lit from inside. His eyes ran along the length of it. A man was leaning on a rail, staring down at him, a drink in his hand. It was Slovak.

Groczek hurried back up the steps and made his way to the entrance to the restaurant building. He raced up the steps and entered the door. He stopped and looked along the length of the room. Slovak was no longer standing by the rail but was in the act of disappearing through the exit at the far end. Groczek couldn't understand it. Was Slovak merely playing with him? Had he got him there merely to taunt him or had Slovak mistaken Groczek's intention and was, himself, on his way down to meet him?

He hurried after him, breaking into a small run as he again felt the panic rising up in him. The place was crowded and he had difficulty in threading his way through the milling throng of people, but he reached the exit and raced down the stairs. He emerged at the rear of the stadium and found himself once again among the crowds of people moving up to betting windows to place bets or collect their winnings. There was no sight of Slovak. Groczek broke into another run but stopped, after a few yards, turning this way and that, searching desperately for Slovak. The man was playing a game with him. But why? He felt a surge of helpless fury rush through him, so helpless that he felt pinpricks of tears in the corners of his eyes. He was about to move off in another direction when he saw something that froze him in his tracks.

A figure was hurrying across his line of vision, a figure he recognised and the sight of which hardened Groczek's jaw, suddenly, and tightened his mouth into a thin line. It was the old clerk. He scurried along, like the White Rabbit, as if desperately late for an appointment, and Groczek watched him, moving at an acute angle away from him. The anger that surged through Groczek had the effect of unfreezing him. All his pent-up hatred for Slovak suddenly burst and flowed in the direction of that small figure that seemed to concentrate, in itself alone, the source of all Groczek's misfortunes. He leapt after him – but stopped again, almost at once.

Slovak had appeared from behind a pillar and the old man had stopped and was speaking to him. Slovak was listening and nodding as the old man went on. Then Slovak pulled from his pocket an envelope which he gave to the old man. The old man took it and said something and Slovak turned and walked away, disappearing among the crowds. The old man pocketed the envelope and then hurried off in the direction of the car park.

For the first time, in a long time, Groczek felt a ray of hope suddenly warm him. In that brief moment of meeting, he knew, beyond any doubt, that he was right, had been right all along, and that the drugs had been stolen in the court. It no longer mattered what Webster thought or what Webster was doing. Here was the living proof of what he had known since that shattering moment that the drugs had disappeared – that Slovak had lifted them with the help of the clerk. A weight was lifted from his chest and he felt himself breathe again. He was not finished, as he had thought. The game was not yet over. He hurried after the clerk, keeping him in sight up ahead of him.

He saw him scurrying out of the stadium and into the car park. He saw him weaving his way between the cars and stopping beside a small, dark blue saloon. Groczek quickened his step. The old man unlocked the door of the car and stepped inside. He put the key in the ignition and was about to turn it when he saw Groczek with his hand on the handle of the door. The old man's hand moved quickly to lock it but he was too late and Groczek pulled the door open and said, 'Move over.'

The old man hesitated for a moment and then moved into the other seat. Groczek got quickly in beside him. For a brief moment he sat there, looking at him. Then, he pulled the old man's jacket aside and took out the envelope. He opened it. There was a thick wad of dollar bills inside. Groczek looked at him. 'You bastard,' he said, quietly, 'what's this, a down payment?' The old man didn't answer, just sat there staring at him. 'Where's he gone?' Again no answer. And then, something broke inside Groczek. He grabbed the old man by his jacket and slammed him back and forth against the car door. 'Where's he gone?' he shouted, 'tell me! You bastard, I'll kill you! Where's the junk? Where's he got it? *Tell* me!' With each blow against the door the old man's head snapped forward and his mouth hung open wider so that his upper plate fell out and landed on Groczek's lap. Groczek stared down at it. It had an oddly calming effect upon him, bringing him back to a sense of reality. The old man was gasping, trying to catch his breath in great heaving spasms while at the same time trying to clutch the denture on Groczek's lap with his outstretched, shaking hand.

He retrieved it, finally, and put it back into his mouth. For a moment, his teeth chattered uncontrollably. Groczek, unmoved by the sight of the old man's helplessness, drew the revolver from his pocket and pointed it at the old man's head. 'Now, you listen to me,' he said, coldly. 'Webster thinks I took those drugs. He thinks I was in it with Slovak. I've already been suspended. But I'm not spending ten years in my own city jail. I'd rather be dead. So if my life's worth nothing to me, yours is worth even less, you understand? Now, where's he got the stuff?'

There was a long pause. There was something so deathly

265

calm about Groczek, now, that the old man could be in no doubt of the firmness of his intention. He swallowed hard and said, 'He's – he's gone to the airport with it. He's got a private plane waiting. He's selling it in South America – somewhere like that. It's a big deal. He's got it all laid on.'

'How will he get it through customs?'

'I don't know,' the old man said, 'but that's no problem to him.'

Groczek could see that the man was telling the truth. He put his hand on the handle of the door and opened it, but paused, and looked again at the old man. 'Tell me something,' he said, 'how was it done? How could Slovak get the cans of chalk into that room and the heroin out in so little time without being seen?'

Again the old man swallowed nervously as if afraid the truth might revive Groczek's anger all over again, but he said, 'It wasn't done like that. I brought the cans of chalk in a little at a time the day before. I stored them in the cupboard. When your men brought the heroin in, it took only a minute to put it in the cupboard and put the cans of chalk back on the table. The real stuff was in the cupboard when you were in the room. Only, naturally, you thought it was on the table.'

'Then you got the heroin out the same way,' Groczek said, 'bit by bit during the day?' The old man nodded. It was all so simple but he hadn't thought of it. As in all good tricks, the magic was done before the audience arrived.

'Of course,' the old man went on, 'we'd no idea you were going to tumble to it so fast.' Groczek nodded. At least, he hadn't been all wrong. 'You'll leave me out of it?' the old man whined. 'I need the money! I'm retiring and the pension's worth nothing, nothing!'

Groczek flung the envelope with the money at him, leapt out of the car and slammed the door. He raced across the car park towards his own car, hearing the clerk's voice shouting

266

at him as he went, 'It's the inflation! There's the criminal! Look at the price of coffee! You bought any coffee lately? Those growers ought to be shot, all of them! Shot!'

He reached his own car and flung himself into it, gripped by a surge of excitement. He was getting near now. He felt like a policeman again. He was on a trail. It had opened up unexpectedly in front of him and he could see the end of it. He saw where he was going and what he had to do. The heroin was within reach for the first time since it had been brought into court. Slovak was within reach. He would bring the heroin back. With luck, he might bring back Slovak as well.

His foot was hard down on the gas pedal and his car streaking along the road out to the airport. He sat solidly at the wheel, gripping it hard, his face alternately light and dark as it was illuminated by the passing headlights. He seethed with impatience to be there. Slovak had, by now, a good start on him. He prayed he would not be too late to prevent him taking off.

It had started to rain and he switched on the wipers. He could see all the glittering lights of the airport up ahead of him and could hear the drone of planes coming in to land or taking off above him. He swung off the main highway and onto the approach road to the complex of buildings that con- stituted the airport. He had to find out which part of the airfield Slovak's plane was taking off from. He hadn't much time. It was unlikely that Slovak had chartered the plane in his own name and precious minutes would be consumed in locating which one it was. He brought the car to a halt out- side the main building and ran inside. Without waiting for the elevator, he raced up the stairs to the administrative offices above. He opened the first door he came to. Girls sat typing at desks. 'Which office deals with private charters?' he shouted above the clatter.

'Third on the right, sir,' the girl nearest to him replied,

turning and giving him a radiant smile, her fingers continuing to clatter on the keys.

He ran out, closing the door, and raced along the corridor to the third door. He flung it open and went in. Clerks were at work at their desks or searching cabinets for files. 'Is there a private plane taking off from here in the next few minutes?' he asked.

All the clerks seemed to stop work at once and stare at him. For a moment no one moved. Then the clerk at the filing cabinet nearest to him said, 'Are you Chief Groczek? Edward George Groczek?'

Groczek felt a slight shock run through him at the mention of his name. How did they know that? Had they recognised him? He stared at the clerk. 'Yes, I am,' he said.

'The pilot's waiting, sir. On runway 14. You'd better hurry or your departure will be delayed. It's on the west side of the airport.'

Groczek stared at him incredulously. What was he saying? Whose departure? Why did they imagine that he was leaving? 'Who chartered the plane?' he asked.

'Why, you did, sir. It's in your name. All the papers have been cleared. Your luggage went through customs earlier.'

Once again, the mist came down. There was an air of unreality about the room, as though he had been given an unexpected distorted view of it. Everyone was looking at him. Groczek saw that they were wondering if he had heard what had been said to him and if so why he was not immediately obeying the instructions given to him. He backed towards the door. The information he had received frightened him and their attitude frightened him. He could make no sense of it. The clerk who had spoken to him said, 'You'll need a car to get out there.' Groczek turned and bolted out of the room, hearing the fading voice of the clerk calling after him, 'Don't forget to go through immigration, sir.'

He raced down the stairs and out into his car. He drove

it round the main building and onto the tarmac road that led out to the runway on the west side of the airfield, waving his identity at the barrier and shouting, 'Police, let me through!' They let him through. The car hurtled through the rain and the dark towards the western edge of the airfield. It was bewildering. Had Slovak taken leave of his senses in chartering the plane in Groczek's name, or had he been exceedingly clever, perhaps too clever? What had he hoped to gain by it? The use of any name would have presented no problem to a man of Slovak's resources. Why had he chosen Groczek's? Was it just another aspect of the man's ironic humour? By doing it, was he putting his thumb, for the last time, to his nose as a farewell gesture? If he were, he had under-estimated Groczek. Groczek was closer behind him than Slovak dreamed.

The headlights of his car picked out the dark shape of a hangar up ahead of him and there on the runway, some distance off, the executive jet waiting motionless. He swung the car towards it but as he neared it, stopped as he saw into the interior of the hangar. It was totally dark, but standing on the floor in the centre of it was a red light that winked slowly on and off. It was curious. Groczek could not understand why it was there. He turned the car and drove it towards the hangar. He stopped and got out. He approached the entrance to the hangar and stared at the winking red light in the middle of the dark interior.

He had to see what it was. It seemed to have no reason to be there. He walked towards it, as if drawn by an invisible thread and as he neared it he saw two shapes on the ground beside it but could not make out what they were in the dim light. As he neared them, however, he saw that they were two suitcases. He stared down at them puzzled. What were they doing there? He knelt down beside them, put his hand to the lamp and turned the switch to a steady, white beam. He saw now, that the suitcases were familiar to him, but

269

could not think why. He raised the first case onto its edge. Clearly marked between the locks were his initials – E.G.G. The case was his own. He looked at the other and saw that it, too, was his. He stared down at them dumbfounded. What did it mean? He put his fingers on the locks of the first case and snapped them open. He lifted the lid and stared down at the contents. All his clothes were neatly packed inside. On top was a passport and a large envelope. He opened the passport. It was his. He put down the passport and opened the envelope. He pulled the papers out from inside and looked at them. He saw that they were tickets and documents relating to the chartering of a private plane – all made out to him.

He put them back in the envelope and closed the case. His heart was beating wildly and his hands were trembling. He snapped open the locks of the other suitcase and lifted the lid. It was packed with cans that were, by now, utterly familiar to him. He could see through the plastic lids to a whitish powder – and he was in no doubt that this was part of the heroin haul. He stared down at it, stunned. Then he began backing away from it as he saw all the implications of it at once. A voice came out of the darkness at him, 'Groczek, this is Webster! Stay where you are!'

He twisted round in the direction of the voice. He saw the hangar full of dark shadows and figures emerging from them like spectres. He knew who they were – policemen, his own policemen, led by Webster and Bradley closing a circle round him. He pulled the revolver from his pocket.

He heard Webster say, 'Don't be a fool! Groczek! Put it down!'

A rising tide of panic gripped him and he backed away from the suitcases. He shook his head like a fighter getting up and shaking the blood from his eyes. He saw it all, in a flash, saw the end of it all. 'Oh, that bastard,' he said, 'that clever bastard!' He gripped the revolver hard.

He heard Webster shouting, 'Give me that gun!'

270

'The bastard,' Groczek repeated, and saw it all again in great flashes of light, saw how even the little court official had been used to lure him to the airport. He laughed – it was so clever. He put the muzzle to his temple. He heard Webster shout again. The last message his brain transmitted was to his finger. It jerked, and the hangar exploded into endless reverberations of noise.

Webster paused, fractionally, in his advance on Groczek as the sound waves hit him, then ran forward to the body as it hit the ground and rolled over. 'Christ,' Bradley said, 'oh, for Christ's sake!' They both stared down at the body and Bradley said, 'He didn't have to do that!'

Webster looked at Groczek and thought of him sharing a cell in his own prison with men he'd sent there, heard the prison drums tapping out the message, 'He's coming! He's coming in!' He nodded. 'Oh, yes,' he said, 'yes, he did.' He looked around the hangar, at its darkened shadows then turned and walked slowly to the end of it and stood looking out into the landscape of night and airport lights. It was foolish, but he felt a presence somewhere near, Slovak's presence, as if he had watched the whole episode from some chosen spot. An overpowering sense of hatred for Slovak overcame him, quite irrational in its intensity. He had never felt quite like that before about any criminal.

He walked back to the body. Bradley bent down and opened one of the suitcases. It was full of heroin. 'That's only half of it,' he said to Webster, 'Slovak has the rest and I'll bet, by now, he's out of the country.'

Webster stared abstractedly down at Groczek then shook his head slowly. 'No,' he said, 'not Slovak. That's not his way.' There was a pause and then he said again, 'No, that's not his way.'

They left two policemen with the body to wait for the ambulance and drove back to the city in silence. Webster's mind was full of Slovak. He knew that at that moment he

271

was ready to commit his life to putting Slovak away. He recognised it as the onset of an obsession. On an impulse he told the driver to leave the road at the next junction and drive in the direction of Slovak's house. 'He won't be there,' Bradley said.

Webster shrugged but didn't reply. They reached the driveway of the house and turned into it. A small light was on in the living room. Someone was there. The cars came to a halt and Webster and Bradley got out. They walked over to the front door. It was standing partly open which surprised him. He went inside followed by Bradley.

He went into the living room. Only the lamp on the desk in the corner was on. The room appeared, at first, to be empty and then he saw the figure of Slovak sitting in an armchair. He walked over to him and stood facing him. Slovak's eyes pierced his own with a peculiar intensity but other than that he registered nothing on his face of Webster's presence. Webster said, 'Your partner's dead, Slovak. He opted out – with his own gun.' Slovak didn't move. Webster nodded to emphasise the point. 'You want my advice?' he went on. 'Do the same. Because I'm going to get you, Slovak, if it takes me the rest of my life I'm going to put you away. From now on, wherever you go, wherever you are, just keep looking over your shoulder because I'll be somewhere around, do you understand? *Do you understand me*?'

He leaned closer to him. Slovak made no reply, though his eyes remained fixed on Webster and flickered as though what Webster had said had disturbed an innermost train of his thought. The gaze was intense, like that of a man who had suddenly been robbed of the power of speech but was trying to tell him something important. Then, abruptly, as if out of the very depths of him, as if the power to speak had suddenly been returned to him, he said, 'Little fish. Play in the rushes. I might never know you're there.'

Webster stared at him, puzzled, then looked at Bradley

272

who shrugged. He looked back at Slovak. 'What did you say?' he asked, but Slovak only laughed, once and then resumed his look of searching intensity.

'It doesn't matter what he said,' a voice said behind them, 'it doesn't mean anything any more.'

They turned. They saw a young, auburn haired woman who had just entered, standing watching them. Clearly she had been in the house when they arrived for she had no outdoor clothes on. 'Who are you?' Webster asked.

'I'm Margaret Phillips,' Maggie said, 'I own this house.'

There was a short silence. Webster stared at her, trying to sum her up. 'Is he – a tenant or a friend as well?'

'A friend,' Maggie answered, 'as well.'

Webster nodded. He remembered that Groczek had mentioned her in passing but in what context he could not now recall. 'What did you mean,' he asked, 'a moment ago when you said, "It doesn't matter what he said"?'

'His mind has gone, can't you see?' Maggie replied. 'He's lost.' She came over to Slovak and put a hand on his shoulder. He seemed not to notice it. 'I've seen it coming for a long time,' she went on, 'I'm not surprised.'

'What are you doing here now?'

'He called me about an hour ago. He sounded odd. It frightened me. It had happened – once before. So, after he'd hung up I decided to come over here. I found him like that.'

Webster turned and looked again at Slovak. He leant forward to him. 'Who are you?' he asked. 'Do you know who you are?'

Slovak appeared to consider the question very seriously, not so much as if he were searching for his name but rather whether he should answer the question at all. Then he said, 'If you snap at me I'll swallow you whole.'

Clearly the man's plight was very serious and Webster suddenly felt a wave of sympathy flow over him. It was obvious they had no way of penetrating into the meaning of

273

what he said if, indeed, what he said had any meaning at all. They were lost or, rather, he was lost and probably what he said was no more than fragments of some half remembered conversations that had relevance in a totally different time and place. Probably they floated about haphazardly in his mind and he merely clutched the nearest as it drifted by.

There was a sound in the doorway and they turned. A young man stood there, looking at them. Maggie said, 'This is my fiancé, Dr. Baron. I called him when got here. These men are policemen,' she added to Phillip.

He nodded to them and went over to Slovak. He examined him briefly for a moment, looking for any signs of physical injury and at the same time speaking to him, his voice increasingly taking on the tone of someone talking to a man who was there but separated by the walls of a thick sarcophagus in which he lay sealed. Slovak made no response to any of the questions. It was as if he had never heard them.

And then, as Webster watched him, he literally saw the light dying in Slovak's eyes. It was an extraordinary experience, something Webster had never seen before. It was like the going down of the sun, the fading of a bright light. He felt that he actually *saw the twilight enter the man's soul,* felt he could see him shrinking before his very eyes, not physically but spiritually, the spirit falling lower and lower in him like mercury in a tube. It was as he had once visualised the dying of a star, its great mass contracting slowly, getting smaller and smaller until it was no more than a hardened lump hanging in black space, unseen, lighting nothing, warming nothing – a single, pulsing object. Webster saw this happen in front of him.

'What is it?' Webster asked. 'What's happening to him?'

Phillip shrugged. 'It looks like a catatonic stupor,' he said, 'but I'm no expert.'

'Could it happen that fast?'

'Fast?' Phillip shook his head. 'I should think it's been

coming a long time. A long time. Somehow, he's been staving it off, though. Maybe he wasn't ready for it – till now.'

'Do you know who he is?' Phillip shrugged and looked at Maggie. Webster turned to her. 'How well do you know him?'

'I know him very well.' Her tone was defiant, challenging.

'Then you know what he is?' She didn't answer. 'Well, do you?'

'I don't know what that means.'

'Well, I'll tell you,' Webster said, 'he's a criminal. Not an ordinary one. A brilliant one, as a matter of fact. He came here to do a job, did you know that?' She didn't answer. 'You know that $10,000,000 worth of heroin was stolen recently from the police?' He pointed at Slovak. 'He did it. In collaboration with the city police chief – who's now dead. We've recovered half the heroin. Where's the rest of it?'

'How should I know?'

'You want me to tear the place apart?'

'Tear it apart.'

Webster sighed. Clearly he would get no co-operation from her. They'd have to go over the place with a fine toothcomb but he already had a feeling they'd never find it.

'I'll phone for an ambulance,' Phillip said.

'No need,' Webster answered, 'we'll take him.'

'Are you arresting him?' Maggie asked.

Webster shook his head. 'No. I've got nothing on him – yet. You can come along if you want to.' He turned to Bradley. 'I want a couple of men in here. I want the place turned over.' Bradley nodded and went outside. Webster turned back to Slovak. The man was an oddly moving sight sitting there so still. He took him by the arm and lifted him to his feet. Unresisting, almost like a child, Slovak went with him.

Webster put him in his own car and Bradley got in beside him. Maggie and Phillip followed behind in their own cars.

275

When they came up off the road and out onto the main highway that led to the city, they fell in behind the ambulance carrying the body of Groczek back from the airport. It seemed fitting they should travel together.

He had pursued him, like the Hound of Heaven, down the nights and down the days, down the arches of the years and the labyrinthine ways of the mind. It had been a battle, a titanic struggle, as of angels wrestling. He was exhausted. The victory had been his but the cost had devoured it.

He had brought off everything, brought it off brilliantly. He had planned everything, foreseen everything, except that one moment when Groczek had taken him by surprise. Apart from that he had dazzled himself with his invention and his resource. He had accomplished nothing like it before, not quite like it. He would accomplish nothing like it again.

He bore no hatred for Groczek as Groczek bore for him. Groczek's intention had been from the first nothing less than to bring about his destruction – but that was understandable. Groczek, in a way, had no alternative. From the moment Slovak had arrived he had perceived in Slovak a deadly enemy, perceived that both could not continue to exist at the same time and in the same place. But in a way, wasn't that the very reason that Slovak had come to the city? And if he did not know it *then*, didn't he know it now?

If he bore no hatred for Groczek it was because he recognised that he deserved Groczek's enmity, yes, *deserved* it – had, in fact, looked for it. And then, having found it in Groczek he had proceeded to create him in the image of his own deadly executioner and challenged Groczek to bring that execution off. Groczek had perceived this, and hit upon it with striking intuition when Slovak had confronted him in his house and across his desk. In coming to the city Slovak was testing Providence, teasing it. He had come, in fact, looking for his own destruction. And why? Because he had

276

come to understand that all his life he had betrayed himself, betrayed the powers he had been given. He was, indeed, a betrayer of gifts.

He had seen that with increasing clarity over the years and knew that ultimately he must be punished for it. He couldn't escape that. Groczek, too, had seen it. He had come closer than anyone ever before to penetrating into the core of his being. He had possessed insights that matched Slovak's own. So remarkable, in fact, had Groczek's penetration been that he seemed actually to have got inside Slovak, to be taking him over, so that there were times when he had confused Groczek with himself, times when, in trying to destroy Groczek he had had a clear sense of trying to destroy himself.

He had returned to the house from the stadium. He had felt strange, separated from something – he was unsure what. It was a feeling that he had experienced many times over the past year, a feeling of being separated. The feeling had come and gone and then come again, but now he felt that it would not go away, that it was here to stay. It was different. It was as if that Herculean labour he had undertaken had somehow damaged something permanently inside him and that his mind would never be the same again. It frightened him.

He stood in front of the mirror on the wall and stared into it. There was nothing in it, nothing, just the empty room. He took the small white marble bust off its rest and hurled it at the mirror. The mirror shattered but the pieces remained in the frame. He saw himself now, clearly reflected in the mirror – but as a portrait painted on a jigsaw puzzle. He was disjointed, conceived in pieces, and that seemed to him to be proper, a proper reflection for the very first time. It showed him as he was, as he *knew* himself to be, not as others saw him. Nothing about him had ever been in its correct relationship – heart, head or will. Everything was there but nothing had been brought properly together. It was a mess. He was a mess. Nothing worked right, not as it should.

His head worked, worked brilliantly, his heart and his will – but never together. That had been the trouble. A woman might have done it, a woman might have put the pieces into the right shape, a woman who loved him. Maggie might have done it. She had loved him once. No, that wasn't true. She hadn't loved him, not *him*, not his real self, only the false one. She was like all the rest when it came to it – you couldn't trust her with your real self.

He had dreamed, dozing in the chair. It was a strange dream. He had found himself in a frozen world. The sky above was black but a pale, blue light illuminated his way across a frozen tundra. He was looking for something, something that was alive but everything had been frozen solid. Even the air had frozen, trapping the little flakes of snow half way to the ground so that they hung there like polka-dots. At last, he had seen a figure in the distance but as he approached he saw that it, too, wasn't alive. Neither was it real. It was made of shiny black metal and looked like a knight in armour but he knew it was a robot. The robot said to him, 'Everything is frozen, nothing has been left alive. You, too, will soon be the same. You will soon be solid.'

He had awoken in a panic and lain there in the dark for a while. He was soaked in sweat, the dream had seemed so real. Lying there, in the dark, he could sense that his brain was gradually freezing from the outside inwards, layer by layer, and that if he didn't get up soon it would be too late, that the cold would have penetrated through to the centre.

He had phoned Maggie. She had answered the phone but the conversation had been sporadic, almost incoherent. He couldn't think why he had phoned her and found himself with nothing to say. And then he realised why he had phoned. It was to hear her voice, to calm the panic of his dream. Her voice had calmed him but he couldn't remember what they had said to each other. He only remembered that when he had replaced the receiver he had discovered that he was crying. His cheeks were wet with tears. Where were they coming from? Who was crying them? He hadn't shed tears since he was a child. Who, then, could be shedding them now – through him? And why? They flowed down his cheeks in great rivulets. They rose up inside and flowed over the edge and he couldn't stop them. They were unrelated to any pain he felt. It was simply as if his tear ducts had been lanced.

He heard the lock of the front door click but he didn't move from his chair. The door into the room opened and he saw Maggie standing there. She was looking at him, first this way and then that. She said, 'Frank? Frank? What is it?' but he didn't answer her. He wouldn't answer her, ever again. He didn't trust her, not any more. She was trying to search him out.

After a time she left the room but he continued to sit there. He felt that while he didn't move he was safe, safe from everyone, that he was on the verge of finding a way of eluding them all for ever.

There was a man standing in front of him whom he recognised as Webster. Webster was talking to him, saying something about Groczek being dead, but that didn't surprise him. Why was he making such a fuss about it? He had contrived it, *he*, Slovak. Why had Webster come here to tell him that? What was the true significance of his visit? Clearly he, too, like Maggie and all the rest, was trying to trap him.

Webster was saying to him, 'I'm going to get you, Slovak, if it takes me the rest of my life I'm going to get you.' He was going on and on, saying it over and over. Now why was Webster saying all that? What was Webster to him or he to Webster? His business was with Groczek. He had come to the city to seek him out, to make of Groczek his own executioner – *if* Groczek could do it. Groczek had tried but Groczek had failed and Groczek was now dead. Slovak had won again. But this time it was different. In destroying Groczek he felt that he had, in a way, destroyed himself. The two had become linked in his mind. He could no longer disentangle them. But this Webster, who was he or who did he think he was? Did he aspire now to stand in for Groczek? If that were so Slovak must put him in his place as he had once put Groczek. So Slovak said to him, 'Little fish. Play in the rushes. I might never know you're there,' which was what he had said to Groczek.

This clearly puzzled Webster for he asked Slovak to repeat what he had said which only made Slovak laugh.

Maggie then came into the room and he could see her talking to Webster. They were obviously discussing him for every now and then they glanced in his direction and then looked away. Then Webster came over to him and said, 'Who are you? Do you know who you are?'

The question took him aback for a moment. Did Webster imagine that he didn't know who he was? No, that wasn't possible. Then why had he asked the question? Was Webster trying to fool him? Was he trying to slip past his guard and confront that other, secret person that he truly was? Was he trying to do what Groczek had done? He felt that he was so he warned him as he had once warned Groczek. He said to him, 'If you snap at me I'll swallow you whole.'

But he was losing interest in them. Someone else came into the room, a man. He had seen him before but couldn't now remember who he was. They were all talking together, all conspiring to find out who he truly was but they would never find that out, now, and he was losing interest in them. He was losing interest in everything.

It was strange. The lights inside him were going out one by one. It had started with the sun which had gone cold and then gone out and then the stars, one by one, like candles winked and disappeared. Everything was cold, the cold was spreading everywhere through him, turning everything numb. He could feel his mind beginning to thicken, and his blood. Darkness was descending. All over there was nothing but the palest of blue, flickering light. He welcomed it, welcomed it. He was alone in there, dark and pulsing. He lived again, safe from them, from their gaze that sought to find him. In here he was secure. They couldn't reach him. They wouldn't even notice him. For them he wouldn't be alive and so they would ignore him. Only he knew that he pulsed in there, everything reduced to a single heart beat and nothing more. Nothing more was needed, neither movement nor activity nor brain waves beating. Only the heart pulsing, the whispered beat that told him he lived where none could enter. They might search but would never find him. They might walk past him and over him but never know he was there. That was good, it was such a relief. For what was turning solid was the rottenness in him. All that would be left, soft and living, was a tiny pulse that told him he was still alive but had nothing more to fear. No more lies were needed. He was shrouding himself in darkness and quietness, wrapping himself round in it, switching off everything. He would play dead. Let them think of him as dead, it was an old trick. In a way, he *was* dead, *he* was dead, he had murdered him and all that was left was that single, pulsing beat that was really him, that was the pure diamond of him, the ray serene that shone with a solitary light in the dark cavern he had entered. It was the pure truth of him at last. But *he* wasn't dead. *He* lived. Deep inside him, *he* lived.